Malachi's Understanding of Unfaithfulness in Covenantal Marriage Relationships is a masterpiece that digs deep into the text of Malachi 2:10–16 to provide a detailed analysis of the theme of faithfulness within the context of covenantal marriage. The book offers a meticulous, careful, and scholarly examination of the passage, throwing light on the significance of faithfulness within the sacred institution of marriage.

The author's careful exegesis and thoughtful interpretation of the text make this book a useful resource for Bible students, scholars, theologians, pastors, and anyone interested in understanding the profound implications of covenantal marriage relationships. Through thorough research and reflection, the author presents a convincing argument for the importance of faithfulness in marriage as a reflection of God's love and faithfulness towards his covenant people.

I highly recommend this book to anyone seeking a deeper understanding of the biblical teachings on marriage, faithfulness, and covenantal relationship. It is a must-read for those who truly wish to explore the timeless truths of the Bible and apply them to their lives today.

Ayuba Asheshe
General Secretary,
ECWA (Evangelical Church Winning All)

This book on unfaithfulness in marriage relationships is a thorough study of Malachi 2:10–16 in the context of contemporary application. In this work Stephen Oluwarotimi Baba, presents a theological interpretation of the marriage relationship in the Old Testament prophetic corpus, surveys the existing interpretations of the passage, and points out that while unfaithfulness in the marriage relationship led to divorce among the Jews, God never approved divorce between his children. From the evangelical point of view, Stephen Baba challenges the contemporary church to faithfulness in and lifelong commitment to marriage. This work is well written, logically presented, and simple to follow. I have no hesitation in recommending this work to scholars of religion and other interested members of society. By making this work available, Dr. Baba has rendered a great service to society.

George O. Folarin, PhD
Professor of New Testament and Christian Theological Studies in Africa,
Obafemi Awolowo University, Nigeria

I have reviewed this dissertation on covenantal marriage and find it appropriate and useful for addressing the increasing rate of divorce in Nigeria. Therefore, I endorse this scholarly work for publication so that it may enjoy wider circulation and benefit academics.

Musa A. B. Gaiya, PhD
Professor of Church History,
University of Jos, Nigeria

Scholars have offered various interpretations of Malachi 2:10–16 concerning marital unfaithfulness leading to divorce. Stephen's dissertation employs the historical-grammatical exegetical method of inquiry and provides valuable insights into the meaning of unfaithfulness as used in Malachi 2:10–16. As far as the covenantal marital relationship is concerned, God abhorred unfaithfulness in the postexilic community and continues to do so. This dissertation proposes a contextual theology of faithfulness in covenantal marriage relationships as an antidote to frivolous divorces and as a means to sustain family piety. I strongly endorse this work for its scholarly and spiritual contributions.

Haruna Kuje Ayuba, PhD
Vice-Chancellor,
Bingham University, Nigeria

Marriage is a covenant between a couple that ultimately mirrors the covenant relationship between God and his people. Unfaithfulness in marriage is arguably one of the gravest offences in a marriage, often leading to divorce and many other negative consequences. Just as unfaithfulness negatively affects the marital relationship, it also destroys God's relationship with his people. Dr. Stephen O. Baba's exegetical study of Malachi 2:6–10 emphasizes that unfaithfulness violates the bond between God and his people in the same way that is breaks a marriage bond. In the modern age, where marriages are crumbling due to unfaithfulness, the author's serious study on this subject makes it a valuable tool for pastors, Bible teachers, students, marriage counsellors, couples, and even intending couples. This study is an important wake-up call!

Samuel Waje Kunhiyop, PhD
Former General Secretary,
ECWA (Evangelical Church Winning All)

Malachi's Understanding of Unfaithfulness in Covenantal Marriage Relationships

Stephen Oluwarotimi Y. Baba

© 2025 Stephen Oluwarotimi Y. Baba

Published 2025 by Langham Academic
An imprint of Langham Publishing
www.langhampublishing.org

Langham Publishing and its imprints are a ministry of Langham Partnership

Langham Partnership
PO Box 296, Carlisle, Cumbria, CA3 9WZ, UK
www.langham.org

ISBNs:
978-1-78641-056-6 Print
978-1-78641-281-2 ePub
978-1-78641-282-9 PDF
DOI: https://doi.org/10.69811/9781786410566

Stephen Oluwarotimi Y. Baba has asserted his right under the Copyright, Designs and Patents Act, 1988 to be identified as the Author of this work.

All rights reserved. No part of this publication may be reproduced, stored in a retrieval system or transmitted, in any form or by any means, electronic, mechanical, photocopying, recording or otherwise, without the prior written permission of the publisher or the Copyright Licensing Agency.

Requests to reuse content from Langham Publishing are processed through PLSclear. Please visit www.plsclear.com to complete your request.

All Scripture translations are the author's own unless otherwise indicated

Scripture quotations marked (NET), are from the New English Translation (NET). NET Bible® copyright ©1996–2006 by Biblical Studies Press, L.L.C. www.bible.org. Used by permission. All rights reserved worldwide.

Scripture quotations marked (NRSV) are taken from the New Revised Standard Version Bible, copyright © 1989 National Council of the Churches of Christ in the United States of America. Used by permission. All rights reserved.

Scripture quotations marked (NIV) are taken from the Holy Bible, New International Version®, NIV®. Copyright © 1973, 1978, 1984, 2011 by Biblica, Inc.™ Used by permission of Zondervan.

British Library Cataloguing-in-Publication Data
A catalogue record for this book is available from the British Library

ISBN: 978-1-78641-056-6

Cover & Book Design: projectluz.com

Langham Partnership actively supports theological dialogue and an author's right to publish but does not necessarily endorse the views and opinions set forth here or in works referenced within this publication, nor can we guarantee technical and grammatical correctness. Langham Partnership does not accept any responsibility or liability to persons or property as a consequence of the reading, use or interpretation of its published content.

To God, the one who is too faithful to fail, for his faithfulness.
To my loving wife, the queen of our home, Mrs. Cecilia Olaitan Baba, Jerusalem Pilgrim, and the children whom God has blessed us with.

Contents

List of Abbreviations xi

Acknowledgments xv

Abstract xix

Chapter One 1
   Introduction
      Background to the Study 1
      Statement of the Problem 1
      The Research Questions 4
      The Purpose of the Study 5
      Presuppositions 6
      Scope of the Study 6
      Summary of Chapters 7
      Conclusion 7

Chapter Two 9
   A Survey of the Intepretative History of Malachi
      Introduction 9
      History of the Interpretation of Malachi 9
          Charles Cutler Torrey 9
          Adams C. Welch 11
          Abel Isaksson 12
          Julia M. O'Brien 15
          Elizabeth Achtemeier 17
          Beth Glazier-McDonald 18
          Richard A. Taylor and E. Ray Clendenen 21
          Pieter A. Verhoef 22
          Gordon P. Hugenberger 24
          Andrew E. Hill 28
      Summary of the Chapter 28

Chapter Three 31
   Study Methodology
      Introduction 31
      Description of Methods 31
          Literary Criticism 31
      The Historical-Grammatical Exegetical Method 32

    A Description of Historical-Grammatical Exegesis 32
    Stages of Historical-Grammatical Exegesis 34
    Characteristics of Hebrew Poetry 38
  Malachi's Use of Poetic and Rhetorical Stylistic Features 39
    Parallelism 40
    Chiasm 40
    Simile and Metaphor 40
    Rhetorical Questions 41
    Contrasts 41
    Repetition 42
    Allusion 42
  Justification for the Use of Historical Grammatical Method 43
  Summary of the Chapter 45

Chapter Four 47
God's Teaching on Marital Fidelity in the Wider Biblical Text
  Introduction 47
  The Context of Malachi 47
    The Name, Author, and Superscription of the Book 47
    The Recipients/Readers of Malachi 48
    The Date and Place of Writing of Malachi 48
    Malachi as a Name and as a Prophet 49
    The Literary Form of Malachi 50
    The Literary Structure of Malachi 51
    Explanation of the Structure of Malachi 53
    Malachi 2:10–16 in Its Biblical-Theological Context 55
    God's Relationship with Israel in the Torah 56
    Expectations of the Covenant Relationship in Malachi 58
    Responsibilities in Covenant Relationships 60
    Consequences in Covenant Relationship 60
  Malachi 2:10–16 and the Issue of Marital Unfaithfulness in
    the Prophets 61
    Yahweh's Relationship with Israel as Reflected in Hosea's
      Marriage 61
    Yahweh's Covenant Relationship in Isaiah 50:1 63
    Yahweh's Covenant Relationship in
      Jeremiah 2:1–25 and 3:1–23 64
    Yahweh as a Faithful Husband and Israel as an Unfaithful
      Wife in Ezekiel 16:1–63 and Ezekiel 23:1–49 65
  Marital Unfaithfulness: A Historical Parallel (Ezra-Nehemiah) 68
  Summary of the Chapter 73

Chapter Five 75
Exegetical Understanding of Malachi 2:10–16
   Introduction 75
      Text and Translation of Malachi 2:10–16 76
   Exegetical Outline of Malachi 2:10–16 81
      Text-Critical Problems in Malachi 2:10–16 82
   Exegetical Analysis of Malachi 2:10–16
   (An Overview) 85
      Exegetical Study of Malachi 2:10–12 88
      Exegetical Study of Malachi 2:13–16a 99
   Distinctive Use of Marriage and Kinship Imagery in Malachi
   2:10–16 118
      The First Pair: Love and Hate (אָהֵב and שָׂנֵא) 118
      The Second Pair: Father-Son Imagery (אָב and בֵּן) 119
      The Third Pair: Husband-Wife Imagery (בַּעַל and אִשָּׁה) 120
   Insights from the Exegetical Study of Malachi 2:10–16 121
      God as Creator and Father 121
      Judgement for Covenantal Unfaithfulness 122
      The One-Flesh Relationship of Marriage 122
   Chapter Summary 123

Chapter Six 125
Malachi 2:10–16 and Its Implications for Pastoral Ministry in Africa
   Introduction 125
   Exegesis of Malachi 2:10–16: Issues Related to Marriage 125
      Unfaithfulness in Covenantal Marriage 125
      Separation in the Marriage Union 126
      Divorce or Sending Away of the Wife of One's Youth 126
      Divorce and Intermarriage 127
   Malachi 2:10–16: Implications of Marital Unfaithfulness for
   the African Church and Society 127
   God's Standard for Marriage: A New Order for the Church in
   Africa 128
      The Permanence of Marriage as an Unbroken Covenant 129
      Marriage: A High and Holy Calling 129
      Faithfulness within the Marriage Union 130
      Faithfulness: Crucial for Family Unity in the African Church 130
      Intermarriage: Prohibited on a Theological Basis 131
   Malachi's Theology of Marital Faithfulness: Implications for
   Personal Family Piety in the African Church 131

Chapter Seven 135
    Conclusion and Recommendations
        The Contributions of This Research 137
        Areas for Further Research 139

Bibliography 141

List of Abbreviations

ABC	Anchor Bible Commentary
AfOB	Archiv für Orientforschung: Beiheft
AJBS	*African Journal of Biblical Studies*
AnBib	Analecta Biblica
ASJL	*American Journal of Semitic Languages and Literature*
BAR	*Biblical Archaeology Review*
BDB	Brown, Driver, and Briggs, *A Hebrew and English Lexicon of the Old Testament*
BH	Biblical Hebrew
BHQ	*Biblia Hebraica Quinta*
BHS	*Biblia Hebraica Stuttgartensia*, edited by K. Elliger and W. Rudolph
BibOr	*Biblica et Orientalia*
BSac	*Bibliotheca Sacra*
BT	*The Bible Translator*
CBC	Cambridge Bible Commentary
CBQ	*Catholic Biblical Quarterly*
CTJ	*Calvin Theological Journal*
CTR	*Criswell Theological Review*
CurBS	*Currents in Research: Biblical Studies*
DCH	*Dictionary of Classical Hebrew*
EvT	*Evangelische Theologie*
ExpTim	*Expository Times*
HAT	Handbuch Zum Alten Testament
HB	Hebrew Bible

ICC	International Critical Commentary
IEJ	*Israel Exploration Journal*
Int	*Interpretation*
IJR	Ife Journal of Religions
ITC	International Theological Commentary
JAOS	*Journal of the American Oriental Society*
JBL	*Journal of Biblical Literature*
JETS	*Journal of the Evangelical Theological Society*
JPOT	*Journal of the Palestine Oriental Society*
JSOT	*Journal for the Study of the Old Testament*
JSOTSup	Journal for the Study of the Old Testament: Supplement Series
KAT	Kommentar zum Alten Testament
LB	*Linguistica Biblica*
LXX	Septuaginta, A. Rahlfs, ed. (Septuagint)
MT	Masoretic Text
NAC	New American Commentary
NCB	New Century Bible
NICOT	New International Commentary on the Old Testament.
NIDOTTE	*New International Dictionary of Old Testament Theology and Exegesis*
OT	Old Testament
OTL	Old Testament Library
Presb	*Presbyterion*
RevExp	*Review and Expositor*
SBLSP	*Society of Biblical Literature Seminar Papers*
SJLA	Studies in Judaism in Late Antiquity
Tg	Targum (The Bible in Aramaic), edited by A. Sperber
TBC	Torch Bible Commentaries
TBT	*The Bible Today*
TDOT	*Theological Dictionary of the Old Testament*
TJ	*Trinity Journal*
TOTC	Tyndale Old Testament Commentaries
TWOT	*Theological Wordbook of the Old Testament*

TynBul	*Tyndale Bulletin*
Vg	Biblia Sacra: Vulgata, B, Fisher, et al., eds (Vulgate)
VT	*Vetus Testamentum*
VTSup	Supplements to Vetus Testamentum
WBC	Word Biblical Commentary
ZAW	*Zeitschrift fur die alttestamentliche Wissenschaft*

Acknowledgments

Thanking everyone who has contributed towards the completion of this dissertation is certainly no easy task. This dissertation could not have been completed without the sacrifices of several people. My supervisor, Rev. Prof. Cephas T. A. Tushima, Deputy Provost (Academics), Jos ECWA Theological Seminary, despite his tight schedule of teaching, research, and family responsibilities, took time to go through my work, and provided helpful suggestions. I am equally grateful to Dr. James A. Crouch, who guided me throughout this work. I appreciate the efforts of both these men, without whose scholarly contributions this dissertation would not be in its present form. I am also grateful to their wives and family members, who might have been deprived of quality time during their supervision of my work. I am grateful to them all.

I am also indebted to the leadership – both past and present – of Jos ECWA Theological Seminary, for the fellowship my family and I have enjoyed with them over the years and for all the support we received, either directly or through the Seminary, during the course of my training at JETS. I am also grateful to them for their continued support for my family and ministry in ECWA. I appreciate the leaders in ECWA for supporting me in my pursuit of further studies. I sincerely thank my loving wife and children for being there for me and for all their contributions – physically, morally, and spiritually – to my success. May the grace of God be sufficient for them all.

I also thank individuals who have contributed to my success at ECWA Theological Seminary, Igbaja, Jos, and in other places. I appreciate Dr. Herbert Jones and Marcilla Jones and all their friends in the USA for their spiritual, parental, and moral support in my ministry. I also appreciate the late Rev. Dr. David Abodunde Buremoh, who was a father to me in the area of Christian counselling in Nigeria. I am indebted to the following individuals, who have served as my mentors: Professor Scott Cunningham (USA), Dr. Dwight Singer, Dr. James A. Crouch (JETS), Professor Yusufu Turaki (JETS), Dr. Mark Nickens (USA), Professor Danfulani Kore, Professor Victor Babajide Cole, Dr. and Mrs. Sunday Agang, and Professor Luke Ekundayo Edungbola. May the good Lord reward them richly.

I thank the examiners, both internal or external, who have laboured during the period of the final assessment. I am greatly indebted to the PhD Committee members, past and present – this dissertation would have been impossible without their support. My special thanks to Professor Randee Morphe Ijatuyi, Professor George Janvier – the former director of the PhD programme – and Dr. J. C. Lee, the current director of the PhD programme. I also thank a provost of JETS, who was a former ECWA General Secretary, Rev. Professor Samuel Waje Kunhiyop, another former Provost, Rev. Dr. Bulus Galadima, and his wife, Dr. Mrs. Rose Galadima, and the current Provost, Rev. Dr. Bauta Motty, for all they have done for me.

I sincerely thank my wife, Mrs Cecilia Olaitan Baba (a Lecturer at the Faculty of Education, Bingham Universty, Karu, Nasarawa State, Nigeria) and all my Children, (Elizabeth Inioluwa, Oreoluwa Nathanyahu, and Gold Olaoluwa), as well as the following people, Pastor and Mrs. M.N. Tsado (ETSI), Pastor James O. Adeyanju (ETSI), Dr. Richardson Oyediran, Dr. Henry Iwarere, Rev. Dr. and Mrs. Peter O. Awojobi, Rev. Professor Samuel P. Ango, and the late Rev. Dr. James Folaranmi, ECWA Trustee, for their support. I also thank Mr. John Hunt, Dr. Scott Cunningham, and Dr. Dwight C. Singer, who are like fathers to me and supplied most of the books for this work. My profound gratitude goes to my friends: Pastor Timothy Kafang, his wife, and their family; Pastor Nathan H. Chiroma, his wife, and their family, who took care of me during my doctoral research at the Faculty of Theology, University of Stellenbosch, South Africa; and Professor Oyetunde and Dr. Judith Patrick, who patiently read the manuscript. I appreciate you all.

In the same vein I appreciate the contributions of the Board of Governors of ECWA Theological Seminary, Igbaja, and all the Provosts – past and present – at ECWA Theological Seminary, Igbaja. This study was made possible by the willingness of the Board of Governors of ECWA Theological Seminary, Igbaja, to grant me study leave with pay. I also thank SIM/ECWA for their assistance. In addition, I thank my home church, Evangelical Church Wining All (ECWA), and my mission organization, SIM International, for their prayers and financial support in this noble ministry of producing future Christian leaders for the church and the nation Nigeria. I am also grateful to all my professors – Yusufu Turaki, Bulus Y. Galadima, Wolfgang Bleudorn, and Mrs. Mbowdman – and my spiritual fathers – Dr. Rick Calenberg and Dr. Scott Cunningham – for all their contributions.

I must also thank Associate Professor Julius B. Lawal, Mr. Michael Ajide, Dr. and Mrs. Jogunola, Architect Olukayode Abogunrin, Elder and Mrs. J. Ogunlowo, Rev. and Mrs. Anthony O. Farinto, former ECWA President. I thank the following people, Rev. Dr. and Mrs. Adams Shaba, Col. Simon K. and Mrs. Margaret Bargo, Rev. Dr. and Mrs. Ogunmola, Mr. and Mrs. Moses Kolawole (ECWA Finance Director), Elder and Mrs. Lanre Bebeyi, Mr. Aremu (ECWA Fate Tanke, Ilorin), Chief and Mrs. J. A. Ogundeji (former Deputy Governor of Kwara State), Rev Dr. and Mrs. Ebere Ukah, Pastor and Mrs. Alexander Abafi, Dr. J. O. K Abioye, Rev. Gideon and Mrs. Ganyilo (of blessed memory), Dr. Mrs. E. O. Abogunrin, Rev. Stephen and Mrs. Panya Baba, Rev. Dr. and Mrs Stephen Sunday Ajise, Kris Gnadson, Honourable Samuel Bulus Adamu (former Chairman Shongom LGA and Commissioner of Tourism, Gombe State), and the Bebeyis, for all they have done for me. I also appreciate all the lecturers at ECWA Theological Seminary, Igbaja.

I acknowledge the support of eight ECWA local churches in Nigeria for their financial support for my studies: First ECWA Church Ilorin, ECWA Church Idoba-Araromi, ECWA Chapel Igbaja, ECWA Fate/Tanke Ilorin, ECWA Wuse II Abuja, ECWA Maitama Abuja, ECWA Abuja Central, and ECWA Church Kubwa. Thanks be to God for the ministry of Back to the Bible International and Overseas Council for providing various scholarships at every level of my theological education.

My success in this work is a testimony to God's goodness, his divine providence, and his provision through Igbaja Seminary, ECWA/SIM, and SIM missionary friends in the USA to bless me. I also thank my colleagues in the programme – Rev. Dr. Bitrus A. Sarma, Rev. Dr. Joel K. T. Biwul, Pastor Dr. Mathew Michael, and Pastor Ishaku Bulus Kubgak – for peaceful coexistence and dynamic interactions in the class.

I thank all the staff members of the libraries of Jos ECWA Theological Seminary, Jos, and ECWA Theological Seminary, Igbaja. I also appreciate the contributions of the faithful staff of the Faculty of Theology Library, the Main Library (J. S. Gericke or Lower Level Library), and Umarga Library

(Humanities Computer Supported Area) at the University of Stellenbosch, South Africa, who helped me in obtaining material for this study. I acknowledge the support of Professor Hendricks Bosman and Professor C. H. J. Van der Merwe (University of Stellenbosch) in every way. My thanks also go to my extended family member in Nigeria: Mr. and Mrs. Jolayemi, the late Elder John Sunday Baba (popularly known as Engineer), his wife, and their children, as well as Grace Monishola, Rev. Joseph and Mrs. Mary Awoyemi, Mr. and Mrs. Adedire, and others. I thank them all for their phone calls and words of encouragement. My sincere appreciation also goes to my past and present professors, colleagues, and friends.

Finally, I appreciate everyone who has stood by me in everything. May God reward everyone who has contributed to my life and to the success of this dissertation one way or another.

Abstract

God designed marriage to be a covenantal love relationship characterized by deep unity and permanence. This study focuses on the subject of marriage as a covenant, with particular reference to Malachi 2:10–16 in the context of the prophetic corpus. A key factor prompting this research was the differing interpretations of Malachi 2:10–16 by scholars with regard to the issue of faithlessness leading to divorce.

At the time of writing this work, the interpretation of Malachi 2:10–16 remains clouded with uncertainty. This uncertainty arises mainly from the noticeable corruption in the text. What, then, is the authorial intent of this passage? The literature review reveals that the place of faithfulness within the covenantal marital relationship has not been adequately explored.

Since this is a theological inquiry, the study employs the historical-grammatical exegetical method of inquiry to better understand the meaning of faithlessness as discussed in Malachi 2:10–16, with reference to both the postexilic Jewish faith community and contemporary society. In the development of this argument, the work places Malachi 2:10–16 within the biblical context of both the Torah and prophetic traditions.

The findings of this research on Malachi 2:10–16 reveal God's abhorrence of unfaithfulness or faithlessness in the postexilic community. The study discovers that throughout the book of Malachi – and particularly in this section – Yahweh continues to be the covenant-keeping God, who expects covenant obedience from his people. It is also clear that Yahweh's faithfulness stands in stark contrast to the faithlessness of his people. The people were failing in their covenant obligations to the Lord by being faithless to one another, particularly in the area of marital fidelity. The prophet rebukes three types of disloyalty in the people's covenant relationships: disloyalty to the spiritual unity of the national family, disloyalty to the family of faith, and disloyalty to the marriage partner to whom one had pledged covenantal loyalty before Yahweh.

Though this work is primarily academic, since the function of true exegesis is to lead to hermeneutics, the study explores the pastoral implications of Malachi 2:10–16 for the contemporary faith community. This study proposes a contextual theology of faithfulness in covenantal marriage relationships as an antidote to frivolous divorces and stresses the need for a contextual theological appropriation of faithfulness in covenantal marriage within contemporary secular and faith communities with a view to safeguarding personal family piety.

CHAPTER ONE

Introduction

Background to the Study

The issue of marriage and divorce receives considerable attention in the Old Testament. While divorce did occur in the OT (Deut 22:13–19, 28–29), a husband was compelled to provide a certificate of divorce to his wife (Deut 24:1–4). In Deuteronomy, sanctions were imposed on God's people in response to violations of the terms of the covenant Yahweh had made with them. These sanctions were intended to deter divorces, which were frequent and numerous. In the postexilic community, however, stricter measures were introduced to safeguard the marriage bond. Despite these measures, marital unfaithfulness continued to be one of the major issues that the OT prophets spoke against.

Some prophets in Israel played a significant role in addressing the issue of unfaithfulness in covenantal marriage relationships. Malachi was among those prophets who spoke out against divorce within a covenantal marriage union. The question may be asked: Is the prophet Malachi, in his book, advancing a new or different opinion on divorce compared to the views espoused by earlier OT prophets?

Statement of the Problem

Both in the past and in the present, scholars have explored Malachi 2:10–16. A survey of the issue of divorce in covenantal marriage relationships in the

OT reveals that various commentaries on Malachi 2:10–16 offer several perspectives.[1]

In one approach, scholars deny any reference to divorce in the text.[2] They argue that Malachi is not dealing with the issue of divorce in general but, rather, with the mistreatment of Jewish women as a result of Jewish men marrying foreign wives. These scholars conclude that Malachi's main focus is cultic matters. Other scholars also do not see the issue here as divorce but, rather, an attack against apostasy or an alien cult.[3] They argue that a reference to divorce in Malachi 2:10–16 is improbable, claiming that the text and its meaning are too uncertain to address the issue of divorce. Abel Isaksson interprets some sections of Malachi 2:10–16 – especially the phrase "married the daughter of foreign god" (2:11 NRSV) – as referring to worship of a female idol. He argues that "the daughter of a foreign god" is "a foreign cult or pagan idol or goddess."[4] Julia M. O'Brien claims that this section of Malachi has nothing to do with intermarriage and divorce but is a rebuke against idolatry alone. She argues that Malachi 2:10–16 accuses the people of worshipping other deities and does not concern itself with intermarriage and divorce.[5] Another interpretation views Malachi 2:10–16 as requiring or permitting divorce – though only divorce of heathen wives – or recommending divorce as the lesser of two evils.[6] Yet another interpretation sees the text as an absolute prohibition of divorce.[7] As a result, there is ambiguity in understanding the text.

---

1. A summary of previous engagements with Malachi 2:10–16 is found in Torrey, "Prophecy of 'Malachi,'" 4–5; and compare Isaksson, *Marriage and Ministry*, 31–32; Ahlstrom, "Joel," 49–80. For a helpful discussion of these arguments, see also Ogden, "Figurative Language," 223–230, and Smith, *Micah–Malachi*, 323.

2. Van der Woude, "Malachi's Struggle," 66, 71. See also Isaksson, *Marriage and Ministry*, 31–32.

3. For specific literature that denies any reference to divorce in the text, see Isaksson, *Marriage and Ministry*, 32. Compare Van der Woude, "Malachi's Struggle," 66, 71. See also Baldwin, *Haggai, Zechariah, Malachi*, 241; Verhoef, *Haggai and Malachi*, 275, 278; and Ogden, "Figurative Language," 223–230.

4. Isaksson, *Marriage and Ministry*, 32. See also Baldwin, *Haggai, Zechariah, Malachi*, 241.

5. O'Brien, *Priest and Levite*, 72–73.

6. Von Bulmerincq, *Der Prophet Maleachi*, 306. See also Baldwin, *Haggai, Zechariah, Malachi*, 241, and Westbrook, "Prohibition on Restoration of Marriage," 403.

7. Verhoef, *Haggai and Malachi*, 278.

C. C. Torrey was the first to raise this issue of ambiguity in the interpretation of Malachi 2:10–16, observing that this passage is one of the most difficult pericopes in the book of Malachi.[8] Other commentators have also commented on the difficulty of this section. J. M. P. Smith was also of the opinion that "this section is hopelessly obscure."[9] Adam Welch writes, "The verses [2:10–16] cannot form the basis of any sure conclusion."[10] This implies that the text is so corrupt and the sense so uncertain that these verses cannot form the basis of any sure conclusion on the issue of divorce. J. G. Baldwin observes that "the text becomes difficult . . . [and that] it is impossible to make sense of the Hebrew as it stands and therefore each translation, including the early versions, contains an element of interpretation."[11] Commenting on the difficulty of interpreting this passage, R. C. Dentan expresses his utter frustration, saying, "In Hebrew this is one of the most obscure verses [15] in the entire Old Testament, almost every word raises a question."[12]

Some other scholars regard this section of Malachi as an interpolation that requires emendation.[13] Therefore, they present interpretations that do not relate to the issue of unfaithfulness leading to divorce.[14] Such scholars face the challenge of fitting this text into the overall message of Malachi because they feel that this passage does not align with the central theme of the book. This shows that interpretative problems surround the understanding of divorce in Malachi 2:10–16, which points to the need for an investigative study.

Though some previous studies focused on the difficulties in interpreting Malachi 2:10–16, a few scholars have accepted the idea that Malachi 2:10–16 speaks of Israel's unfaithfulness to the covenant relationship with Yahweh, especially in relation to Jews being wedded to foreign or strange cults. Others have accepted that Malachi 2:10–16 speaks against marital unfaithfulness and

---

8. Torrey, "Prophecy of 'Malachi,'" 10.
9. Smith, *Haggai, Zechariah, Malachi*, 54.
10. Welch, *Post-exilic Judaism*, 120
11. Baldwin, *Haggai, Zechariah, Malachi*, 240.
12. Dentan, "Malachi," 1136. See also R. L. Smith, who cited Dentan in Smith, *Micah–Malachi*, 321, and Verhoef, *Haggai and Malachi*, 275.
13. Wellhausen, *Die Klein Propheten Übersetzt*, 80. See also Rudolph, W " *Haggai, Sacharja 1–8*, 270, and Fuller, "Text-Critical Problems," 54.
14. Rudolph, *Haggai, Sacharja 1–8*, 270; see also Smith, *Micah–Malachi*, 324–325; Van der Woude, "Malachi's Struggle," 65–71; O'Brien, *Priest and Levite*, 127; O'Brien, "On Saying No," 208.

not just religious infidelity.[15] While the various views posited by scholars on this passage are plausible, the primary aim of this work is not to continue the scholarly debate on whether the issues of marriage and divorce in the text are literal or figurative. Instead, the focus of this work is to clarify how the prophet Malachi deals with the issue of marital unfaithfulness and consider how this serves as a guide for resolving marital problems within the faith community and contemporary society.

This book aims to show that the prophet Malachi, along with several other biblical authors, understood the issue of unfaithfulness resulting in divorce discussed in Malachi 2:10–16 as an act of betrayal or unfaithfulness (faithlessness) against the covenant marriage partner. This kind of betrayal not only violates God's original plan for the marriage covenant but also has pastoral implications for believers in the universal church. It is based on this claim that the present study uses a historical-grammatical exegetical method of inquiry in interpreting the Hebrew text of Malachi 2:10–16.

The focus of this work extends beyond the debate of tying the issue of unfaithfulness to either idolatry or physical human marriage as discussed by preceding scholars. Instead, the focus of this study is the exegesis of Malachi 2:10–16 and its pastoral implications for the church in Africa. First, the research will show that Malachi viewed God's covenant relationship as the as the foundational factor in God's relationship with Israel., as well as between a man and a woman. Therefore, the key issue in Malachi 2:10–16 is the failure in the bond of covenantal relationship. Second, this study will argue that unfaithfulness to covenantal obligations within the marriage union destroys the distinctiveness of God's covenant people. Therefore, God's people must strive to be faithful to their covenant obligations and to purify themselves from anything that can cause disunity in their homes.

The Research Questions

The background to this study and the problem stated led to the formulation of four research questions. The research problem will be investigated using the following four questions as guides:

---

15. Baldwin, *Haggai, Zechariah, Malachi*, 238; Achtemeier, *Nahum–Malachi*, 181; Verhoef, *Haggai and Malachi*, 269–270.

1. What is the central issue Malachi addresses in 2:10–16, and how does he deal with the issue of unfaithfulness resulting in divorce in the covenantal marriage relationship described in the text?
2. What is the historical and cultural background of the book of Malachi?
3. How does Malachi, in 2:10–16, develop his theological themes to fit within the literary context of the book and the broader context of the entire OT?
4. How can insights from Malachi's theology of faithfulness in Malachi 2:10–16 be applied in a pastoral context to strengthen marital unity and and to make divorce less appealing in contemporary society?

The Purpose of the Study

Over the years, the interpretation of Malachi 2:10–16 has proven difficult, with some scholars emending the text to suit a particular interpretation while neglecting the others. Scholars continue to acknowledge the difficulties in interpreting Malachi 2:10–16.

Therefore, the first purpose of this work is to determine the central issue that the prophet Malachi addresses in Malachi 2:10–16 and consider how he deals with the problem of unfaithfulness within the covenantal marriage relationship. The second purpose is to examine the historical and cultural background of the book of Malachi. The third purpose is to determine whether the text can be read literally as Malachi's charge of unfaithfulness. In this regard, the study seeks to locate the discussion within its proper exegetical context, using a literary method of inquiry to understand the issue of unfaithfulness related to divorce in Malachi 2:10–16 and consider its pastoral implication for the church.

The fourth purpose is to determine the theological themes developed in this passage and discuss how these themes relate to other books of the Torah, the prophetic books of the OT, and the ancient Near Eastern culture. In this regard, the study uses the text as a starting point to reassess the issue of divorce and the covenantal nature of marriage in order to ascertain how Malachi was influenced by pentateuchal sources. This is necessary because the whole relationship of God with Israel is centred on the covenant and the Torah, which he had made and given with both their ancestors as well as the nation.

Finally, this research will highlight the dangers inherent in marital unfaithfulness and examine its pastoral implications for the church with the aim of providing a deeper understanding of the text and drawing lessons from the issue of divorce in Malachi. Ultimately, it is hoped that these findings will offer helpful guidelines for protecting marriages and preventing marital unfaithfulness.

Presuppositions

This study assumes that the Bible is theological and inspired and that the historical-grammatical exegetical approach can overcome the limitations of the historical-critical method that is often used in the interpretation of Malachi 2:10–16. Using this method in engaging with the text provides an alternative reading of the text and the issues of unfaithfulness resulting in divorce that are raised in the text. This approach is helpful in addressing marital unfaithfulness in contemporary society and understanding its pastoral implication for future generation.

Scope of the Study

This study is a literary analytical inquiry, not a field survey. There is a wealth of scholarly material on the book of Malachi, with some scholars focusing on specific themes or chapters, while others provide exhaustive commentaries on the entire book. Since this work is not intended to be yet another commentary on the book of Malachi, it has a limited scope. While acknowledging the value of the numerous works that will be cited, it is important to note that this study does not deal with methodology in great detail. In addition, the study does not address the issue of unfaithfulness in covenantal marriage relationships by exploring the entire Bible; rather, the scope of this work is limited to an exegetical study of Malachi 2:10–16 and its pastoral implications for contemporary readers.

Summary of Chapters

This dissertation consists of seven chapters. Chapter 1 sets out the background for the study. It introduces the problem, describes the research questions that guide the research, and discusses the purpose of the study.

Chapter 2 is a review of the interpretative history of scholarly writings on the issue of unfaithfulness leading to divorce in the covenantal marriage relationship. This chapter reviews academic literature pertaining to the study, identifying key authors, explaining their views, and critiquing their positions.

Chapter 3 discusses the study methodology used in examining the issue of unfaithfulness resulting in divorce in Malachi 2:10–16. In it I argue that historical-grammatical exegesis is an effective method for the reading and interpretation of Malachi 2:10–16.

Chapter 4 is a brief introduction to the book of Malachi. I explore the form, genre, and structure of the book, as well as the background to God's teaching on marital fidelity in the biblical text. This background is traced through the Torah, the Prophets, and the Writings in order to understand how unfaithfulness fits within the overall story of the Bible and the context of God's relationship with his people.

Chapter 5 presents my own translation of Malachi 2:10–16 from Hebrew to English. An exegetical outline of the passage is given, along with an exegetical study using the historical-grammatical exegetical approach to Malachi 2:10–16. Theological themes developed from this exegesis are then summarized.

Chapter 6 discusses the key issues raised from the interpretation of Malachi 2:10–16 and draws implications for the church in Africa.

Chapter 7 concludes the study and offers recommendations. It discusses the pastoral implications of unfaithfulness for Christians in the contemporary church. I summarize the findings, present my conclusions, and offer a recommendation for further research.

Conclusion

In the first chapter, the study presents the background to the study. The issue of marriage and divorce receives considerable attention in the OT. The problem identified for investigation is the inadequate attention given by other scholars to the understanding of Malachi 2:10–16, particularly in relation to the lack of faithfulness in the marriage relationship between a man and a woman.

CHAPTER TWO

A Survey of the Intepretative History of Malachi

Introduction

The pursuit of this work began with the introduction in the previous chapter, where the primary concern of the study was laid out. In this chapter, a review of the relevant literature on the interpretation of Malachi 2:10–16 is presented.

History of the Interpretation of Malachi

During the closing years of the nineteenth century a history of religions approach was used in the interpretation of Malachi 2:10–16, emphasizing the abomination of intermarriage between the people of Israel and non-Jews in the postexilic period.[1]

Charles Cutler Torrey

This cultic interpretation of Malachi 2:10–16 began with Charles Cutler Torrey in 1898.[2] Torrey observes that, in the past, several commentators had translated Malachi 2:10–16 as "a rebuke of the custom of intermarriage with gentiles; at least since the first centuries of the Christian era that the historical setting of this prophecy is to be found in the narratives contained in the

---

1. For such an approach, see Hill, *Malachi: A New Translation*, 228.
2. Torrey, "Prophecy of 'Malachi,'" 1–15.

book of Ezra."[3] However, Torrey claimed that this method of interpretation was no longer tenable.[4] He proposed a fragmentary theory, which emphasized various independently existing sources that were later joined together.[5] Torrey observed that the prophet's attack is not against mixed marriages and divorce at all, arguing that the "rebuke is directed against the encroachment of some foreign cult in Israel."[6] He claimed that translating words like בָּגַד (faithless), חָלַל (profane), בַּת־אֵל נֵכָר (daughter of a foreign god), and בְּרִית אֲבֹתֵינוּ (covenant of our fathers) literally is ridiculous.[7] He also said that the phrase בַּת־אֵל נֵכָר (the daughter of a foreign god) leads him to conclude that "the daughter of a foreign god is a foreign cult or pagan idol or goddess."[8]

This interpretation led Torrey to argue that the only way to translate and understand this section is to assume that the prophet Malachi uses figurative language. Torrey interpreted the Hebrew words בַּת־אֵל נֵכָר (daughter of a foreign god) metaphorically because he restricts the connotation of the term "daughter of foreign god" solely to idolatry. He views Judah as being unfaithful, betraying the covenant with Yahweh by going after a strange god, like a faithless husband who betrays the wife of his youth.[9]

In essence, Torrey read and interpreted Malachi 2:10–16 not as referring to divorce but as a figurative expression or metaphor for idolatry by the priesthood. It was his use of source-critical methodology for interpreting Malachi 2:10–16 that led Torrey to claim that the passage deals only with unfaithfulness at the cultic level – that is unfaithfulness to Yahweh – and not marital unfaithfulness leading to divorce among the people of Judah. His main conclusion is that Malachi 2:10–16 focuses solely on the issue of unfaithfulness resulting in idolatry.[10]

Torrey's work became the bedrock of almost all research on the book of Malachi during the rest of the nineteenth century. To a great extent, his work is still used as the definitive point of departure for many scholars who use the

---

3. Torrey, 9.
4. Torrey, 9.
5. Torrey, 4–5.
6. Torrey, 5.
7. Torrey, 5.
8. Torrey, 4, 9–10. See also Hvidberg, *Weeping and Laughter*, 121–122.
9. Torrey, "Prophecy of 'Malachi,'" 9–10.
10. Torrey, 4.

historical-critical approach for the study of Malachi. However, the pastoral implication of Malachi 2:10–16 – that is, the issue of marital unfaithfulness leading to divorce – remains unexplored.

This study does not follow Torrey's interpretation of unfaithfulness in Malachi 2:10–16 as referring to idolatry alone, or his refusal to accept that unfaithfulness leading to divorce in the marriage covenant is being addressed in Malachi 2:10–16.[11] The study observes that the expression בַּת־אֵל נֵכָר – translated "the daughter of a foreign god" – as used in Malachi 2:10–16 could refer to many goddesses.[12] Although Torrey's work was remarkable, he neglected the concept of covenant. He failed to recognize Israel's covenantal election – first introduced in the book of Exodus – which refers to the people addressed in Malachi as God's chosen people who share the same divine fatherhood.

Adams C. Welch

In 1935, Adams C. Welch followed in the footsteps of Charles Torrey, opposing the literal traditional view that Malachi 2:10–16 refers to actual human divorce because he held to a figurative view of the passage.[13] Welch claims that the evil rebuked in this passage refers to the Israelites being wedded to a foreign or strange cult, which undermined their covenantal position before Yahweh.[14] His major problem relates to the interpretation of "the daughter of a foreign god," and he questions whether this expression refers to marrying a foreign woman or to worshipping a female deity. Similarly, Welch also finds the identity of "the wife of one's youth" problematic and questions whether this refers to husbands divorcing their wives or to Israel's unfaithfulness to the covenant religion.[15]

Welch offers several reasons for his figurative view. Since the meaning of the two evil acts (marrying "the daughter of a foreign god" and divorcing their "wives") in Malachi 2:10–16 is unclear, he declares that the text is

---

11. Shields, "Syncretism and Divorce," 72–73. Shields concludes that those who interpret this oracular unit figuratively tie their understanding to strong cultic associations. Therefore, he, along with others mentioned, favour a figurative interpretation.

12. H. Haag, "בַּת" in *TDOT*, 1:333–334.

13. Welch, *Post-exilic Judaism*, 119–121.

14. Welch, 119–121.

15. Welch, 120.

corrupt and has no meaning. He also observes that it is far more relevant to connect these two "evil acts" with the period preceding the restoration of the temple rather the period following it.[16] Welch proposes an early date of around 520 BC, claiming that Malachi is a continuation of Haggai and Zechariah. Therefore, he is not convinced that the temple had been rebuilt by the time of Malachi.[17] Based on these reasons, he concludes that Malachi 2:10–16 has no reference to unfaithfulness, divorce and mixed marriages but only to the issue of worship of a foreign deity.[18]

Welch's figurative approach, by dismissing a literal interpretation, also neglects the social context of Malachi's time. It is inadequate to reduce the entirety of Malachi 2:10–16 to the cultic context alone when the literary evidence within the text suggests that Malachi was addressing social and moral problems arising from marital unfaithfulness leading to the breakdown of marriage.

By contrast this study emphasizes that the biblical teaching on divorce should never be studied in isolation and must always be interpreted within the broader context of the biblical understanding of the covenant marriage relationship in the entire OT.

Abel Isaksson

Abel Isaksson's book, which was originally a doctoral dissertation, begins with a reaction to the ongoing discussion of divorce in his time. He observes that all interpretations of Malachi 2:10–16, from Jerome to the present day, have seen two evils rebuked in the text: marrying heathen women and being wedded to a strange cult. While these two interpretations are, in a sense, literal, Isaksson suggests that the issue of divorce in this passage should be seen as a metaphor for worshipping a foreign goddess or an alien deity.[19] He

---

16. Welch, 113–125.
17. Welch, 118–119.
18. Welch, 119–121.
19. Isaksson, *Marriage and Ministry*, 27–29, 30–33. For other scholars who hold similar views to Isaksson, see Peterson, *Zechariah 9–14 and Malachi*; Shields, "Syncretism and Divorce," 68–69; Milgrom, *Cult and Conscience*, 134. Isaksson argues that this oracular unit cannot be identified with marriage as covenant because it lacks the oath used in covenants. Similarly, Ogden observes that "the failure of the present generation of priests to live by the demands of the priestly code" was the issue addressed and that the text does not discuss the social reality of marital unfaithfulness resulting in divorce. Ogden, "Figurative Language," 223.

offers five major arguments in support of his thesis. First, in his exegesis of Malachi 2:10–16, he observes that the interpretation of verse 16 is problematic and that the OT concept of covenant is incompatible with the understanding of marriage during that period.[20]

Another of Isaksson's arguments is based on the phrase "covered the altar of Yahweh with tears" (Mal 2:13). Isaksson proposes that this phrase must allude to ritual mourning, leading him to conclude that the interpretation of tears in Malachi 2:10–16 is figurative and not literal.[21] Based on his observation of textual variants, Isaksson notes that the writers of the Septuagint (LXX) and the Targum (T) did not see verse 16 as a prohibition against divorce; instead they interpreted this verse as granting a continual permission to divorce one's wife.[22]

Isaksson presents his five major arguments as follows: He argues that the meaning of שָׂנֵא שַׁלַּח is unclear because no subject is given for שָׂנֵא and no object is mentioned for שַׁלַּח. Second, he claims that the OT concept of בְּרִית (covenant) is incompatible with the idea of marriage in the OT. Third, he argues that the term "covered the altar of Yahweh with tears" in verse 13 must be an allusion to ritual mourning. Fourth, he argues that neither the LXX nor the T interpret verse 16 as a prohibition against divorce but, instead, treat this verse as granting permission to divorce one's wife. Finally, he concludes that the interpretation that expresses the teaching in Malachi 2:10 mainly as an attack on apostasy to an alien cult is basically in view. He claims that the association of this verse with an alien cult is entirely in agreement with the rest of the book of Malachi since "the Prophet's attention is concentrated on

---

20. Isaksson, *Marriage and Ministry*, 68.

21. Isaksson, 32.

22. Isaksson, 32. For other scholars who hold this view, see Ahlström, *Joel*, 49–50; Matthews, "Tammuz Worship," 47; and Hvidberg, *Weeping and Laughter*, 121–122. Hvidberg argues that the issue is related to a heathen cult. In his interpretation of Malachi 2:10–16, he adopts the view that marriage is not a covenant. He carries this interpretation to an extreme, as demonstrated in his interpretation of two specific phrases in verses 11 and 13. He states that "the expression *bath 'el nackar* in verse 11 undoubtedly cannot – as generally mentioned mean – 'eine Auslander,' 'Heiden'" translated as "A daughter of a god is a goddess." Therefore, Hvidberg connects this phrase with the phrase "covering the altar with tears, weeping and groaning" (Mal 2:13). I believe that Hvidberg reads into Malachi 2:13 things that are not present in the text.

the true religion."[23] Therefore, Isaksson maintains that "Malachi is a priestly reformer, not a prophetic renovator of the ethics of marriage."[24]

This study disagrees with Isaksson's five arguments, particularly his claim that there is no issue of unfaithfulness leading to divorce in the human covenantal marriage relationship in Malachi 2:10–16. Isaksson's arguments are not persuasive, and this text can be interpreted differently for the reasons set out below.

First, the speaker of the words שָׂנֵא שַׁלַּח (he hates sending away) is clearly יְהוָה. (Yahweh). This translation is preferable. Since the verbal adjective is used as a participle, the pronominal subject need not be present but can be inferred from the context.[25]

Second, the idea of בְּרִית. (covenant) is prominent and is used in the OT not only in a cultic context but also in relation to marriage.[26]

Third, in response to Isaksson's third argument regarding ritual mourning, it is relevant to note that while ritual mourning is found in the OT, the only positive reference to such cultic tears is found in Ezekiel 8:14, where women weep for the goddess Tammaz. However, the tears in Malachi 2:13 are the tears of the divorced wives in the postexilic community.

Fourth, as revealed by Douglas Stuart, most manuscripts of the Septuagint, Targum, and Vulgate avoid the ordinary sense of כִּי (for) and interpret the term כִּי (if) as a conditional "if." Although the text is corrupt and has proven textually difficult for translators, there is no need to emend verse 16. This is because the translation prefers the consonantal text and re-pointing to make "hates" a *qal* active participle and to serve as the subject of sending away.

Finally, there are several weaknesses in Isaksson's argument that the text focuses solely on idolatry. Although much of the book of Malachi critiques the pagan cult, there is clear evidence that the entirety of Malachi cannot be interpreted from this single perspective. While Isaksson's insightful focus on the understanding of covenant relationship relating to cult or idolatry in the text is highly commendable, he places too much emphasis on the cultic

---

23. Isaksson, *Marriage and Ministry*, 32.

24. Isaksson, 32. For another scholar who follows Isaksson's view, see Matthews, "Tammuz Worship," 44.

25. Kautzsch and Cowley, *Gesenius' Hebrew Grammar*, 1165.

26. Genesis 31:50; Proverbs 2:17; Ezekiel 16:8; Hosea 1–2. See also a discussion of *berith* for marriage in the work of Woudstra, "Everlasting Covenant," 25.

context and neglects the theological understanding of the issue of unfaithfulness leading to divorce in human covenantal marriage relationships.

While there is much to agree with in Isaksson's understanding of the cultic context, particularly his excellent insights into the connection between idolatry and the broader context of the book, there are still some areas he neglects. Isaksson ignores the personal and social aspects of the covenant, which are emphasized in both the Torah and prophetic traditions. He also neglects the judgement that will come upon three groups of people mentioned in Malachi 2:10–16 who, according to Malachi 3:5 face the judgement which will come upon those who violate the unity of the common fatherhood in the covenant (2:10), those who violate the unity of the common brotherhood in the covenant, and those who fail to uphold the covenantal obligations of the human marriage bond.[27]

Julia M. O'Brien

Julia M. O'Brien is another scholar who uses a similar form of criticism in her engagement with Malachi 2:10–16.[28] She argues that the central issue addressed in Malachi 2:10–16 has nothing to do with divorce but that this passage takes the form of a *rib* or covenant lawsuit.[29] In the early pages of her book, O'Brien calls attention to the different methods – such as tradition-historical and source-critical approaches – that previous scholars used in their engagement with Malachi 2:10–16. O'Brien, however, employs a form-critical approach by reconstructing the book. She claims that the entire book of Malachi fits "the pattern and mentality of the classical *rib*"[30] and uses this approach to actively engage with Malachi 2:10–16. Her position is that the book of Malachi only rebukes the priests and "accuses the people of worshipping other deities; it does not concern intermarriage."[31]

---

27. Clendenen and Taylor, *Haggai–Malachi*, 321.
28. O'Brien, *Priest and Levite*, 63–80. See also O'Brien, "Malachi in Recent Research," 85.
29. O'Brien, *Priest and Levite*, 63, 79.
30. O'Brien, 63–80. See also O'Brien, "Malachi in Recent Research," 85.
31. O'Brien, *Priest and Levite*, 121–123, 144. See also, Isaksson, *Marriage and Ministry*, 31–32. For a similar view, see also Ahlstrom, "Joel," 49–50, and Ogden, "Figurative Language," 223. Ogden observes that "the failure of the present generation of priests to live by the demands of the priestly code" was the issue addressed and that no social reality of mixed marriages and divorce in the postexilic community was present.

Some aspects of O'Brien's work do present a comprehensive ideological engagement with the various reasons why Malachi should be read as a harsh and abusive book. However O'Brien moves beyond interpretation, instead reconstructing the text's meaning and pointing out how bad, unjust, and ridiculous the text is.[32] A key feature of her argument pertains to the gender shift or the use of feminine gender for Yahweh as a means of feminizing Him in the book of Malachi.[33] O'Brien suggests that there is lack of grammatical agreement for Judah and Yahweh as far as gender is concerned, thereby concluding that Yahweh is a hermaphrodite, with no definite gender.[34]

O'Brien's argument on gender shift in her interpretation of Malachi 2:10–16 is her way of explaining to readers the disparity in God's gender as portrayed in the text. She finds this gender shift problematic and maintains that if God is feminine, then he is not a father at all.[35] Therefore, she offers a literary method in the form of deconstruction for interpreting gender and power hierarchies in Malachi.[36] She asserts that it is clear to her that "deconstruction was a way to resist that rhetoric."[37] The term "deconstruction" is a literary method most often associated with Jacques Derrida, who influenced Western literary studies between the late 1960s to the 1990s.[38] O'Brien's approach to biblical studies shifts the focus away from authorial intention, to presenting her own meaning and, thereby, undermining attempts to approach the text from its author's intended meaning. Those who use this deconstruction method teach that "no one, whether author, speaker, or God, is present out there to ground the meaning of a text"[39] and argue that an interpreter presents their own meaning.

---

32. O'Brien, *Priest and Levite*, 111–121.

33. O'Brien, "On Saying No," 208. See also O'Brien, "Judah as Wife," 247–250 and O'Brien, "On Saying No," 112–113.

34. Robert Jeffrey Ratner observes that lack of gender agreement is not uncommon in biblical Hebrew. Ratner, "Gender Agreement."

35. O'Brien, "Judah as Wife," 249.

36. O'Brien, "On Saying No," *Semeia* 72, 112–113, and O'Brien, "On Saying No," 208.

37. O'Brien, *Priest and Levite*, 113. See also O'Brien, "Judah as Wife," 113.

38. See Longman, *Literary Approaches*, 42. See also Baker and Arnold, *Old Testament Studies*, 108.

39. Baker and Arnold, *Old Testament Studies*, 107–108.

On the issue of historical connection, O'Brien does not agree that the book of Malachi bears any connection to the books of Ezra-Nehemiah.[40] She argues that the oracular unit of study in Malachi 2:10–16 is not an attack on divorce but an attack against idolatry and insincere worship.[41] O'Brien's key concern is the interpretation of the phrase בַּת־אֵל נֵכָר (daughter of a foreign god) where she suggests that this phrase describes a goddess in Malachi 2:10–16[42] and that the issue described in this passage is "a modification of the marriage metaphor used elsewhere in the Prophets."[43] Therefore, the text does not address the issue of unfaithfulness leading to divorce but, rather, Judah's profanation of the very holiness of Yahweh by marrying "the daughter of a foreign god."[44]

O'Brien's form-critical approach articulates a set of norms that call for a deconstruction of the book of Malachi, particularly Malachi 2:10–16. This study however aims to interpret Malachi in the context of the whole biblical canon, and from this persepctive O'Brien's approach, which interprets Malachi in isolation from other books in the biblical canon is fundamentally lacking. In addition, O'Brien demonstrates extreme scepticism about the possibility of meaning in Malachi 2:10–16.

Elizabeth Achtemeier

Elizabeth Achtemeier's interpretation of Malachi 2:10–16 departs from the existing tradition-historical, source-critical, and form-critical approaches discussed earlier in this work.[45] She observes that the key issue in this oracular unit concerns "the dailiness of life, obeying God's commands in daily relations with neighbours and friends."[46]

---

40. O'Brien, *Priest and Levite*, 122, 133. O'Brien rejects the idea of external historical controls on Malachi.

41. O'Brien, 122, 144. See also Ogden, "Figurative Language," 223. Ogden follows previous scholars and their interpretative approach, especially in tying the oracular unit to figurative interpretation. He argues that "the anomalies produced by a literal reading of Malachi" [do not concern themselves with] "the failure of the present generation of priests to live by the demands of the priestly code."

42. O'Brien, "Historical Criticism," 57–79. See also O'Brien, *Priest and Levite*, 66–69, and O'Brien, "Judah as Wife," 249.

43. O'Brien, "Malachi in Recent Research," 88.

44. O'Brien, 57–59.

45. Achtemeier, *Nahum–Malachi* , vii.

46. Achtemeier, 175.

In her study of Malachi 2:10–16, Achtemeier links the central theme to "the vitality of the covenant relationship."[47] She argues that the form used in this passage is a court setting that combines the genres of prophetic disputation and prophetic Torah.[48] Achtemeier observes that "if there was no covenant, Israel's life had no purpose and God was not acting to save his world."[49] She claims that the covenant that God, the divine lover, made with Israel's forefathers must be given central importance, pointing out that God was a witness to this covenantal marriage union.[50]

For Achtemeier, the concept of marriage as a covenant furnishes the leading motif for this passage in Malachi[51] and she disagrees with scholars who link Malachi 2:10–16 exclusively to Deuteronomic origins. Achtemeier also asserts that the other books of the Pentateuch and prophetic traditions form the background that shapes this oracular unit.[52]

A significant contribution of Achtemeier's book is her understanding of the background to Malachi 2:10–16, which includes not just Deuteronomy but other books in the Torah. Her book contains many other helpful insights, especially her call for further investigation into the covenantal relationship as described in other books of the Pentateuch and prophetic traditions. A weakness of her work is her failure to deal with the historical background of Malachi and provide a thorough grammatical explanation of Malachi 2:10–16. Her call for further investigate provides impetus for a fresh perception of the passage using historical-grammatical exegesis for a better understanding of Malachi 2:10–16.

Beth Glazier-McDonald

Beth Glazier-McDonald's work departs from the well-worn path of the historical-critical method. Glazier-McDonald has done extensive work on the interpretation of Malachi. Her first work focuses on Malachi 2:12 and takes a

---

47. Achtemeier, 176.
48. Achtemeier, 172.
49. Achtemeier, 176.
50. Achtemeier, 182.
51. Achtemeier, 182.
52. Achtemeier, 172, 181–182. For a similar position see also Klein, "Introduction to Malachi," 27. Others who advocate for a similar position include Fishbane, *Biblical Interpretation*, 332–334; Meyers, "Priestly Language," 232; and Glazier-McDonald, "Ma'ak Habberit," 79.

fresh look at the Hebrew phrase עֵר וְעֹנֶה (everyone who awakes and answers).[53] In subsequent works, she considers the entire unit of Malachi 2:10–16, focusing on intermarriage, divorce, and the Hebrew phrase בַּת־אֵל נֵכָר (daughter of a foreign god).[54] Glazier-McDonald's dissertation, published by the Society for Biblical Literature, is her major work, in which attention is given to the interpretation of the whole book of Malachi.

In Glazier-McDonald's work, which is a standard critical and exegetical resource, she examines the book of Malachi using historical and descriptive literary analysis to defend reading the prophecy as a poetic composition.[55] She demonstrates that the work enjoys a kind of unity and that the book is "held together by parallelism, repetition of grammatical elements, assonance and similar poetic devices."[56] Her translation and commentary on the oracular unit of Malachi 2:10–16 provides a thorough engagement with the issue of divorce. She reviews the interpretative history prior to her[57] and proceeds into text and commentary.

In her text and commentary, Glazier-McDonald concludes that Malachi 2:10–16 deals with the people's unfaithfulness to God in respect to their covenantal obligations in two phases.[58] First, the people sinned against Yahweh by violating the covenant through a treacherous act.[59] Second, this violation goes beyond this first level and also "denotes faithlessness in marriage, deserting one's legal partner and cementing a relationship with someone else."[60]

Glazier-McDonald departs from the existing position of scholars whose key concern was the debate over whether the sole focus of the text is the issue of idolatry or physical human marriage. This is clearly stated in the summary of her position, which states that scholars have adopted two positions in the interpretation of this passage.[61] However, Glazier-McDonald claims that "each

---

53. Glazier-McDonald, "Malachi 2:12," 295–298.
54. Glazier-McDonald, "Intermarriage," 603–611.
55. Glazier-McDonald, *Malachi: The Divine Messenger*, 5.
56. Glazier-McDonald, 4
57. Glazier-McDonald, 99–120.
58. Glazier-McDonald, 84–85.
59. Glazier-McDonald, 85.
60. Glazier-McDonald, 85. See also Glazier-McDonald, "Malachi," 233.
61. Glazier-McDonald, *Malachi: The Divine Messenger*, 120.

of these interpretations is incomplete."[62] Her exegesis reveals that "all three of these nuances of (*begad*), covenant faithlessness, marital faithlessness and faithlessness to Yahweh and his cult, are present in Malachi 2:10–16 and are closely interrelated,"[63] leading to the violation of the bond that unites the people in these three areas. Glazier-McDonald's position is that the three basic nuances of covenant faithlessness – which were mentioned earlier in this work – are related and add "pathos to the text by heightening the severity of the offense. Thus any attempt to penetrate the *ipsissima verba* [exact word][64] of this oracle unit must take both into account."[65]

Glazier-McDonald views the interpretation of the text from two perspectives. Since Malachi is concerned about the purity of the cult, there is an element of figurative understanding of the unit.[66] However, Glazier-McDonald is also concerned about unfaithfulness in human marriage and the issue of divorce.[67] Some commentators follow her line of interpretation, viewing the issue of marriage and divorce in Malachi 2:10–16 from two perspectives. With regard to the use of the term "covenant," they view בְּרִית (covenant) as referring primarily to Yahweh's covenant with Israel and secondarily to the literal marriage covenant.[68]

Glazier-McDonald also responds well to O'Brien's form-critical method. She argues that "Malachi was not the first to employ this question and answer schema. Indeed numerous examples are scattered throughout the OT but Malachi's usage of this form is different because the concise statement of fact that precedes each question is peculiar to Malachi's style."[69] She pays attention to an area that O'Brien neglected – a review of the period's history – and connects Malachi 2:10–16 to the historical situation during the time of Ezra

---

62. Glazier-McDonald, 120.
63. Glazier-McDonald, 85.
64. The literal translation of the German word *ipsissima verba* to English is mine.
65. Glazier-McDonald, *Malachi: The Divine Messenger*, 120. See also Glazier-McDonald, "Intermarriage," 609.
66. Glazier-McDonald, *Malachi: The Divine Messenger*, 115.
67. Glazier-McDonald, 116.
68. Moore, *Haggai and Malachi*, 134. See also Fausset, "Malachi," 738; Glazier-McDonald, "Intermarriage,", 609–610; and Glazier-McDonald, *Malachi: The Divine Messenger*, 119–120.
69. Glazier-McDonald, *Malachi: The Divine Messenger*, 21. And see Clendenen and Taylor, *Haggai–Malachi*, 219. Numerous examples of the question-and-answer format can also be found in other OT books (Deut 29:24–25; 1 Kings 9:8–9; Isa 49:1; 50:1–2; Jer 13:12–14; 15:1, 5; 22:8–9; Ezek 11:21; 18:19; Amos 5:18; Hag 1:9; 2:11–12).

and Nehemiah.[70] While her work commendably defends a poetic interpretation of the prophecy, it does not go beyond the second step in historical-grammatical exegesis. This study, however, goes further, emphasizing the importance of applying the text and considering its pastoral implications for the faith community.

Richard A. Taylor and E. Ray Clendenen

Another interpretation of Malachi comes from Richard A. Taylor and E. Ray Clendenen.[71] They regard Malachi as an "oracle from a divine creator, Redeemer, and Lord."[72] They argue that the book deals with the nature of God and the relationship between the covenant members, setting out their responsibilities to God as well as to the other members of the covenant community.[73]

Clendenen and Taylor deal extensively with issues of authorship, authenticity, dating, and the historical context of the exile and restoration, as well as the economic and political situation in Judah.[74] They link the problem described in Malachi 2:10–16 to the situation prevailing during the time and ministry of Ezra and Nehemiah.[75] They also emphasize the importance of identifying both the genre and structure of the book. In their opinion, the genre should be seen as a prophetic oracle, not through "form-critical markers but as a rhetorical device."[76] They conclude that identification of the rhetoric is helpful in understanding the message of the book. Their work departs from traditional methods discussed earlier in this work, especially the historical-critical method, which tends to overlook the book's unity. Clendenen and Taylor state that the book should not be viewed as "a set of six loosely connected oracles . . . [but as] a unified hortatory discourse."[77] While acknowledging that the failure of the priests of Judah was a significant issue, they argue that the book also addresses other important concerns, such as immoral

---

70. Glazier-McDonald, *Malachi: The Divine Messenger*, 7–13.
71. Clendenen and Taylor, *Haggai–Malachi*.
72. Clendenen and Taylor, 203.
73. Clendenen and Taylor, 204.
74. Clendenen and Taylor, 204–215.
75. Clendenen and Taylor, 216–217.
76. Clendenen and Taylor, 223.
77. Clendenen and Taylor, 229.

behaviour towards one another.[78] In their exegesis of Malachi 2:10–16, they categorically state that

> vv 11–12 concentrate on instances of Judah's violation of their covenant with God, involving marriage to pagan women, [and that] vv 13–15a focus on violations of the marriage covenant. This argues against those who would see vv 10–16 as concerned with only one issue, either spiritual apostasy, marriage to pagan woman, or divorce.[79]

Their work is commendable in the sense that it emphasizes the central concern over treacherous acts against fellow covenant members. However, they do not explain how this central concern can be applied to contemporary readers. By contrast this author's work presents a pastoral guide for solving marital problems in the marriage union in the faith community.

Pieter A. Verhoef

Pieter A. Verhoef was a reformed theologian in Africa, who wrote a scholarly commentary on the books of Haggai and Malachi. His commentary on Malachi is divided into three parts. He begins with a discussion of the book's title and authorship; then, having established authorship and date, he briefly discusses the historical background, placing the book of Malachi in the postexilic period.[80] With regard to the unity and authenticity of the book, Verhoef criticizes previous scholars who claimed that some passages were later additions because of a lack of continuity with earlier prophecy[81] and argues that the book reveals uniformity in language and vocabulary.

Verhoef applies a modest structural analysis to Malachi 2:10–16. This approach involves dividing the book into pericopes, analyzing sentences and discourses, and examining various literary devices. Verhoef divides the entire book – apart from the heading – into seven pericopes and uses verse-by-verse exposition in his interpretation of both the entire book and the particular section of study.[82] He observes that prophecy derives more from

---

78. Clendenen and Taylor, 231.
79. Clendenen and Taylor, 342.
80. Verhoef, *Haggai and Malachi*, 160–161.
81. Verhoef, 163.
82. Verhoef, 171, 265.

divine revelation than from historical events. Although he touches on this in certain parts of the introduction, he shows less interest in the historical dimensions of Malachi and, instead, provides technical exegetical assistance and homiletical suggestions for readers.

In his structural analysis, Verhoef divides the entire book into seven pericopes using God's statements and the people's responses and arranging these in a chiastic structure.[83] In Malachi 2:10–16, he argues that the central theme is the covenant with Levi and that the major focus of this pericope is Israel's intimate relationship with Yahweh.[84] He also observes that the covenantal relationship not only involves God but also certain obligations of the priests towards their office and their community. If this relationship is not safeguarded, it could be "endangered when a foreign element is introduced by way of religiously mixed marriages. Such marriages reflect faithlessness and profane the covenant. The whole spectrum of the covenant relationship is thereby affected."[85] Verhoef concludes that the problem in Malachi 2:10–16 is not just the issues resulting from religious intermarriage but also "the accusation of being unfaithful toward a legal wife [which] is introduced by the well-known pattern of statement-question-answer."[86] I agree with his observation because the people addressed in Malachi 2:10–16 are bound to one another through a covenantal faith in the one true God. In contrast to those who interpret the text figuratively – and see it as pointing to idolatry – Verhoef views marriage as a covenant and divorce as covenant-breaking. He presents a literal interpretation, referring to marriages with heathen women – that is, the daughters of foreign gods – as unholy alliances.[87] One of his strongest arguments is that the evidence for viewing marriage as a covenant and divorce as covenant-breaking is seen in "God's severe displeasure against the culprits who have divorced their legal wives."[88] In addition, the warning against being faithless to the wife of one's youth is another strong objection to those who hold to a merely figurative interpretation of the covenantal relationship in the text. Verhoef claims that the book is prosaic. By contrast the present

---

83. Verhoef, 171.
84. Verhoef, 174–175.
85. Verhoef, 175.
86. Verhoef, 175, 264.
87. Verhoef, 269–270, 274–275.
88. Verhoef, 176. And also compare 279.

work will demonstrate that most of the prophetic texts are poetic including Malachi 2:10–16.

Gordon P. Hugenberger

Another important work on Malachi is that of Gordon P. Hugenberger,[89] who systematically examines the book and focuses on the key critical issues in Malachi 2:10–16. He begins by surveying recent scholarship on marriage in the OT. While acknowledging that a great deal has been done by scholars on various aspects of marriage, he notes that the relationship between biblical marriage law and covenantal concepts has been neglected.[90] He states that he is "not seeking to elucidate the actual practice of marriage in ancient Israel which, no doubt, often fell short of the prophetic ideal" and adds, "Ours is rather a study of that ideal; a study of Old Testament canonical ethics."[91] Hugenberger observes that the book of Malachi originates from the period contemporaneous with the ministries of Ezra and Nehemiah.[92] To justify the need for his work, Hugenberger then considers the interpretative context of Malachi 2:10–16 by examining its historical and literary context[93] and literary structure.[94] On the identification of the issue of unfaithfulness in Malachi 2:10–16 he observes that there have been various interpretations. Some link the issue of marriage as a covenant in Malachi 2:10–16 to ancient Near Eastern law, using the comparative study of religions in the ancient Near East and Israel.[95] A few scholars insist that the marriage described in this passage is not a literal human marriage but a figurative one, symbolizing idolatry.[96] Still others maintain that it is figurative but relates to a covenant with Israel[97] or

---

89. Hugenberger, *Marriage as a Covenant*.
90. Hugenberger, 1.
91. Hugenberger, 12.
92. Hugenberger, 15.
93. Hugenberger, 13–20.
94. Hugenberger, 23–26.
95. Hugenberger, 10. See also Redditt, "Malachi in Its Social Setting," 240–255. See also Verhoef, *Haggai and Malachi*, 180, 182.
96. Hugenberger, *Marriage as a Covenant*, 12. See also Isaksson, *Marriage and Ministry*, 33; Hvidberg, *Weeping and Laughter*, 123; and Torrey, "Prophecy of 'Malachi,'" 1–15.
97. Hugenberger, *Marriage as a Covenant*, 5. See also, Vawter, "Biblical Theology of Divorce," 223–243.

between individuals – that is, the priests in the community during Malachi's time.[98] All these strands represent figurative interpretations of the text.

Hugenberger observes that there are contradictory views even among those who support the identification of marriage as covenant and divorce as covenant-breaking.[99] He evaluates and responds to five major arguments of those who propose a literal interpretation.[100] While surveying the arguments of those who do not view marriage as a covenant and divorce as covenant-breaking, he maintains that the majority of the arguments presented by this group are not persuasive because these scholars place too much emphasis on the cultic context in their interpretation of the text. Noting these issues with the existing interpretative approaches, Hugenberger argues that the primary interpretative problem of Malachi 2:10–16 is whether the text should be understood as referring to a literal marriage or a symbolic one, although he neglects the issue of unfaithfulness, which is also addressed in the text.[101] Hugenberger states that resolving this problem requires an understanding of the literary aspects of obscure phrases such as "the daughter of a foreign god" (2:11 NRSV), "you cover the LORD's altar with tears" (2:13 NRSV), and the even more problematic 2:15, which some scholars regard as one of the most difficult verses in the OT.[102] On the issue of divorce, too, Hugenberger observes that there are diverse interpretations and outlines nine interpretative approaches, which he groups into four major categories.[103]

The first category consists of approaches that deny any reference to divorce in Malachi 2:10–16 because they fail to recognize the certainty of verse 16.[104]

---

98. Ogden, "Figurative Language," 20–22.

99. Hugenberger, *Marriage as a Covenant*, 20–22. See also, Ogden, "Figurative Language," 2–3. See also Van der Woude, "Malachi's Struggle," 68–69, and Rudolph, "Zu Mal 2:10–16," 85–90.

100. Hugenberger, *Marriage as a Covenant*, 27–29. See also, Ogden, "Figurative Language," 20–22.

101. Hugenberger, *Marriage as a Covenant*, 7. See also. Ogden, "Figurative Language," 20–22.

102. Hugenberger, *Marriage as a Covenant*, 8. See also. Ogden, "Figurative Language," 18.

103. Hugenberger, 51.

104. Hugenberger, 51–57. For a detailed discussion of these people, see Ogden, "Figurative Language," 20–22. For other examples of those who hold this view, see Isaksson, *Marriage and Ministry*, 32; O'Brien, *Priest and Levite*, 72–73; Torrey, "Prophecy of 'Malachi,'" 10; and Van der Woude, "Malachi's Struggle," 66–69. Isaksson, Torrey, and Van der Woude maintain that Malachi 2:10–16 does not deal with divorce at all.

Scholars in this group claim that the text and meaning of Malachi 2:10–16 are too uncertain to affirm that the passage addresses the subject of divorce. They maintain that Malachi's intent in verse 16 is not to condemn divorce but, rather, to address the subordination and mistreatment of married Jewish women by their husbands because of foreign, heathen wives.[105]

According to Hugenberger, the second category includes those who interpret the passage as requiring or permitting divorce. Some of those scholars misinterpret the Hebrew word שִׁלַּח (he sends away);[106] others see the term "divorce" as referring only to permission to divorce heathen wives;[107] and still others view divorce as the lesser of two evils.[108] Within this category, there is a significant diversity of views regarding Malachi's precise attitude towards divorce.

The third category comprises those who interpret Malachi 2:10–16 as an absolute prohibition of any kind of divorce because they link the issue in this passage to Deuteronomy 24.[109] These scholars claim that the Deuteronomic law of divorce must be upheld at all times.[110]

The final category consists of those who limit the kind of divorce prohibited in Malachi 2:10–16.[111] This category has two major divisions.[112] Some scholars maintain that Malachi prohibits divorce only when initiated by the woman, while others argue that divorce is prohibited when it is unjustified – that is, divorce based purely on aversion.[113]

Hugenberger specifically states that the purpose of his work is to reassess the existing controversies surrounding the terms "covenant marriage" and "divorce," using Malachi as a point of departure.[114] He rejects the view held by those who do not view marriage as a covenant and divorce as

---

105. Hugenberger, *Marriage as a Covenant*, 52–53.
106. Hugenberger, 58.
107. Hugenberger, 59–60.
108. Hugenberger, 60.
109. Hugenberger, 62–66. Those who hold this view include Rudolph, "Zu Mal 2:10–16," 85–90. Compare Smith, *Micah–Malachi*, 319–210, and Verhoef, *Haggai and Malachi*, 278.
110. Hugenberger, *Marriage as a Covenant*, 64.
111. Hugenberger, 66–76.
112. Hugenberger, 66–67.
113. Hugenberger, 67.
114. Hugenberger, 2.

covenant-breaking, claiming that the OT presents marriage as a divinely protected covenant between husband and wife.[115]

One strength of Hugenberger's work is his argument against the view that interprets the term "daughter of foreign god" in a cultic context. He argues that some scholars who stress affinity with idolatry place too much emphasis on the cultic context of Malachi 2:10–16 while neglecting the issue of unfaithfulness that the passage addresses. He also points out that while the prophet's concern with cult matters may be evident, the fact that the prophet addresses cultic matters does not exclude his concern with personal or social ethics.[116] Hugenberger maintains that the prophet is addressing a historical situation in postexilic Judah.[117]

Another strength of Hugenberger's argument is his interpretation of the Hebrew word שָׁלַח (he sends away). He notes that this verb "is found elsewhere in the Old Testament in the context of marriage where it refers to the attitude of husbands toward their wives."[118] He also emphasizes that the usage of the term "hate" alongside "marriage" as a technical formula is attested to in the Aramaic marriage contracts of the Elephantine Papyri.[119] In the same vein, based on the grammar and context of the oracular unit, he notes that the Old Testament consistently portrays human marriage as a covenant and demonstrates that בְּרִית (covenant) refers to the marriage covenant between husband and wife, rather than solely to religious affiliation.[120] Hugenberger's work on the issue of marriage and covenant is highly commendable, particularly in the way he connects the covenant relationship in marriage to themes found in Genesis and Deuteronomy. However, one weakness of his work is that it does not discuss the issue of unfaithfulness in other pentateuchal sources – Exodus, Leviticus, and Numbers – or the prophetic corpus in the OT.

---

115. Hugenberger, 27–30, 36, 68, 98–101. In chapters 6–8, Hugenberger deals with the notion of covenant as applied to marriage.
116. Hugenberger, 34–36, 47.
117. Hugenberger, 34–36.
118. Hugenberger, 72.
119. Hugenberger, 71.
120. Hugenberger, 29, 47, 340

Andrew E. Hill

Andrew E. Hill argues that the canonicity of Malachi has never been in doubt.[121] Historically, he connects the situation in Judah to the time of Ezra-Nehemiah;[122] literarily, he relates it to the time of Haggai and Zachariah. Hill writes, "Finally, I align myself with those who opt to read Malachi in a larger context, namely Haggai-Zechariah-Malachi corpus."[123] This contrasts with the view held by Julia M. O'Brien, who claims that a covenant lawsuit pertains solely to idolatry.[124] Covenant lawsuit, which is a genre of prophetic disputation, also addresses social and relational problems. Since Yahweh's covenant is comprehensive, it includes provision for both vertical (human-divine) and horizontal (human-human) relationships. Hill upholds the integrity of the pericope and argues that in Malachi 2:10–16, the prophet is not only addressing the issue of idolatry but also unfaithfulness resulting from the people's failure to observe the covenantal regulations – a failure that leads to a breach of faith with the wives of their youth.[125]

Summary of the Chapter

This chapter began with a review of some relevant literature on Malachi. There is an abundance of scholarly material on the structure of the book of Malachi. It is also observed that, in this dispensation, Malachi 2:10–16 is still considered "one of the most important yet most difficult pericopes in the book of Malachi."[126] This brief overview of interpretations demonstrates that various interpretative opinions exist and shows how the text has been interpreted over time.

The dominant scholarly views include those who argue that the passage addresses the Israelites who were wedded to a foreign or strange cult. These scholars do not view marriage as a covenant; nor do they recognize in

---

121. Hill, *Malachi: A New Translation*, 12.
122. Hill, 51–76.
123. Hill, 23.
124. Hill, 31. See O'Brien, *Priest and Levite*, 79.
125. Hill, 43–4, 223, 242–43, 258–259
126. Smith, *Micah–Malachi*, 325. Smith notes that, at the time of writing his statement, the debate on whether the interpretation is figurative or literal was still continuing. This ongoing debate is evident in the work of other prominent scholars who followed after Smith.

Malachi 2:10–16 any kind of unfaithfulness resulting in divorce within the covenantal marriage relationship. Instead, they claim that Malachi 2:10–16 is a metaphor for idolatry, in the form of an unholy alliance formed by Israel with foreign nations. They claim that this passage merely refers to idolatry without adequately addressing the issue of physical unfaithfulness within the marriage union.

There are also scholars who view marriage as a covenant and divorce as a covenant-breaking action.[127] This group includes scholars who link the issue of divorce in Malachi 2:10–16 to the background of the Deuteronomic divorce laws. Others consider this unit a later addition or an interpolation. Some scholars see this unit as having an essential unity within the text. There are also scholars who do not view marriage as a covenant or see divorce as either a covenant-breaking act or as sending away wives.

Within these interpretations there are three essential strands. The first strand is the metaphorical understanding of the passage, in the form of a figurative or symbolic marriage to God, as stated earlier in this work. The second relates to the priestly covenantal relationship. The third strand interprets the passage as a reference to both Yahweh's covenant and, in a secondary sense, the literal marriage covenant.[128] In addition, there are also different strands when it comes to the interpretation of marriage as a covenant and divorce as covenant-breaking. Some commentators argue that this section is a typological allusion to the practice of idolatry – which entered Israel as a result of intermarriage in the postexilic community – and that the issue of unfaithfulness resulting in the breaking of the marriage covenant is not the key issue.[129]

The debate between the metaphorical and literal interpretations remains ongoing.[130] There are two main schools of thought when it comes to the interpretation of Malachi 2:10–16: those who connect the passage to idolatry and those who focus on the literal human marriage relationship. While

---

127. Zehnder, "Fresh Look at Malachi," 228. He argues that the section deals with a conjugal relationship between men belonging to the Yahweh-congregation and their wives. See also Hugenberger, *Marriage as a Covenant*, 98–101. I am indebted to Gordon P. Hugenberger for his sound and dynamic discussion of these arguments. His work is well-documented and responds to this figurative interpretative engagement of Malachi 2:10–16.

128. More, *A Critical Commentary on Haggai and Malachi*, 134; Fausset, "Malachi".

129. O'Brien, "On Saying No," 122.

130. Smith, *Micah–Malachi*, 325. See also Achtemeier, *Nahum–Malachi*, 181.

both sides of the scholarly debate are tenable, the unique contribution of this work is not centred on whether the text is literal or figurative. Instead, it attempts to clarify how Malachi addresses the issue of marital unfaithfulness, offering guidance for solving marital problems within the marriage union and considering the pastoral implications of Malachi 2:10–16 for the church community and society at large.

CHAPTER THREE

Study Methodology

Introduction

The previous chapter reviewed the history of scholarship in Malachi, spanning the period from the late nineteenth century to the dawn of the new millennium. This review considered various scholars and their approaches to studying Malachi. The historical-critical method – along with various tools such as source criticism, form criticism, and the comparative study of religions – was used in the interpretation of Malachi. This review provides the necessary context for the present task in chapter 3.

The preceding chapters discussed the approaches used and the presuppositions underlying the study of Malachi 2:10–16. This chapter will describe the methodological approach of the present work – the use of the historical-grammatical exegetical method, which helps in deriving meaning from the text.

Description of Methods

Literary Criticism

During the last three decades, there have been varied approaches to literary criticism. Cephas T. A. Tushima observes that amid growing dissatisfaction with the use of the historical-critical method for studying biblical texts, a new literary method for engaging with biblical texts was introduced.[1] This method of literary criticism treats the text as a finished piece of writing.

---

1. Tushima, *Fate of Saul's Progeny*, 68.

Literary studies may mean different things to different people. In the past, it referred to the older historical-critical approaches – such as source, form, tradition, and redaction criticism – used by the scholars reviewed in chapter 2 of this work. Such methods are used to dissect texts, especially in the search for their origins and development. But newer methods – such as such as narrative analysis, structuralism, rhetorical criticism, reader response, and ideological readings[2] – focus more on texts as texts. However, some go to the extent of denying that the biblical text has any fixed or determinative meaning. Baker and Arnold observe,

> Since the 1940s, the field of literary studies has passed through successive stages on new approaches to literary texts. Once the connection with authorial was severed, the search was for a new locus of meaning . . . attention moved to the reader (reader-response and ideological reading) and then finally to a denial of any meaning at all.[3]

The Historical-Grammatical Exegetical Method
A Description of Historical-Grammatical Exegesis

Historical-grammatical exegesis as a method of Bible interpretation can be traced back to the time of Origen, was developed further during the Renaissance, was supported by the Reformers, and was formalized in the modern era (the eighteenth to the nineteenth centuries).[4] This method strives to discover the original meaning intended by the biblical authors.[5] It rejects, in varying degrees, the historical-critical method, which, as discussed earlier in this work, dominated the interpretation of Malachi 2:10–16 in the writings of scholars such as Charles Torrey, Adam Welch, and Abel Isaksson. However, with the emergence of new approaches, there is now an alternative paradigm for the interpretation of Malachi 2:10–16 in current scholarship.

---

2. Longman, *Literary Approaches*, 25–45. See also: Baker and Arnold, *Old Testament Studies*, 102–112.

3. Baker and Arnold, *Old Testament Studies*, 100.

4. Longman, *Literary Approaches*, 25–45. See also Longman, "Historical-Grammatical Exegesis," 137–153.

5. Kaiser, *Exegetical Theology*, 33, 88. See also Dockery and Guthrie, *Holman Guide*, 45, and Longman, *Literary Approaches*, 24–25.

For this work, the literary approach used in the interpretation of Malachi 2:10–16 is the historical-grammatical exegetical method. This approach focuses on the text in its final form and serves as a dynamic approach to the study of Malachi 2:10–16. The interpreter studies the historical background of the author and his intended readers – to the extent that this can be determined. This method assumes that events and experiences of people of the past offer lessons that modern readers can apply to their own lives.

This method of interpreting Scripture focuses on what can be derived from the original historical meaning. In the historical aspect of this method, the interpreter tries to determine the identity and location of the author, the intended audience, the date and circumstances of the writing, information about any individuals and places mentioned in the text, social customs, cultural factors, and the world views of the people of that time and place.[6] In other words, historical exegesis involves studying the historical background of the text as well as its historical foreground (events that happened before and after the writing) so as "to discover what the biblical texts meant to their authors in their relationship with their readers."[7]

The grammatical aspect of historical-grammatical exegesis is also very important for interpreting a biblical text.[8] Here, the interpreter analyses the grammatical structure of the passage, identifying nouns, verbs, adjectives, adverbs, and other parts of speech. In essence, this method aims to discover the author's intent by studying the grammar, syntax, literary genre, and textual and historical context of a biblical passage. This approach seeks to discover the plain and normal meaning of a text in its context, taking into consideration the rules of grammar and figures of speech.

Historical-grammatical exegesis is a process that seeks to determine the exact meaning of a passage by ascertaining the meaning of words (lexicography), the form of words (morphology), the function of words (pragmatics), and the relationship between words (syntax).[9] This method assumes that Scripture is divinely inspired by God and that the Bible was written within a specific historical and geographical situation for a specific purpose.

---

6. Terry, *Biblical Hermeneutics*, 181; Kaiser, *Exegetical Theology*, 88; Dockery and Guthrie, *Holman Guide*, 45.

7. Dockery and Guthrie, *Holman Guide*, 45.

8. Dockery and Guthrie, 45.

9. Baker and Arnold, *Old Testament Studies*, 283,

For instance, the book of Malachi was written in Hebrew, following normal grammatical conventions of the language, uses figurative language, and is a unified work. A distinctive feature of historical-grammatical exegesis is that it seeks to comprehend the exact meaning of all the details of a Scripture passage, using principles that help to discover the author's intended meaning.[10]

Stages of Historical-Grammatical Exegesis

This section describes the three basic steps involved in historical-grammatical exegesis. First, the interpreter discusses the general historical background of the text. Understanding the historical aspect is very important because the biblical text, its message, and its claims are anchored in historical events. Therefore, understanding the text requires knowledge of its historical setting. The historical background provides information about the author and his audience, helping to identify who the author is and to whom he is writing. Information about the historical setting also helps in understanding the historical era within which the book was written.[11] It is at this stage that an interpreter considers the prevailing thought at the time of writing and assesses whether the text (in this case, Malachi 2:10–16) is saying something similar to or different from it. Three main elements are considered in relation to this historical background: the sociohistorical and religious-cultural environment, the author and his circumstances, and the audience and their circumstances.[12]

Second, the interpreter studies the literary context of the passage within the broader framework of the book in which it occurs. The ultimate goal of exegesis is to discover the author's intended meaning (what it meant to the original readers) before establishing what it means for contemporary readers. This process of discovering authorial intent requires tracing the author's

---

10. Kaiser, *Exegetical Theology*, 47; Bock and Fanning, *New Testament Text*, 24.
11. Osborne, *Hermeneutical Spiral*, 20.
12. According to Kaiser, "the historical sense is that sense which is demanded by careful consideration of the time and circumstances in which the author wrote. It is the specific meaning which an author's words require when the historical context and background are taken into account," Kaiser, *Toward an Exegetical Theology*, 88.

argument through grammatical-syntactical analysis,[13] lexical analysis,[14] and validation of exegetically significant but problematic phrases or clauses.[15]

The final step in historical-grammatical exegesis involves appropriating the results of the exegesis for both its original recipients and contemporary society.[16] The work does not end with understanding how the first readers would have understood the text but moves beyond to the application of the text: What is the text calling me to do?

In essence, the purpose of historical-grammatical exegesis is to understand, to the extent possible, the author's original intention. Historical-grammatical exegesis is a method of interpretation that requires reading a passage as an organic whole and trying to understand what it expresses in the context of the background of the original human author and the original situation. In the light of the several approaches that has been used for the interpretation of this section, the approach for this study calls for a historical and grammatical understanding of the Bible. The historical background is important in an attempt to grasp the meaning that the author intended to convey through his message, and grammatical exegesis is equally important in an attempt to understand words and relationships between words in their literary contexts.[17] The combination of historical and grammatical exegesis helps this author to ascertain the specific usage of words as employed by Malachi.

However, the literary method has been used by other scholars who have held a different premise. W. K. Wimsatt and M. Beardsley move away from authorial intent in their description of the "intentional fallacy."[18] They argued that "the design or intention of the author is neither available nor desirable as

---

13. See Bock and Fanning, *New Testament Text*, 136–140. A Festschrift in honour of the late Dr. Harold Hoehner, this book is a step-by-step discussion of the exegetical process (part 1) and the application of exegetical principles to selected NT passages (part 2). Though the book is about NT exegesis, the exegetical process it presents is applicable to the OT as well.

14. The goal of lexical analysis is to establish the precise meaning of key terms used in the passage under consideration. To do this, one must recognize the possible range of meanings of the term and then allow the context to determine the appropriate gloss within the semantic field. See Bock, "Lexical Analysis," 136–140.

15. Validation aims to arrive at the most probable interpretation of a text and requires sorting through a variety of possible meanings from commentators and interpreters, evaluating the strengths and weaknesses of each alternative and defending the most probable. For a good description of this process, see Lowery, "Validation: Exegetical Problem Solving," 155–66.

16. Osborne, *Hermeneutical Spiral*, 62.

17. Dockery and Guthrie, *Holman Guide*, 45.

18. Wimsatt and Beardsley, "Intentional Fallacy," 3–20.

a standard for judging the success of a work of literary art; and it seems to us that this is a principle which goes deep into some differences in the history of critical attitudes."[19] T. S. Eliot was another icon for the view that interpretative process is an impersonal one, where the text stands apart from any author.[20] Hirsch also describes a "banishment of the author" theory whose proponents teach that literary texts belong to a distinct ontological realm, where meaning is independent of authorial will.[21]

Those who follow Wimsatt and Eliot also claim "that the author has no control over the words he has loosed upon the world and no special privileges as an interpreter of them."[22] The claim that an author should be banished from his poem led them to believe that the author's intended meaning cannot be known. Eliot rejects the author as the major element in the interpretative process. Hirsch cites a decisive wave of such attacks from Eliot, who claims that he does not believe "that a text means what its author meant."[23] Since Eliot and his contemporaries launched an offensive against authorial intent, their teaching emphasized that the author is not a major element in the interpretative process and that authors have no privileged insights into their own work. Eliot and his contemporaries regarded the best poetry in three ways: as impersonal (with no author), as objective, and as autonomous.[24]

This clamour for meaning independent of the author ruthlessly banishes the author as the determiner of the text's meaning.[25] According to Hirsch, those who hold this view claim that "the best poetry should be impersonal, objective and autonomous; that it leads an afterlife of its own, totally cut off from the life of its author"[26] and that "literature should detach itself from the subjective realm of the author's personal thoughts and feelings."[27] Proponents of the "author-intended meaning cannot be known" theory treat the text as

---

19. Wimsatt and Beardsley, "Intentional Fallacy," 3.

20. Eliot, Thomas Stearns. *On Poetry and Poets*, 1st ed. London: Faber & Faber, 1957, 113–14.

21. Hirsch, *Validity in Interpretation*, 12.

22. Hirsch, *Validity in Interpretation*, 10.

23. Hirsch, 1.

24. Eliot, *On Poetry and Poets*, 113–14. See also Tremper Longman III, *Literary Approaches to Biblical Interpretation*, 25–27 and 53–4.

25. Hirsch, 3.

26. Hirsch, 1.

27. Hirsch, 1.

all-important and the author as being of little contemporary significance. They also claim that it is a fallacy to talk about the author's intention.[28]

Though this theory has been a working assumption for a number of scholars, yet many even in the 1950s and 1960s were not comfortable with this claim and there were several scholars who challenged this and provided a variety of alternative approaches. Hirsch describes the task of Eliot and his contemporaries as "banishment of the author" and the claim that "text and meaning is independent of the author's control" as dangerous.[29] One assumption underlying the banishment of the author from their text is that a poet is unable to make an objective or valid interpretation. Another assumption is that the author is not as important as the poem itself. Proponents claim that "meaning is not what the author meant but what the poem means to different sensitive readers."[30] One major weakness of this view is the claim that the meaning of the text is not the author's meaning. Another weakness is claiming that only the text is important and not the author.

Hirsch defends authorial intention, arguing that the theory of authorial irrelevance and the intentional fallacy ignore "the fact that meaning is an affair of consciousness not of words."[31] He believed that both the poem and the author are important and states,

> A word sequence means nothing in particular until somebody either means something by it or understands something. There is no magic land of meanings outside human consciousness. Whenever meaning is connected to words, a person is making the connection, and the particular meanings he lends to them are never the only legitimate ones under the norms and conventions of his language.[32]

Therefore, Hirsch concludes,

> While it is a fallacy to claim that a particular norm for interpretation is necessarily grounded in the nature of this or that

---

28. Wimsatt and Beardsley, "Intentional Fallacy," 3–18.
29. Hirsch, *Validity in Interpretation*, 1. See also, Longman, *Literary Approaches*, 20–21.
30. Hirsch, *Validity in Interpretation*, 4. See also, Longman, *Literary Approaches*, 20–21.
31. Hirsch, *Validity in Interpretation*, 4.
32. Hirsch, 4.

kind of text, rather than in the interpreter's own will, it is quite another matter to claim that there can be only one sort of norm when interpretation is conceived of as a corporate enterprise. For, it may very well be that there exists only one norm that can be universally compelling and generally sharable.[33]

This norm is that the meaning of a text is to be identified with the author's intended purpose. He also observes that "if the meaning of a text is not the author's, then no interpretation can possibly correspond to the meaning of the text, since the text can have no determinative and determinable meaning."[34] This would mean that no viable normative ideal governs the interpretation of biblical texts.

Hirsch concludes, "No presently known normative concept other than the author's meaning has this universally compelling character. On purely practical grounds, therefore, it is preferable to agree that the meaning of a text is the author's meaning."[35] Therefore, to avoid construing meanings that are different from the author's intended (original) meaning, the historical-grammatical exegesis approach is used in the interpretation of Malachi 2:10–16.

Characteristics of Hebrew Poetry

This section discusses the major elements and characteristics of Hebrew poetry. Poetry is a special use of language in writing.[36] Daniel J. Estes writes, "Poetry is among other things, an attempt to transcend the limitations of normal (prosaic) human language and to give expression to something not easily expressed in words."[37] Robert Alter observes that the artist's purpose is to communicate an expression of the imagination and passion. This spontaneous overflow of powerful feelings is intended to excite readers or hearers and enable them to experience a feeling similar to that which existed in the poet's own heart.[38]

---

33. Hirsch, 25.
34. Hirsch, 25.
35. Hirsch, 25.
36. Bullinger, *Figures of Speech*. See also Kugel, *Idea of Biblical Poetry*, 204–286, and Alter, *Art of Biblical Poetry*.
37. Estes, *Wisdom Books and Psalms*, 144.
38. Alter, *Art of Biblical Poetry*, 3–26.

Alter observes three major features of Hebrew poetry. The first characteristic is the average line length (terseness). Poetry usually has three to four words in each line, each having one beat.[39] It usually communicates its meaning with brevity and uses the best word in the best order. Alter refers to a situation where the poet introduces a term in one line and places further emphasis on it in the next line.

The second feature of Hebrew poetry is parallelism,[40] which is one of its defining characteristics. In parallelism, there are equivalencies of parallel words, thoughts, or sense units.

The final characteristic of Hebrew poetry is that it tends to use more literary devices (figures of speech) than prose.[41] Poetry frequently makes use of such devices. The prophecy in Malachi 2:10–16 evinces a wide variety of poetic forms and figurative language.[42] The next section describes some of these poetic features in Malachi.

Malachi's Use of Poetic and Rhetorical Stylistic Features

Questions have often been raised about Malachi's style. The question remains: Is the book prose or poetry? Various commentators adopt different positions. Walter C. Kaiser maintains that the book is prose.[43] Other scholars, like J. M. P. Smith, argue that some passages appear prosaic, while others seem quite poetic and contain parallelism.[44] It is important to discuss Malachi 2:10–16 in light of its poetic stylistic features since this helps restore literary study of this book through the historical-grammatical exegetical method in the interpretation of Malachi 2:10–16, moving away from interpretive approaches that have fragmented the book of Malachi over the past hundred years. A few of the more prominent poetic stylistic features observed in Malachi are discussed below.

---

39. Alter, 3–26.
40. Alter, 4. See also Bullock, *Old Testament Prophetic Books*, 34–35.
41. Alter, *Art of Biblical Poetry*, 3–4.
42. Bullinger, *Figures of Speech*. See also Bartholomew and O'Dowd, *Old Testament Wisdom Literature*, 62.
43. Kaiser, *Malachi: God's Unchanging Love*, 18.
44. Smith, *A Critical and Exegetical Commentary of Malachi*, 4–5.

Parallelism

> A son honours a father,
> and a servant his master.
> Now if I (am) a father, where (is) my honour?
> And if I (am) a master, where (is) my fear? (1:6)[45]

The arrangement above illustrates parallelism, which is a prominent Hebrew poetic device, in the book of Malachi.

Chiasm

Chiasm is also prominent in the structure of the book. Two examples are as follows:

1. (A) "I have loved you,"
    (B) says Yahweh.
    (B) And you say,
    (A) "How have you loved us?" (1:2)

2. (A) And suddenly he will come to his temple, the Lord,
    (B) whom you are seeking,
    (C) who is the person? The messenger of the covenant,
    (B) whom you are pleased (with).
    (A) Behold, he comes, says the LORD of hosts. (3:1).

Simile and Metaphor

Another major stylistic feature is Malachi's use of both similes and metaphors. These are figurative expressions that take the form of comparisons.[46]

> For he (is) like *fire* of the refiner and like *soap* of the fuller.
> And he will sit (like) a *refiner* and a *purifier* of silver,
> and he will *purify* the sons of Levi,
> and he will *purge* them like *gold* and like *silver* (3:2).

---

45. Translation from Hebrew to English Language is mine.

46. Though both figures of speech are figures of comparison, there is a difference between a simile and a metaphor. A simile completes the truth; a metaphor, however, does not complete a truth but makes a comparison in order to make a point. See Bullinger, *Figures of Speech*, 721–733, 735–743.

> For behold, the day (is) coming, *burning* like an *oven*,
> and all the arrogant ones and every doer of wickedness will be *stubble*,
> and it will *set* them *ablaze*, the coming day,
> ... and they will be *ashes* under the soles of your feet. (4:1, 3)

The use of imagery in the form of figures of speech or figurative language is highly poetic. Here, Malachi uses the imagery of a goldsmith (or blacksmith) or a refiner to symbolize the ministry of purification that Yahweh is about to carry out in the lives of those who are violating covenantal stipulations in the "coming day of Yahweh." Such extended figures are highly poetic and emphatic because they are "pictures made out of words."[47]

In addition to the two poetic features of comparison mentioned above (simile and metaphor), there are also a number of important comparisons that express the relationship between Yahweh and Israel in intensely human terms – for example, father-son, master-servant (1:6).

Rhetorical Questions

The book of Malachi also uses rhetorical questions. This is one of the most important poetic devices since Malachi uses such questions to highlight crucial attitudes and emotions. Examples of Malachi's use of this device are shown below:

> Was not Esau the brother of Jacob? (1:2)
>
> And if I am a father, where is the honour due me? (1:6)
>
> Go ahead and bring it to your governor, will he be happy with you? (1:8)
>
> Am I to accept (such offerings) from your hand? (1:13).

Contrasts

Emphatic contrasts are also used in both positive (2:11) and negative (2:6–10) ways, highlighting the wicked attitudes and behaviour of the Jews by comparing them either with what Yahweh demands in his holy law or with what

---

47. Friedman, N. "Imagery," 363. See also Longman, "Literary Approaches and Interpretation," 121, and Longman, *Literary Approaches*.

will be take place in the future Messianic age. Joyce G. Baldwin observes that Malachi is wrapped up in his message and that he is a fitting mouthpiece of God because forty-seven out of the fifty-five verses in the book are a first-person address by Yahweh.[48]

It is common of Yahweh to speak in the first person in the OT, and this author believes that this presentation allows Yahweh to speak for himself. Here is a righteous and all-powerful God who is, paradoxically, also a merciful and loving Father, calling his delinquent children to repentance.

Repetition

The language of Malachi also contains repetition, which is clearly seen in his use of repetition of both sound and sense. A typical example of such usage by Malachi is shown below:

> *When you present* blind (beasts) for sacrificing
>   there is no harm in that!
> *When you present* the lame and the sick,
>   there is no harm in that! (1:8a)
> Bring it now (-*a'*) to your governor (-*cha*),
>   will he accept you (-*cha*) or
> will he lift up (-*a'*) your face (-*cha*) (1:8b)

Allusion

The prophet also alludes to what God had previously taught his people about keeping faith in their covenantal relationship.

> Did (God) not make one (being), flesh and spirit for him?
>   And what was the one seeking?
> (It was) the seed of God.
> So take heed for your spirit,
>   and do not be unfaithful to the wife of your youth! (2:15)

Here, there is a verbal shift or movement from one verb form to another, to deliberately lay emphasis on the next course of action.

> With a curse you (are being) cursed,
>   for *me* you (are) robbing, *the nation, all of it*! (3:9)

---

48. Baldwin, *Haggai, Zechariah, Malachi*, 216.

> Remember the law of Moses, my servant,
>> which I commanded him in Horeb for all Israel,
> the statutes and the judgements. (4:4)

> A son honours (his) father, and a servant his master.
>> Now if I (am) a father, where (is) my honour?
> And if I (am) a master, where (is) my fear?
>>> says Yahweh of hosts . . . to you, O priests, despisers of my name! (1:6)

In the preceding chapter, the prophet addresses some of the sins of Israel. Here in Malachi 3:5, he begins this section in a forceful manner in order to conclude a larger segment of the text, using specific examples to reveal the root of Israel's problem.

> and I (Yahweh) will be a swift witness
> against the sorcerers and against the adulterers,
>> and against those swearing deceitfully,
> and against those extorting the labourer
>> and (oppressing) the widow and the orphan,
> and those turning away the alien,
>> and they do not fear me!
> says Yahweh of hosts. (3:5)

From the illustrations discussed above, it seems clear that the book of Malachi contains typical poetic literary features, contrary to scholars who argue that Malachi does not have a clear structure.[49] Some scholars even designate Malachi as prose, believing that it lacks any characteristics of poetry.[50] However, Malachi does contain poetic features and displays the typical characteristics of Hebrew poetry.

Justification for the Use of Historical Grammatical Method

Given below are justifications for the use of historical-grammatical method for the study of Malachi 2:10–16. The literary analysis of the final form of

---

49. Welch, *Post-exilic Judaism*, 120, and Baldwin, *Haggai, Zechariah, Malachi*, 214.
50. Smith, *A Critical and Exegetical Commentary of Malachi*, 4–5.

the text is used. This method of historical and grammatical exegesis helps to define the meaning of unfaithfulness in this passage more precisely. In addition, the major metaphors, themes, and symbols projected by the text will be examined. The study traces the development of Malachi's thought in the style, structure, and content of the book to arrive at the authorial intent of Malachi 2:10–16. However, since the study of a text cannot be done in isolation, this work also studies the author within the context of the Torah, God's relationship with his people in other relevant OT prophetic texts, and the historical period of Ezra-Nehemiah.

The historical-grammatical method is the most appropriate for the interpretation of this prophetic oracle. This method does not focus so much on how text came to be written but attempts to account for its content. The task of historical-grammatical exegetical engagement requires knowledge, as much as is possible, of the author and the context of the time of his writing, including the historical, cultural, economic, and political background. Historical-grammatical exegesis is also helpful in identifying literary elements such as parallelism, chiasm, and other stylistic features of poetry. The editors of *Biblia Hebraica Stuttgartensia (BHS)* place the Hebrew text in a poetic configuration. Malachi should be regarded as poetic, both in form or content, because it has a poetic rhythm, which will be explained later in this work. The historical-grammatical exegetical method of interpreting Malachi 2:10–16 helps the interpreter to move away from analysing hypothetical sources in an attempt to go behind the text – the focus of the historical-critical tools of form,[51] source, and redaction criticism.[52] Such tools place greater emphasis on "what lie[s] behind the text in both oral and written stages of development."[53] The historical-grammatical method is used for Malachi 2:10–16 because it will provide a good grasp of the text's truth claims. This method helps the interpreter in exploring the exegetical approach to understanding the exact

---

51. Wilson, *Form-Critical Investigation*, 100–27, and O'Brien, *Priest and Levite*, 122–23.

52. For scholars who use the redaction-critical approach, see Petersen, *Zechariah 9–14 and Malachi*, 197; Dumbrell, "Ezra-Nehemiah Reforms," 45, 47, 51; Coggins, *Haggai, Zechariah, Malachi*, 75–76; and Shields, "Syncretism and Divorce," 66–67. This last scholar removes verse 15a and posits that verse 16 was a later insertion so as to be able to prove that the issue of divorce is not a key concern in Malachi 2:10–16.

53. Yilpet, "Canon Criticism," 29. See also Barton, *Reading the Old Testament*, 20–47, and Baker and Arnold, *Old Testament Studies*, 152.

meaning of the details in Malachi 2:10–16 and presents a means of providing solutions to the various interpretative issues in the text.

The historical-grammatical exegetical approach is significant for this work because our only access to an author is through the text. It also emphasizes the need to study the Bible in light of its historical origin and the final form of the text, contrary to the view held by some scholars who regard the text as having no author, no structure, or being a later addition or interpolation.[54]

Summary of the Chapter

As discussed earlier, the historical-critical method in its various forms has enjoyed dominance in the interpretation of Malachi 2:10–16 since the time of Charles Torrey, Adam Welch, and Abel Isaksson, who interpreted this passage solely along cultic lines.[55] However, their approach no longer enjoys the same prominence because more recent interpreters adopt the view that this text focuses on the physical marriage relationship. The historical-critical method used by the scholars mentioned in chapter 2 fails to consider the contributions of history and language (grammar). Therefore, this approach undermines the coherence of Malachi 2:10–16, either by interpreting it as a later addition or interpolation or by viewing the text as too difficult and uncertain in its meaning and context. This has resulted in neglecting the pastoral implications of Malachi 2:10–16 for future generations of believers.

The historical-grammatical exegesis discussed in this chapter seems more promising because it enables the study to describe the historical circumstances in which a text was written, touching on specific information about the events, time, and place where the material was written. In addition, this approach helps in discussing the implications of Malachi 2:10–16 from the perspective of the author's intention for future generations within the community of faith.

---

54. Baldwin, *Haggai, Zechariah, Malachi*, 214.

55. Baker and Arnold, *Old Testament Studies*, 146. See also. Barton, *Reading the Old Testament*, 81.

CHAPTER FOUR

God's Teaching on Marital Fidelity in the Wider Biblical Text

Introduction

In chapter 3 historical-grammatical exegesis was identified as the method this study will use to understand unfaithfulness in Malachi 2:10–16. In chapter 4, the background of Malachi and similar teachings on marital fidelity in the OT are examined.

The Context of Malachi
The Name, Author, and Superscription of the Book

The understanding of the name "Malachi" has caused many problems for scholars. Some scholars believe that the term was misunderstood and that the proper name originated from a misconception of the word.[1] The prophet is called "Malachi," meaning "my messenger" (Mal 1:1) or a messenger of the Lord. Scholarly consensus seems to point to 432–424 BC as being the time of the book's composition. Therefore, it is unnecessary to consider the historical background beyond 400 BC. It is against this broad background that the setting of Malachi must be understood, and this also requires examining the

---

1. Hinson, *Books of the Old Testament*, 183. See also McConville, *Exploring the Old Testament*, 259.

affairs of the Jewish restoration community to which Malachi belonged and whose problems he addressed.

The Recipients/Readers of Malachi

The question here revolves around the audience of Malachi: What kind of audience is being addressed in Malachi? The prophet begins his message in Malachi 1:1, stating that this message is an oracle (prophetic disputation) from Yahweh directed to his people, Israel. The identity of the audience is Israel, but the question remains: Which period of Israelites history is the message intended for – the exilic period or the postexilic period? As mentioned earlier in this work, this study argues that the book was written for the postexilic restoration community.

The historical background of Malachi reveals that it was addressed to a postexilic restoration community, in which only Judah had returned. This community was a religious community formed after the return from exile. The problems faced by these returning exiles are described in the books of Ezra and Nehemiah, while the hope for a dynamic community is dealt with in the minor prophetic books of Zechariah, Haggai, and Malachi. The book of Malachi is addressed to the community of Judah, comprising the leaders, priests, and people, who together constituted the one people of Yahweh.

The Date and Place of Writing of Malachi

Hosea 1:1 serves as the historical background to the ministry of the prophet Hosea, revealing that his prophetic ministry spanned the reigns of four successive kings of Judah (Uzziah, Jotham, Ahaz, and Hezekiah), as well as the reign of Jeroboam II, king of Israel. Since there is no such direct reference indicating the date of Malachi in either Scripture or tradition, indirect evidence must be used to deduce an appropriate date for this book. The historical background also helps to determine when Malachi commenced his prophetic ministry. Malachi's ministry probably began shortly before Nehemiah's arrival in Jerusalem.[2] While some scholars propose a later date[3] and others remain

---

2. Hinson, *Books of the Old Testament*, 184.
3. Torrey, "Prophecy of 'Malachi,'" 14–15.

uncertain about a specific date,[4] it is clear that Malachi directed his message to his own people – that is, the postexilic Israelite community.[5]

The historical background, including specific events that took place during Malachi's time, is crucial for understanding his prophecy. The book was written during a challenging time for the nation, a period of great political, military, economic, and religious change.[6] Therefore, it was necessary to teach the Jews about Yahweh's faithful love and his coming righteous judgement in order to encourage them to repent and initiate genuine reform within society. Malachi commenced his prophetic ministry in 433 BC, a date that falls between Nehemiah's two visits to Jerusalem. The historical contexts of Nehemiah and Malachi seem to be aligned. This work interprets Malachi against the background of the facts recorded in Nehemiah 10:1–13:31, especially the abuses that Ezra and Nehemiah set out to reform.

Malachi as a Name and as a Prophet

Over the years, it has been argued that Malachi should be regarded as anonymous because the title is seen taken from the prophecy of Malachi 3:1 rather than from Malachi 1:1.[7] However, the priest is the messenger of the Lord of hosts, which means the title is not borrowed from Malachi 3:1 since it is a reference to the function of priest in Malachi 2:7, and "Malachi" is therefore a proper name.[8]

Little is known about the human author, Malachi, and no details are given about his father or mother. He lived, laboured, and prophesied in the small province of Judah. He had no formal training in the school of prophets but was called directly by God to be his messenger. Prophets were God's spokespersons and enforcers of the covenant. They were officers appointed by God. The book's author, Malachi, was called or chosen by God himself. He is referred to as the messenger of God. One could see the analogy of the

---

4. Baldwin, *Haggai, Zechariah, Malachi*, 213.
5. Smith, 302. See also Baldwin, *Haggai, Zechariah, Malachi*, 299–300.
6. Smith, 302. See also McConville, *Exploring the Old Testament*, 259–260, and Zuck, *Biblical Theology*, 428.
7. Verhoef, *Haggai and Malachi*, 154, share the idea held by some Jewish scholars and church fathers who saw Malachi as an anonymous prophet, an angel who appeared in human form.
8. C. Hasell Bullock, *Old Testament Prophetic Books*, 335–336.

titles of other prophetic books in which reference is made to the author (Jer 1:1; Hos 1:2; Amos 7:14–15). Similarly, when the expression *beyad* (literally, "in or through the hand of") is used to introduce the human instrument of God's revelation, it is normally followed by a proper name (Isa 20:2; Jer 50:1; Hag 1:1; 2:1, 10).

The different messages in the book of Malachi were communicated by God through his "hand" (*beyad*). Malachi prophesied to his own people at a time when the nation was facing significant problems. This period was characterized by great political, military, economic, and religious change. The prophet's name signifies "salvation," "deliverance," or "help." There is compelling evidence from Scripture to support the idea that Malachi prophesied to the returned exiles who had settled in the small province of Judah. A striking feature of the book is Malachi's keen insight into the religious, social, and political conditions of his day, demonstrating that he had intimate knowledge about the things he spoke about and a close and intimate relationship with the people of Israel.

The Literary Form of Malachi

The classification of literary genres in the OT includes law, narrative, poetry, and prophecy.[9] However, one should not be dogmatic or stereotypical in these classifications because different genres can sometimes be found within a particular category.[10] For example, poetry may be found within a narrative passage.

The Scriptures contain literary artistry as well as historical and theological truth, and the writer of Malachi employs various literary conventions at his disposal in formulating and expressing his message. Therefore, understanding the literary structure of Malachi is important because this helps readers to study this study the text within its literary context. The genre of Malachi has been identified as a disputation oracle presented in a question-and-answer format.[11] The prophet builds his argument in the form of a series of dialogues involving Yahweh and his people, in which God addresses their unfaithfulness to him. The prophet states his proposition, followed by objections that might

---

9. Tucker, *Form Criticism*, 25, 54–66.
10. There may sometimes be a fluidity of genre in a particular text.
11. Hill, *Malachi*, 41. See also Murray, "Rhetoric of Disputation," 95–121.

be raised by those he addresses, and concludes by reasserting his original thesis. This form adds vividness to the argument.

The Literary Structure of Malachi

Some scholars argue that Malachi does not employ any literary structure and that the arrangement of his material is haphazard.[12] However, the contrary view seems more convincing because any written material must have some kind of structure. In Malachi, the genre is a series of disputation speeches,[13] and the rhetoric is dynamic. The way Malachi uses words in the text helps to convey his message to the readers, especially when words are interpreted in their context.[14]

Prohibiting marriage to foreign women was one of the basic stipulations given to protect people from possible unfaithfulness (Exod 21:8; Deut 7:3–6). When the priests returned to the land after the exile, they were involved in various activities such as rebuilding the city walls, teaching the law of God, and leading the religious duties of the nation. However, over time, the priesthood had deteriorated, which adversely affected the people, both spiritually and morally.[15] Walter C. Kaiser observes that "since the spiritual level of leadership was low, it could not be expected that the spiritual attainment of the people would be any higher."[16] Therefore, the followers, like the leaders, also failed to be faithful. Since there was failure on the part of both leaders and followers, this study disagrees with those who see Malachi 2:10–16 as an interpolation, a later addition, or as not fitting the context, arguing that such a view arises because they fail to read the text as a coherent whole.

The book of Malachi has poetic stylistic features embedded within it. As asserted earlier, contrary to the view of scholars such as Adam C. Welch and Joyce G. Baldwin,[17] Malachi displays the typical characteristics of Hebrew poetry. The rhetorical method is used effectively by Malachi to convey the message of Yahweh's covenant relationship with his people.

---

12. Baldwin, *Haggai, Zechariah, Malachi*, 214.
13. Clendenen and Taylor, *Haggai–Malachi*, 218.
14. Silva, *Foundations of Contemporary Interpretation*, 139.
15. Clendenen and Taylor, *Haggai–Malachi*, 315–20.
16. Kaiser, "Divorce in Malachi 2:10–16," 74.
17. Welch, *Post-exilic Judaism*, 120, and Baldwin, *Haggai, Zechariah, Malachi*, 214.

Previous scholars have used the concept of dispute to discover that there are six discussions which each have three sections involving Malachi, Yahweh and the addressees.[18] Based on the Masoretic signs (Parassah Setumah) in the text, the book of Malachi may be divided into three sections: (1) 1:1–2:13, (2) 1:14–2:16, and (3) 2:17–3:24.[19] However, the larger structure of Malachi – apart from the superscription (1:1) – is outlined in this work, showing the six disputations as follow:

(1) first disputation, 1:2–5,
(2) second disputation, 1:6–2:9,
(3) third disputation, 2:10–16,
(4) fourth disputation, 2:17–3:5,
(5) fifth disputation, 3:6–12, and
(6) sixth disputation, 3:13–21.

In addition, there are two appendices that appeal to ideal OT figures – Moses (3:22) and Elijah (3:23–24).

The structural pattern that reveals how Malachi addresses the issue of God's love for people who are unfaithful in fulfilling their covenantal obligations in various areas – including worship and marriage – is clearly seen in an oracle presented as disputation speeches. The structure of this oracle is shown below:

Introduction: Yahweh's word introduced by his messenger (1:1)
A. Yahweh is a faithful God, who has a deep covenant love for his people (1:1–5)
B. The priests are failing to fulfil their covenantal obligations and to model covenant-keeping for the rest of the Jews through the teaching of the Mosaic law (1:6–2:9)
C. Yahweh judges those who are faithless or unfaithful in the covenantal love relationship with their fellow covenant members and in the marriage union (2:10–16)
D. Faithful Yahweh comes in judgement against his faithless or unfaithful people as a Purifier and Refiner (2:17–3:5)

---

18. Smith, *Micah–Malachi*, 299. See also Wendland, "Linear and Concentric Patterns," 108, Clendenen and Taylor, *Haggai–Malachi*, 227.

19. The divisions given being that of the Masoretic Text. Elliger and Rudolph, *Biblia Hebraica Stuttgartensia*, 77.

E. Yahweh's judgement comes on those who fail to obey his covenantal obligations (3:6–12)

   F. Yahweh establishes a kingdom of righteousness (3:13–21)

This structure is followed by two appendices: Malachi 3:22 and Malachi 3:23–24. In this structure, we can see that Malachi places Malachi 2:10–16 as the third disputation using a chiastic pattern, as revealed by Hugenberger.[20]

Explanation of the Structure of Malachi

Malachi begins his book with a superscription (1:1). The first oracle, presented in the form of a disputation, opens with a tender reference to the love shown by Yahweh to Judah and the everlasting hostility towards Edom (1:1–5).

The second oracle, also in disputation form, is directed to the priests of Judah (1:6–2:9). Here, Yahweh addresses the priests, who, despite being called to lead the people in the way of Yahweh and his covenant, were unfaithful. God indicts the priests because they were directly responsible for the moral and spiritual condition of the people in Judah. He reprimands them for slacking in their duties by offering polluted and blemished sacrifices on Yahweh's altars, thereby despising Yahweh (1:6–10). Yahweh can do without their worship, for the time will come when the whole heathen world will worship him (1:11). Malachi concludes with a warning that if the priests do not heed this admonition, punishment will come upon them (2:1–9).

The third oracle (2:10–16) begins Malachi's discussion of God's covenantal love and the unfaithful response of his people, addressing the issue of marital unfaithfulness through three rhetorical questions (2:10–16). In this section, the prophet expresses pastoral concern for a restored community of leaders, priests, and people, who make up the "one" people of Yahweh. Here, Malachi shows that God opposes those who had been unfaithful to their fellow Jews, as well as those who had abandoned their Jewish wives to marry heathen women. He clearly states that Yahweh, as the righteous and final judge, will purify the social and religious lives of the community.

The central theme of the fourth oracle (2:17–3:5) is judgement and purification. Here, the prophet speaks of Yahweh as the righteous and final Judge, who will deal with the unrepentant ones – those guilty of unfaithfulness to a

---

20. Hugenberger, *Marriage as Covenant*, 99

covenant member or disloyal to a marriage partner – by bringing judgement on them. This oracle teaches about the Day of Yahweh (the Day of the Lord) as a day of judgement for evildoers within the ranks of the covenant people. This is also a day when Yahweh will bless the remnant and make them his treasured possession. Malachi concludes with the announcement that the messenger of Yahweh will come to prepare the way for him by purifying the social and religious life of the people (3:1–4).

The fifth oracle (3:6–12) is a call to repentance. The disputation begins with a compound declaration: "I have not changed" (3:6) and "return to me" (3:7). There are three basic subunits in this disputation: the summons to repentance (3:7ab), the indictment and challenge (3:7c–11), and the aftermath (3:12). Malachi summarizes this by inviting all who have gone astray to return to Yahweh and receive his blessings.

The sixth oracle (3:13–21) is also the final one. In this disputation, there is a three-part pattern of prophetic discussion in the form of declaration, audience rebuttal, and prophetic refutation. This oracle is a summary of the prophet's previous discussions, where he contrasts the faithful with the faithless. Malachi warns Judah to be aware that, at the end, the messenger of Yahweh will come in the final judgement. He reiterates that the faithful will be blessed, while those who persist in disobeying God's law will be punished (3:16–21).

There are two appendices to this section. The epilogue appeals to two ideal OT figures: Moses as the lawgiver (3:22) and Elijah as the prophet (3:23–24). These two postscripts to the book of Malachi constitute a summary of the role of the prophets as enforcers of the Mosaic law and serve as the closing theme of Malachi's prophecy, which is eschatological in nature. The messenger of Yahweh will come like the prophets of old, who are represented in these verses by Moses and Elijah, and will regenerate the people and restore them to union with Yahweh. He will also call to judgement all those – including the priests – who have transgressed the moral law and failed to observe the rituals, and to show a pastoral concern.

The text of Malachi is cohesive and is structured around the theme of unfaithfulness, beginning with the prophet's exhortation to the priests to remain faithful in honouring God (1:2–2:9). Judah is exhorted to faithfulness, both in their marital relationships (2:10–16) and in their relationship with God (3:7–14). The anticipation of the coming Day of the Lord brings to an end Malachi's disputations. In Malachi 2:10–16, which fits perfectly into the structure of whole book, Malachi describes the continuing unfaithfulness of the people of God.

Malachi 2:10–16 in Its Biblical-Theological Context

With regard to the placement of Malachi 2:10–16 in its context, some previous commentators had referred to this section as an interpolation or "a latter addition."[21] Since scholars who hold to a figurative interpretation believe that the concerns elsewhere in Malachi focus only on syncretism or apostasy, they maintain that Malachi 2:10–16 was not initially part of the book.[22] Others, however, consider only a smaller part of the passage as being an interpolation or later addition. They conclude that the problem in 2:10–16 should be interpreted in the broader context of the issues Malachi addresses.[23] This study argues that Malachi 2:10–16 expands the scope of the message to embrace not only the priests but all the people. This section is a single unit, the work of a single author, that does not contradict the teaching of the rest of the book. This text addresses the priesthood, but it also applies to the entire people, declaring that sincerity towards a loving God and a holy lifestyle with regard to faithfulness in fulfilling covenant obligations is absolutely essential in the presence of Yahweh. In other words, if the people are to receive Yahweh's blessings, they must live up to their higher calling as a holy nation, awaiting the Messiah who will come both as a judge who is a purifier (2:17–3:5) and a judge who will bless his people at his coming (3:6–12). This God is Israel's hope of a righteous judge who will reward those who obey when the day of judgment comes.

This study argues that Malachi 2:10–16 is not an interpolation or a later addition. The section fits well within the series of problems addressed in the book of Malachi for several reason. First, the text is not an interpolation because its literary form continues the prophetic disputation with which Malachi began in chapter 1. Second, Malachi connected his material together closely. From the beginning, the prophetic disputation shows that Malachi is dealing with history. He reminds the people of Israel that it was at Sinai

---

21. Wellhausen, *Die Klein Propheten Übersetzt*, 80, and Fuller, "Text-Critical Problems," 54.
22. Shields, "Syncretism and Divorce," 66. See also, Rudolph, *Haggai, Sacharja 1–8*, 270.
23. Shields, "Syncretism and Divorce," 66.

that God established a covenant with Israel, chose the nation in fulfilment of his promises to Abraham (Exod 2:24), and promised to establish them as a kingdom of priests and a holy nation (Exod 19:4–6). The Lord gave Israel both the Ten Commandments (unconditional principles) and the books of the law (written in the form of casuistic law), with punishments prescribed for specific violations of these laws.

This theme continues in succeeding books. In Leviticus, the covenant is reaffirmed with Israel. This theme is carried over into the book of Deuteronomy, which clearly states that God will bless an obedient nation (Deut 28:1–14) and punish a disobedient nation (28:15–68). To fulfil its identity, Israel would have to obey God's law in three ways. First, the people of God were to purge idolatry from their midst. Second, they were to follow God's sacrificial laws. Third, they were responsible to obey the purity laws. All these laws were intended to strengthen the relationship between Yahweh and his people.

God's Relationship with Israel in the Torah

Prior to the time of the prophets, the Torah had already addressed the physical marriage relationship, which was instituted by God in the creation story in Genesis 1–2. The narrator says that God saw that both man and woman were "very good" and then proceeds to describe God's the physical relationship God intended for them in Genesis 2: "a man leaves his father and his mother and cleaves to his wife [not wives], and they become one flesh" (Gen 2:24 RSV).

This shows God's intention for marriage to form a "one-flesh" union. God intended marriage to be a monogamous institution for the purposes of companionship and procreation (Gen 2:18, 24; see also Psalm 128) that, once entered into, is a covenant dissolved only by death (Matt 19:6; Mark 10:9). This was God's ideal plan and purpose for marriage. The OT speaks about marriage as a covenant in its own right. Solomon, in Proverbs 2:17, calls marriage the "covenant" of God, perhaps because it is superior to all human contracts and because God himself participates in its formation.

Any discussion of covenant in the Bible must begin with a proper conception of who God is and what he has done for those with whom he has bound himself in covenant. The concept of a covenant relationship must be understood within the context of the Torah, where it all began. Yahweh's covenant relationship with individuals goes as far back as Genesis 6:18. In

Genesis 9:1–17, God initiates a new covenant relationship with Noah. This covenant contain instructions about what people must and must not do (Gen 9:1–7) and what God promises to do (9:8–17). Hamilton sees this type of covenantal relationship as bilateral.[24]

God's covenantal relationship continued in the call of Abram in Genesis 12:1–20, where the election of Abram was based on God's divine choice and promise. Although the term "covenant" is not mentioned until Genesis 15, there were promises prior to the implementation of that covenant. Yahweh's relationship with human beings began with Abram, but Abram was a transmitter of this divine promise to others.

The essence of God's covenant with Abram is found in Genesis 15. Although God declared his enduring love for his people even before the birth of Israel as a nation, Genesis 15 marks a specific development of God's covenantal relationship with Abram through a word of divine self-disclosure (Gen 15:1–6) and the performance of covenantal ceremonies (15:7–21). The text contains a mysterious rite in which the Lord literally "cut a covenant" with Abram. He instructed Abram to prepare a sacrificial offering, which Abram did, and Abram then experienced God's presence in the form of fire and smoke.

Wenham observes that there are two aspects to this covenant: the terms of the relationship and the terms of the covenant that must be kept.[25] However, Hamilton argues that the covenant is unilateral since Abram did not pass through the carcass.[26] Instead, what passed through was the theophanic appearance of the presence of God in form of a smoking fire pot and the flaming torch.

In tracing the concept of בְּרִית (covenant), Alan J. Avery-Peck defines covenant generally as "a formal agreement between two parties, in which one or both make promises under oath to perform or refrain from certain actions stipulated in advance."[27] Hugenberger defines it as "an elected, as opposed to natural, relationship of obligation established under divine sanction."[28] In

---

24. Hamilton, *Book of Genesis*, 319.
25. Wenham, *Genesis 1–15*, 332.
26. Hamilton, *Book of Genesis*, 437.
27. Avery-Peck, "Covenant," 136. For another scholar who sees covenant as oath, see Tucker, "Covenant Forms," 488.
28. Hugenberger, *Marriage as a Covenant*, 215.

Judaism, the covenant is the agreement made between God and the people of Israel at Sinai, and the people of God are required to fulfil their covenantal obligations as set out in the law.

Thus, the covenant and Torah are key shaping factors for the relational identity of Yahweh and his people. These people, who are the recipients of both the covenant and Torah in the OT, are invited by God to enter into covenant with him (Gen 6:18a; Exod 6:7; Lev 26:9, 45; Deut 26:16–19; 29:13; 2 Sam 7:24; Jer 7:23; 31:33–34; Hosea 2:18–20).

Expectations of the Covenant Relationship in Malachi

The relationship of Yahweh and his people, Israel, can be traced back to the early understanding of the covenantal relationship as expressed in various formulas, beginning with the pre-Deuteronomic version of the Sinai events (Exod 24:12–18; compare Deut 4:13, 23). The Lord covenanted with his people from the beginning (Gen 6:18a).

Though the emphasis of Yahweh's covenant is promissory, he also expects his people to faithfully fulfil their covenantal obligations to their covenant-maker. Immediately after the exodus from their bondage in Egypt, the people of Israel, under Moses's leadership, entered into a covenant with Yahweh. This covenant clearly states that God would be their God and that they would be his people (Exod 6:7; Lev 26:12).

Some scholars note that the covenant follows a pattern found in the ancient Near East. In covenants between the two parties known as suzerains and vassals, the vassal received blessings for keeping the covenant and curses for breaking it.[29] However, the covenant between God and his people is unique. It entails faithfulness to covenantal obligations, but this agreement is between a superior – that is, God – and an inferior – that is, the people of Israel. The promises inherent in this covenant are threefold: the promise of land for Abram and his descendants (Gen 15:18–21), the promise of a great nation (Gen 12:2), and the promise that Abram and his descendants would be blessed and be a source of blessing to all other nations (Gen 12:2–3).

In dealing with his people the Lord gave them the law at Mount Sinai (Exodus 19–24). John J. Davis observes that the main purpose of the law "was

---

29. Yamauchi, "Cultural Aspects of Marriage," 241–243. See also Matthews, "Marriage and Family," 7.

to restrain wrong behaviour in order to protect the integrity of the moral, social and religious institutions of Israel."[30] While there is truth in what Davis says, the purpose of the law was far greater than merely restraining wrong behaviour. Even before giving the Ten Commandments, God had already declared that Israel was his prized or treasured possession (Exod 19:4–6). The law was meant to maintain the purity of Israel's relationship with the Almighty God, who was also their Redeemer (Exod 20:1–5). In Exodus 20, the monotheistic assertion is explicit: "The religion of Israel from this time onward is to be unambiguously monotheistic."[31]

Thus, from the beginning, there was a covenant between Yahweh and individuals, and later between Yahweh and Israel as God's chosen people (Gen 12:1–3; Deut 7:7–8). The intimacy of this covenant relationship is sometimes described in terms of a father-son relationship. A covenant always involves mutual obligations (Gen 15:17–21 and 17:1–14), and the OT includes many such covenant stipulations. For example, Israel was commanded not to have any other gods (Exod 20:3; cf Jer 1:16; 7:9; 9:14; 13:10; 16:10–13; 17:1–4; 19:1–4, 13; 22:8–9; 25:4–7; 32:26–29; 44:1–6). In the Pentateuch, an important stipulation was the prohibition against marrying foreign wives since this was essential for the people of God to maintain a cordial relationship with him.

W. L. Moran claims that God expected Israel to respond to his love, which Moran interprets as a covenantal term involving loyalty, service, and, on the human level, obedience.[32] The people were expected to love God because the covenant was based entirely on God's promise. As a people graciously elected by God, Israel was expected to respond by acting as a covenant community. God expected them to follow his law, which was embodied in the Torah. The covenants with the patriarchs were legally binding on all generations, even those not yet born. Israel was expected to keep the terms of the covenant as God's people, be obedient and loyal to the covenant-maker, and united as one people.

For this community, which began with a distinct promise and covenant relationship with Yahweh, the concept of covenant, in the form of both promise and law, was their defining mark, and the people were responsible for

---

30. Davis, *Moses*, 207.
31. Davis, 207.
32. Moran, "Ancient Near Eastern Background," 77–87.

transmitting the covenantal stipulations in the Torah to future generations, including those yet unborn. This covenantal relationship provided a unique identity and a distinct theology. Their way of life and their exclusive loyalty to God set them apart as different from other nations. Therefore, the people addressed in the book of Malachi were to have no allegiance to anyone other than God; any unholy relationship would violate their covenant obligations.

Responsibilities in Covenant Relationships

As observed earlier, God established a harmonious relationship between himself and Israel. Right from the beginning, scholars have seen the term covenant as an agreement between two parties, ratified by an oath. Later, however, there was a shift in the concept and בְּרִית (covenant) was viewed as "the all-embracing symbol for expressing the religious relationship, and is no longer qualified by other images."[33] Thus the covenant became the key shaping factor for the relational identity of Yahweh and his people, who were the recipients of both the promise and the law.

In response to God's promise and the law of the covenant, the people had responsibilities. Beginning with Noah, Abraham, and others who followed after them, God expected the continuation of their relationship with him (Gen 15:18; 17:2; Exodus 24). The people were responsible for keeping the covenant, especially the regulations set out in the Mosaic covenant, which governed the life of the Israelites.

In all these covenants, whether made with individuals or with the entire nation of Israel, specific responsibilities were outlined. As the elect people of God, who were in covenant relationship with him, the Israelites were required to conform to God's law. God's sovereignty demanded that Israel obey God and walk in his ways.

Consequences in Covenant Relationship

As stated earlier, God invited Israel in order to establish his covenant with them (see Exod 6:7; Lev 26:3, 12; Deut 26:16–19; 29:13). Israel was expected to obey God or, in covenantal terms, to be faithful to the covenant. The consequences for violating the covenant were set out in the Torah (Lev 26:27–33; Deut 4:25–31; 8:19–20; 28:36–37, 62–68). Time would reveal that while God

---

33. Eichrodt, *Theology of the Old Testament*, 55.

upheld his part of the covenant,[34] Israel failed to do so,[35] and these violations resulted in punishment. Hill claims that God is a God of promise, a covenant-keeper who is always faithful and unchanging, extending mercy to his own (3:6) and punishing those who violate the covenant's stipulations (3:5, 18, 21).[36] However, Eichrodt notes, "The people responded to God's love with disloyalty, disobedience and disservice, not just towards God, but also towards their fellow man."[37] The people of Israel breached the covenant by their disregard of Yahweh, the covenant-maker.

Malachi 2:10–16 and the Issue of Marital Unfaithfulness in the Prophets

The OT contains a significant amount of material that directly or indirectly relates to instances of either physical or metaphorical marital unfaithfulness. The development of the biblical canon was a complex process, spanning several millennia. In the next section, the portrayal of the issue of marital in other prophetic genres within the biblical canon is examined.

Yahweh's Relationship with Israel as Reflected in Hosea's Marriage

It is not surprising to find that the OT employs different metaphors to describe the marriage relationship. This is evident in selected passages from the OT prophetic books, which include metaphorical references to marriage and unfaithfulness. Taking Hosea's marriage to an unfaithful woman as the starting point for his prophecy and metaphor, God declares that Israel is bound in an exclusive covenant relationship with Yahweh. He likens Israel's infidelity to that of an adulterous wife. In addition, the land is personified as a woman acting like a prostitute – in other words, she is sexually unfaithful.

There are striking parallels between Hosea's audience and Malachi's audience. Hosea uses the metaphor of a woman's unfaithfulness to express Israel's infidelity against Yahweh. God is portrayed as the husband and Israel as the

---

34. Hill, *Malachi*, 25–31.
35. Eichrodt, *Theology of the Old Testament*, 55.
36. Hill, *Malachi*, 47.
37. Eichrodt, *Theology of the Old Testament*, 414.

wife. Yahweh has chosen Israel and made a covenant with her, instructing Israel to refrain from entering into relationships with foreigners or women of foreign faiths. This is in line with earlier warnings to God's people against intermarriage with foreigners (see Deut 7:3–4). Leo G. Purdue observes that marriage to foreigners was prohibited mainly on religious grounds because "the foreign wife would maintain her own alien culture, especially her pagan religion, especially her pagan religion (Exod 34:11–16; Num 25:1–2; Deut 7:3–4; Judg 3:5–6 and Neh 13:23–27) which would lead [first] the household and, by extension, Jews to adopt the ways of foreign cultures and their gods."[38]

In Hosea, there is also the narrative of Hosea's physical marriage. Hosea 2:2–23 is centred on the historical narrative of his physical marriage and the restoration of that broken marriage through reconciliation with his unfaithful wife. God tells Hosea to marry a woman whom he knows will be unfaithful to him and also instructs Hosea to forgive her. The message and ministry of Hosea begins with the formation of a physical relationship that involves the difficult and costly commitment of taking a prostitute as his wife and having children with her.

There has been debate over whether God would ask a prophet to marry a prostitute. While some scholars oppose this idea, the description of Gomer in the text as a prostitute is clear and indisputable. The narrator makes it clear to readers that Gomer was a prostitute when God told Hosea to marry or "take" her (Hos 1:2). The Lord blesses their marriage with offspring, and they have three children (Hos 1:2–9). But along the way, there is a problem in Hosea and Gomer's marriage. He has no one to confide in except his children, and he urges them to rebuke their mother for her prostitution (2:1–2).

Although Hosea thought he could use some physical means to bring Gomer back (2:6), he is not able to do so because the luxury and fulfilment she receives from her lover clouds her thinking and prevents her from acknowledging that her husband is her true provider. The physical marriage union of Hosea and Gomer, acted out in a memorable way, serves as an illustration of the relationship between God and his people. Witte and Nichols observe:

> In the Hebrew Bible, Yahweh's special covenantal relationship with Israel is analogized to the special relationship between

---

38. Leo G. Purdue, "The Israelite and Early Jewish Family," 183.

husband and wife, and that covenant relationship entails faithfulness. Israel's disobedience to Yahweh, in turn, particularly its proclivity to worship false gods, is frequently described as a form of playing the harlot. Idolatry, like adultery, can lead to divorce, and Yahweh threatens this many times, even while calling his chosen to reconciliation.[39]

From chapter 4 onwards, Hosea's own marriage is used as a metaphor for the relationship between God and Israel. It reveals that Israel has been unfaithful to its covenantal obligations by pursuing other gods. Gomer's unfaithfulness to Hosea parallels the people's unfaithfulness to Yahweh. The marriage metaphor illustrates that Israel has broken its covenant promises and stands under God's judgement because of its "idolatry-adultery." However, the restoration of this relationship is to be demonstrated in the life of the prophet. Hosea is to "Go again, love a woman who is loved by another man and is an adulteress, even as the Lord loves the children of Israel, though they turn to other gods and love cakes of raisins." (Hosea 2:1). He is to love her as Yahweh loves the Israelites in spite of their apostasy.

This gracious action illustrates that God will maintain and restore Israel's position not by her own righteousness but because of his own compassion, grace, and love. Several passages in the OT use marriage and unfaithfulness as metaphors of Israel's covenant relationship with God. What is demonstrated through Hosea's life is God's instruction to Israel to refrain from relationships with foreigners or women of foreign faiths.

Yahweh's Covenant Relationship in Isaiah 50:1

Earlier in this book we observed that Yahweh had made a covenant with Israel on Mount Sinai (Exod 24:12–18; see Jeremiah 11), establishing a special and significant covenantal relationship with them. He demanded an exclusive relationship with his people, using the bride-husband model, which is reflected in Hosea's life. Isaiah adopts a metaphorical understanding of the covenantal relationship between Yahweh and his people, likening apostasy and idolatry to unfaithfulness within the marriage union.

---

39. Witte and Nichols, *Covenant Marriage*, 17.

Isaiah reiterates that the covenant Yahweh made with Israel demands their obedience and exclusive loyalty. The worship of other gods violates of Israel's covenantal obligation of exclusiveness and justifies Yahweh's revocation of his promise of provision and protection. Isaiah portrays Yahweh as the husband and Israel as the unfaithful wife who prostitutes herself with other gods and commits spiritual adultery. Israel's failure to honour its covenantal obligations is seen as treachery. Isaiah employs the marriage metaphor using the concepts of divorce and debt against Israel's sinfulness in order to make the people realize their infidelity and repent, and in turn, to act in a way acceptable to Yahweh, who was their husband.

Yahweh's Covenant Relationship in Jeremiah 2:1–25 and 3:1–23

There are two main texts in the book of Jeremiah that explicitly refer to the marriage metaphor. In these passages, the prophet pictures Yahweh as the husband and Jerusalem as the representative of the people of God. In Jeremiah 2:2, Yahweh remembers with regret the happiness he once enjoyed with his bride. He reflects on what life was like when they were young and in covenantal relationship and regrets that those days are now gone. In other words, there is a break in the once-happy relationship between God and his people. From verses 2 to 20, the prophet builds up the suspense, finally revealing the current state of Yahweh's relationship with his bride, Israel. The bride is no longer what she used to be; now "You lay down [playing] the harlot" (Jer 2:20).

The expression "lay down as a prostitute" (NIV) or "playing the harlot" (KJV) in verse 20 signifies the change in the relationship, showing that the people who were once faithful to their covenantal relationship are now disloyal and unfaithful to Yahweh. The prophet uses various images to show that the people had departed from their original covenantal loyalty and rebelled against Yahweh, and he contrasts their current apostasy with their faithfulness during the wilderness wanderings.

The Sinaitic covenant, which required that Yahweh alone should be worshipped, was still in place (Deut 28:15, 58–59; 30:17–19). However, instead of giving Yahweh – Israel's husband – happiness, the people rejected the covenant and worshipped idols (Jer 32:34). Jeremiah notes that the people's rebellion through alliances with foreign nations and abandonment of Yahweh as their true husband led to God's wrath against them in their daily lives. Jeremiah predicts judgement on Judah for rejecting the Sinaitic covenant, which required that the people abide by its stipulations (Jer 11:3; compare Exod 24:7).

In Jeremiah 3:1–23, the marriage metaphor is very clear. In this text, too, God is portrayed as the husband and the people are depicted as his wife. Although the wife has engaged in prostitution with many people, she expects her husband – Yahweh, the faithful one – to take her back even though she breached the covenant. It is important to remember that Israel's main sin was abandoning Yahweh and worshipping idols (Jer 2:11).

In denouncing a woman who leaves a man and marries another man, Jeremiah denounces the sins of both adultery and idolatry. He claims that returning to such a man constitutes an unclean act (Deut 24:1–4; Lev 18:20). He observes that the reunion of such an unclean woman causes problems for the land. Jeremiah metaphorically portrays the adulterous wife as defiling the land and then in Yahweh issuing a writ of divorce. He depicts Yahweh as a human husband who has provided for his wife but been disappointed by her adulterous behaviour. Her failure to maintain her covenantal obligations will result in misery and shame (Jer 4:2–4). However, Yahweh forgives his wife, erasing the shame of her youth as he erases all memories of his wife's unfaithfulness and renews their covenant, extending grace that goes beyond the law.

Yahweh as a Faithful Husband and Israel as an Unfaithful Wife in Ezekiel 16:1–63 and Ezekiel 23:1–49

In the preceding prophetic texts, the prophets use the marriage metaphor in dynamic ways. The OT marriage metaphor originates with Hosea. Isaiah builds on this, asking for Judah's certificate of divorce but also emphasizing God's mercy and his willingness to take back his unfaithful people. Jeremiah shows that Israel was unfaithful in her marriage covenant because she failed to uphold its terms (Prov 2:17).

Jeremiah describes Israel as being unfaithful to her husband (Jer 3:20). He wonders whether Yahweh can take her back after so many adulteries (3:1–5) but concludes that Yahweh acts beyond the law through grace. Ezekiel takes up the marriage metaphor where the other prophets leave off and expands on it in two basic texts: Ezekiel 16:1–63 and Ezekiel 23:1–49.

Ezekiel 16:1–63

In chapter 16, Ezekiel begins with the introductory prophetic formula, "and again the word of Yahweh came to me, saying, son of man" (Ezek 16:1). From this point, the prophet moves on to a denunciation of Jerusalem – which represents Israel – depicting her as Yahweh's wife – who is representative of the people.

In other words, Jerusalem, which represents Israel, is depicted as Yahweh's unfaithful wife. The prophet helps Jerusalem to recognize her abominations (16:2) by reminding her of her origins (16:3–5) and the initial situation when things were going well. He uses the imagery of a pagan baby girl who had been neglected by her parents and denied normal care (16:6). Yahweh had rescued this helpless baby, saved her, covered her nakedness, and provided for her (16:6–8, 9–14).

In this first marriage metaphor, Ezekiel links the various stages of the relationship between Yahweh and the pagan girl to key periods in Israel's history. The metaphor is very clear: Yahweh found an uncared-for girl, loved her, married her, and spread his garment to cover her nakedness. But now, this young girl whom Yahweh loved and cared for is misbehaving. She has become an adulterer and behaves like a harlot.

Nelly Stienstra views this as the worst possible betrayal in a relationship – a breach of trust. The people of Israel had betrayed Yahweh in many ways and in different situations.[40] Ezekiel calls on Israel to remember the day of her youth as a reminder that Yahweh's wife had totally failed her husband and declares judgement on her for the failure to uphold her covenantal obligations. This chapter describes how God fulfils all the terms of his marriage covenant, contrasting this with Israel's failure to keep the terms outlined in the laws of Moses (Ezek 16:1–7; see Exod 21:10–11). Israel breaks all the laws, especially the promise to be faithful, by committing adultery. Ezekiel concludes the allegory affirming God's immutable faithfulness to his covenants (16:59–63).

Ezekiel 23:1–49

In this chapter, the prophet Ezekiel once again takes up the marriage metaphor, this time with reference to two sisters. He describes how these two women misbehave right from the beginning, failing to preserve their virginity

---

40. Stienstra, *Yahweh Is the Husband*, 134.

(23:1–3) and refusing to mend their ways, and warns that they would be punished for their fornications (23:22–35).

An important question arises: Is Yahweh marrying two wives? In light of the injunction in Leviticus 18:18, we should not conceptualize Yahweh as marrying two wives. The two sisters are not wives of Yahweh but symbolically represent the two kingdoms of Israel. Ezekiel uses this imagery of Yahweh marrying two young girls to refer to the division of Israel into the northern and southern kingdoms. Yahweh is not a polygamist but a monogamist who remains the faithful husband of his undivided people, Israel, as Ezekiel reiterates in other passages where he predicts the reunion of the two kingdoms (Ezek 16:59–63).

The two sisters had sinned wilfully and become depraved because of their failure to uphold the covenant entered into between Israel and God at Sinai, where Yahweh had his marriage with His people. It was there that he became the husband of his people, with the whole nation of Israel as his bride (Exodus 24). Despite portraying Israel as an unfaithful wife, who faced judgement and shame, the chapter also offers words of comfort, reconciliation, and forgiveness, promising that the unfaithful wife would be restored to her former position as God's wife.

Ezekiel wants his readers to understand that the two sisters misbehaved by committing adultery (Ezek 23:5–8). They defiled themselves by engaging in harlotry with both the Assyrians and the Egyptians. Ezekiel also asserts that the misbehaviour of one sister is greater than that of the other (23:11). While both sisters broke Yahweh's laws and would be judged (23:18), the sin of one is more grievous. This is made clear from verses 32–36, where it is revealed that they committed adultery, which is a sin committed against their husband, Yahweh, for which they would be punished (23:32–39).

Throughout this chapter, Ezekiel employs the language of harlotry to depict the unfaithful wife, using the marriage metaphor to denounce the people of Israel for their unfaithfulness to God and describe the punishment that would follow. From the foregoing, one can see marriage as a covenant relationship from different parts of the OT, in which marriage is seen, both metaphorically and literally, as a sacred covenant that is blessed by God and seen as honourable among all people (Gen 2:24; Prov 5:18; 18:22; 19:14). This concept of covenant relationship, which depicts Yahweh as a covenant-keeping God, is also found elsewhere in the Bible (Isa 50:1; 54:4–6; Jer 2:1–3; Ezek 16:6–22; 23:1–49; Hos 2:1–20).

Marital Unfaithfulness: A Historical Parallel (Ezra-Nehemiah)

This section is very important to the study of Malachi because it examines the issues and situations faced by the Jewish restoration community of which Malachi was a part. The Ezra-Nehemiah narrative forms an important background to the book of Malachi. As noted earlier, the people of God disobeyed him, acting contrary to what was stated in the law and ignoring the warnings of the prophets about the consequences of disobedience to Yahweh (Isa 6:8–13; Jer 1:13–15; 6:11–12, 22–26; 7:30–34; Ezek 7:21–27; 16:59–63; Mic 4:10). The prophets made known to the people of Israel the charges against them: they had violated the covenant stipulations and refused correction. The inevitable result was exile (Jer 25:1–11).

In 605 BC, Nebuchadnezzar defeated Pharaoh Neco at the battle of Carchemish and was crowned king of Babylon.[41] That same year, Nebuchadnezzar's army besieged Jerusalem for the first time. They deported some of the young men of the nobility and removed some of the gold articles from the temple (Dan 1:1–4). In 604 BC, when Nebuchadnezzar took control of the Philistine plain, Judah became a vassal of Babylon (2 Kgs 24:7). This signalled Judah's downfall, which would culminate in exile.[42] The death of King Josiah at the hands of Pharaoh's forces at Megiddo brought to an end his programme of religious and political reforms.[43]

Just three months later, Judah's brief period of interdependence came to an end. It became a vassal of Egypt and was forced to pay heavy taxes (2 Kgs 23:33; 2 Chr 36:3). The pharaoh set up Eliakim, the son of Josiah, as a puppet king, changing his name to Jehoiakim as a sign that he was under the pharaoh's authority. From the time of the battle of Carchemish to the time of the final deportation to exile in Babylon in 586 BC, there were three deportations

---

41. Wiseman, *Chronicles of Chaldeans Kings*, 25–26, 66–69; Craigie, Kelly, and Drinkard, *Jeremiah 1–25*, 46. See also Childs, *Biblical Theology*, 163, and Kafang, *Intertestamental Period*, 7–8.

42. Childs, *Biblical Theology*, 161–163.

43. Malamat, "Last Kings of Judah," 137–156; Malamat, " Twilight of Judah," 123–145.

from Jerusalem to Babylon.[44] The first deportation is mentioned in Daniel 1:1–6.[45] The Babylonians began deporting members of the royal family, and Daniel, Hananiah, Mishael, and Azariah were given a royal scholarship to study at the royal academy and were provided with royal food. Some of the golden articles were removed from the temple during this deportation.

Nebuchadnezzar attacked Jerusalem with full force and besieged the city again, and Jehoiakim became his vassal for 3 years (2 Kgs 24:1). Jehoiakim rebelled against him (2 Kgs 24:1), and other nation's raiders attacked Judah (2 Kgs 24:2).[46] Finally after Jehoiakim's son Jehoiachin had reigned for 3 months, Nebuchadnezzar re-launched his attack against Jerusalem again and was successful (2 Kgs 24:10–11).[47] The city surrendered to the Babylonians. The Babylonians captured Jehoiachin, his mother, his captains, his officials, and craftsmen and deported them to Babylon, together with the rest of the larger golden items from the temple (2 Kgs 24:12–16).

Nebuchadnezzar then made Jehoiachin's uncle, Mattaniah, the king, renaming him Zedekiah (2 Kgs 24:17). Zedekiah reign was marked by two key problems. First, the experienced men who had served his predecessor were no longer there to help him. Second, he was never accepted as a legitimate ruler by the people, who continued to regard Jehoiachin as their king. In 586 BC, Jerusalem was besieged for the third time and fell into the hands of the Babylonians (2 Kgs 25:1–26; Ezek 21:18–29), and Zedekiah was captured, blinded, and deported.[48] The city, palace, and temple were burned, and its walls were cast down, and Gedaliah was appointed governor of Judah (2 Kgs 25:4–21; Jer 26:18; 32:1–5; 39:8–10; 52:12–27).

The nation was destroyed, and the people were carried off into exile. This marked the end of Israel's existence as an independent, sovereign nation. The

---

44. For reference to the three deportations see Archer, "Daniel," 31–33, and Bruce, *Israel and the Nations*, 88. See also Pritchard, *Ancient Near Eastern Texts*, 308; Bright, *History of Israel*, 323; and VanGemeren, *Interpreting the Prophetic Word*, 323.

45. Archer, "Daniel," 31–33. See also a reference to this deportation in Whiston, "Antiquities of the Jews," 281.

46. VanGemeren, *Interpreting the Prophetic Word*, 322. See also Bruce, *Israel and the Nations*, 88.

47. Katzenstein, "'Before Pharaoh Conquered Gaza," 249–251. See also VanGemeren, *Interpreting the Prophetic Word*, 307.

48. Pritchard, *Ancient Near Eastern Texts*, 308. See also Bright, *History of Israel*, 328.

exiles were distressed and disillusioned in their so-called new homes. Donald E. Gowan describes their psychological trauma with these words:

> Many must have been isolated individuals, still in shock from seeing their loved ones die, or frantic with anxiety because they did not know what had become of husband or child, wife or parent. And they walked, day after day, for months. The route from Jerusalem to Babylonia is about 700 miles. They walked, and more died, and they found themselves in a strange and forbidding land, not hilly and wooded like Palestine, but a flat alluvial plain, marked only by great rivers and an extensive network of canals watering fertile fields, and there what seemed to them to be immense walled cities, with temple towers looming into the heavens.[49]

The people of God were in a state of disillusionment and their "devotion to Yahweh was threatened less by apostasy and idolatry, largely dealt with by the cataclysm of exile and more by lax worship and loose morals."[50] But in the midst of all of this, there was the hope of restoration.

The cause of their misfortune was their failure to uphold their covenantal obligations. Israel had breached the law of the covenant, under which God relates to his people as a husband and they were to respond as his faithful wife. There had been a warning issued in Deuteronomy 28:64–65, but Judah had ignored it. Since the God of justice would never overlook the sin of his people, he punished them. Babylon and other nations were God's instruments of judgement against his people, but there was still hope of restoration. Although the invading Babylonians were God's tool of judgement (Jer 25:12–14), what befell Judah was not outside of God's purpose (Lam 2:17). God's people had to return to the covenant, and this is emphasized in Jeremiah 31:31–34.

The important question is this: Was there any future hope for the exiles? Would the generation of the exile be restored in their land? Would Judah's history end with the exile now that the temple, priesthood, kingship, and land were gone? Three key issues are raised here: the future of the temple,

---

49. Gowan, *Prophetic Books*, 122. See also Ackroyd, *Exile and Restoration*, 230–231.
50. Johnston, "Malachi," 260.

the future of the Davidic kingship, and the future restoration of the exiled generation back to the land.

The restoration began with the edict of Cyrus and included the period of Ezra and Nehemiah.[51] The remnant that returned from exile became the nucleus of the postexilic people of God. L. H. Brockington observes that in 549 BC, Cyrus revolted against the king of the Medes, of whom he was a vassal, and became the king of both the Medes and the Persians.[52] Jeremiah had prophesied concerning the seventy-year period of the exile (Jer 29:10; and see 25:1–11). The restoration began with the edict of Cyrus.[53] Brockington says,

> In 546 he defeated Croesus king of Lydia and in 538 Babylon fell to him without serious fighting. It was from this point that the chronicler dated the reign of Cyrus, since only then did he become ruler over Palestine. The title, King of Persia was retained after the conquest of Babylon and after the Persian Empire was formed.[54]

Cyrus reversed the policies of the great rulers before him – the Elamites, Hittites, Assyrians, and Babylonians – by allowing conquered populations to return to their homelands and practise their own religions instead of deporting them and their gods.[55]

As mentioned earlier, the deportations took place in three stages. Similarly, the restoration was also in three phases. The memoirs of Nehemiah and Ezra chronicle the beginning of the return of the Jews who were exiled in Babylon. The returns were led by three prominent figures: Zerubbabel, Ezra, and Nehemiah. However, only a small percentage of the people actually returned when the period of the exile was technically over (Neh 7:4–69; Isa 6:13; 10:20–23), and the problem of divorce and intermarriage became evident during this time.

The temple was completed by 515 BC, and it may be assumed the cultus was carried out according to Mosaic prescription, while the state as a whole

---

51. Bright, *History of Israel*, 360–362. See also Yamauchi, *Persia and The Bible*, 89–92.
52. Brockington, *Ezra, Nehemiah and Esther*, 76.
53. Brockington, 76.
54. Brockington, 76.
55. Albertz, *History of Israelite Religion*, 444–450. See also Drinkard, "The Socio-historical Setting of Malachi," 385–387.

functioned in an orderly manner, at least for a few years. However, with the arrival of Ezra in 458 BC, it became evident that all was not well and that reformatory measures were already necessary (Ezra 7:21–26).

One of the problems Ezra had to deal with was the issue of mixed marriages, a clear violation of the Mosaic laws of separation and purification (Ezra 9:1–4). This breach of covenant was not only serious in itself but also symptomatic of a more widespread spirit of compromise and unfaithfulness, including in marriage relationships (Ezra 9:1–2, 14). The situation did not improve very much during the years between Ezra's reformation (Ezra 9:5–10:44) in 458 BC and the arrival of Nehemiah in 444 BC. To address these and other problems, Nehemiah assembled the people for a great ceremony of covenant renewal (Neh 7:73–9:38). In his prayer of public confession, Nehemiah refers to the sins of the people, including unfaithfulness in marriage relationships, which were detrimental to the spiritual vitality of the community (9:36–37). These issues were more clearly spelled out in the response of the people (10:28–39), who pledged to avoid intermarriage with pagans.

When Nehemiah's returned from Susa to Jerusalem after a period away, the same religious and social disorder continued. He responded to these issues by taking steps to restore order in the house of Judah. Although Nehemiah did not demand divorce as Ezra had done (Ezra 10:1–4), he expressed his intense displeasure over the matter and threatened dire consequences if such marriages should be contracted in the future (Neh 13:23–27).

Although the author of Malachi never identifies himself, except by two references to his name, and never links his work to a precise historical situation like some other OT prophets, what we know of Persian and biblical history in the fifth century suggests links between that time period and the message of Malachi. The conditions that existed during the time of Malachi's predecessors, Haggai and Zechariah, seem to have continued in his own time as well. The exile was a matter of the past, the temple had been rebuilt, and sacrifices were being offered (Mal 1:10; 3:1–10).

Malachi reflects the spirit of his generation. The people God loved had strayed from their covenantal obligations and relationship with him and sought to hide their restlessness by an attitude of indifference and mockery. The exiles had been disillusioned to discover that the land of their fathers was now a wilderness, and the experience of drought, locusts, and failed harvests (3:10–11) had deepened their discontent. Although Yahweh's sanctuary had been rebuilt, their situation had not improved; they were growing impatient and sought proofs of Yahweh's love (1:2).

Under pressure of these unfavourable circumstances, both priests and people had neglected to show Yahweh the honour due to him (1:6). Malachi stresses the people's insincerity in their relationships and warns that if Yahweh's rights are not honoured, the inevitable day of judgement, the Day of the Lord, will prove to the sceptical that devotion and fear of God are not in vain for they will see the unfaithful punished but the faithful preserved from Yahweh's dreadful judgement. Malachi writes of the moral degeneracy of his time, a time marked by adultery, false swearing, and oppression of the hired workers, the widow, and the fatherless (3:5). During this time, several other ethical injustices had also resulted in violence against members of the covenant community in Israel.

Malachi speaks sternly to those who had married foreign women and sent away the wives of their youth (2:11–16). He emphasizes that the priest, as Yahweh's messenger (2:7; 3:1), must strictly observe the law of Moses (3:22). He also stresses the brotherhood of the covenant community and calls all people to fulfil their religious duties to God and their social duties to one another, especially in the home.

Summary of the Chapter

Since Malachi 2:10–16 cannot be studied in isolation, this chapter has examined the background of God's teaching on fidelity in marriage in order to provide a basis for a better understanding of the prophet Malachi's message. This chapter is very important because it enables us to study the author within the context of fidelity in the covenant relationship in both the Pentateuch and the Prophets, as well as in the historical period of Ezra-Nehemiah and in God's relationship with his people as presented in other OT texts.

This section provides the necessary background for a thorough understanding of God's relationship with his people and how Malachi 2:10–16 functions within its larger biblical context. It also recognizes that God's relationship with his covenant people is the broader framework within which the marriage covenant operates. This insight forms the foundation for exegetical engagement with Malachi 2:10–16 in the next chapter.

CHAPTER FIVE

Exegetical Understanding of Malachi 2:10–16

Introduction

The previous chapter, discussed the background to the book of Malachi and explained the various covenantal relationships in the Torah, Nevi'im, and Ketubim. This chapter exegetically studies Malachi 2:10–16 and employs the literary-historical-grammatical exegetical approach to determine its meaning. Here text-critical issues in Malachi 2:10–16 are discussed and various exegetical problems are evaluated in order to arrive at the most probable meaning of the text under consideration.

The language of the text is studied by considering the words in the text, the grammar, the literary elements, and their meanings. Attention is paid to both the immediate and broader contexts of the text. Word studies of key terms in the text are presented in order to examine these words and their usage for contextual understanding. Finally, the entirety of the text within the context of the full history of God's revelation to the church is examined.

Furthermore, the place of history in situating the text within its context is vital. The literary analysis of the final form of the text is used. The historical-grammatical method of exegesis that is employed to engage the text helps to define the meaning of unfaithfulness in Malachi 2:10–16 more precisely. Careful attention is given to the major metaphors, themes, and symbols contained in the text. Finally, the contemporary significance of the text as it speaks to the needs of modern listeners is presented.

Text and Translation of Malachi 2:10–16

Text: Malachi 2:10–16

Verses 10–12

הֲלוֹא אָב אֶחָד לְכֻלָּנוּ הֲלוֹא אֵל אֶחָד בְּרָאָנוּ מַדּוּעַ נִבְגַּד אִישׁ בְּאָחִיו לְחַלֵּל בְּרִית אֲבֹתֵינוּ:

בָּגְדָה יְהוּדָה וְתוֹעֵבָה נֶעֶשְׂתָה בְיִשְׂרָאֵל וּבִירוּשָׁלָ͏ִם כִּי | חִלֵּל יְהוּדָה קֹדֶשׁ יְהוָה אֲשֶׁר אָהֵב וּבָעַל בַּת־אֵל נֵכָר:

יַכְרֵת יְהוָה לָאִישׁ אֲשֶׁר יַעֲשֶׂנָּה עֵר וְעֹנֶה מֵאָהֳלֵי יַעֲקֹב וּמַגִּישׁ מִנְחָה לַיהוָה צְבָאוֹת:פ

Verses 13–16

וְזֹאת שֵׁנִית תַּעֲשׂוּ כַּסּוֹת דִּמְעָה אֶת־מִזְבַּח יְהוָה בְּכִי וַאֲנָקָה מֵאֵין עוֹד פְּנוֹת אֶל־הַמִּנְחָה וְלָקַחַת רָצוֹן מִיֶּדְכֶם:

וַאֲמַרְתֶּם עַל־מָה עַל כִּי־יְהוָה הֵעִיד בֵּינְךָ וּבֵין | אֵשֶׁת נְעוּרֶיךָ אֲשֶׁר אַתָּה בָּגַדְתָּה בָּהּ וְהִיא חֲבֶרְתְּךָ וְאֵשֶׁת בְּרִיתֶךָ:

וְלֹא־אֶחָד עָשָׂה וּשְׁאָר רוּחַ לוֹ וּמָה הָאֶחָד מְבַקֵּשׁ זֶרַע אֱלֹהִים וְנִשְׁמַרְתֶּם בְּרוּחֲכֶם וּבְאֵשֶׁת נְעוּרֶיךָ אַל־יִבְגֹּד:

כִּי־שָׂנֵא שַׁלַּח אָמַר יְהוָה אֱלֹהֵי יִשְׂרָאֵל וְכִסָּה חָמָס עַל־לְבוּשׁוֹ אָמַר יְהוָה צְבָאוֹת וְנִשְׁמַרְתֶּם בְּרוּחֲכֶם וְלֹא תִבְגֹּדוּ:

Translation of Malachi 2:10–16

> 10. Have we not all one father?
>
> Has not one God created us?
>
> Why are we acting treacherously[1] a man with his brother,

---

1. The BHS editors in BH textual apparatus indicate that in verse 10 the term נִבְגַּד (act faithlessly) should probably be rendered as *nibgod*, a *qal* imperfect first-person plural to be pointed with *holem* instead of *patakh*. Various commentators claim that the Hebrew is bad. Baldwin observes that the text gives no indication of a change in speaker. Baldwin, *Haggai, Zechariah, Malachi*, 236. Nor does the writer identify with the sinners he was condemning anywhere else in the book. Redditt, *Haggai, Zechariah, Malachi*, 153. In arguing for the propriety of translating the imperfect conjugation form נִבְגַּד to mean "to deal faithlessly with," vocalization of the Hebrew נִבְגַּד (to deal faithlessly) as *niphal* creates an unusual usage. Other commentators observe that there is no linguistic reason to describe the Hebrew as bad and argue that Malachi includes himself in the indictment of unfaithfulness as a means of identification with his audience. Tate, "Questions for Priests," 402. Clendenen, "Structure of Malachi," 328). The pointing of the בגד (act faithlessly) with *patakh* rather than *holem* is idiosyncratic. Some commentators claim that the pointing better fits the context and hence that it is accepted as fitting since the range of meanings of בגד (act faithlessly) includes betray, be disloyal, prove untrustworthy, and a failure to live up to an agreement or expectation. Botterweck and Ringgren, *Theological Dictionary*, 1:470; Verhoef, *Haggai and Malachi*, 266; Alden, *Malachi*, 718; Ogden

by profaning the covenant of our fathers?

11. Judah has acted treacherously[2]

and an abomination has been committed in Israel and[3] in Jerusalem.

For Judah has profaned the sanctuary of the Lord, which he loves,

when he married the daughter of a foreign god.

12. May the Lord cut off the man out of the tent of Jacob, the witness and testifier,[4]

---

and Deutsch, *Joel and Malachi*, 94. All these commentators argue that there is no reason to exclude the prophet because the prophet includes himself as he speaks to his readers.

2. The editors of BHS, in the textual apparatus, indicate that the Hebrew term used in verse 11 should probably be read as בָּגַד, a *qal* perfect masculine singular instead of the *qal* perfect feminine singular form בָּגְדָה. One major problem with the text raised by commentator is why a grammatical gender shift. Why is it that the first half of the verse is the feminine singular verb בָּגְדָה (she acted faithlessly) and the second half the predominantly masculine singular verb חִלֵּל "to profane"? O'Brien, "Judah as Wife," 247. Is this a grammatical problem or a copy error? Stuart says that there is no need for an alternative reading contrary to the Masoretic Text and that "rather than being the result of a copy error, this is in all probability an intentional merism by which the entire population, male or female, is indicted." Stuart, "Malachi," 1331. Glazier-McDonald, Verhoef, Van der Woude, and Stuart claim that the treacherous act of the inhabitants of Judah – who are grammatically feminine – is that they have become faithless. These scholars conclude that there are instances in the OT where nations are referred to as either feminine or masculine. Glazier-McDonald, *Malachi*, 89; Van der Woude, "Malachi's Struggle," 67; Verhoef, *Haggai and Malachi*, 267–268; Stuart, "Malachi," 1331.

3. The editors of BHS indicates that the Hebrew words, וּ בְיִשְׂרָאֵל (in Israel and), should be deleted because this was likely an expansion by a later editor. The LXX reads "in Israel and in Jerusalem." Jones calls for deletion of "in Jerusalem" since Judah is mentioned in the preceding context as suggested by the editors of the BHS. Jones, "LXX of Malachi 2:16," 683–685. Some other commentators hold an opposing view. J. M. P. Smith claims that the term "in Israel and" is outside Malachi's interest but that Malachi is alluding to Deuteronomy 17:4, which states that such things that had been done in "Israel" (in the past) were now being practised in Jerusalem. Smith, *Critical and Exegetical Commentary*, 45; Clendenen and Taylor, *Haggai–Malachi*, 331. However some commentators note that locating the abomination in Israel rather than in Judah seems surprising since the being people addressed were the postexilic community. Smith, *Critical and Exegetical Commentary*, 48, and van der Woude, "Malachi's Struggle," 67. Verhoef asserts that the Masoretic rendition fits the context because Jerusalem is both the capital city and the religious centre of God's people. This "Israel" has committed a detestable thing in this "Jerusalem," which is the promise and the Holy City, and now faithlessness is practised everywhere in the city. This work agrees with Verhoef, *Haggai and Malachi*, 268, and Jones, *Haggai, Zechariah and Malachi*, 221, that deletion of "in Israel and in Jerusalem" is without warrant because this idiomatic expression is used to denote totality (See: Deut 32:36; 1 Kgs 21:21; 2 Kgs 9:8; 14:26; Zech 9:8). Thus Malachi shows that faithlessness is widespread.

4. In the textual apparatus, the BHS editors indicate that from כִּי (for) in verse 11 to the end of verse 12, was not original or that it was uncertain and had probably been added. Smith observes that the Hebrew of the two coordinated particles עֵר וְעֹנֶה (everyone who awakes and answers) is complicated and does not seem to have a clear meaning. Smith, *Micah–Malachi*,

even though he presents an offering unto the Lord of hosts.

13. And second thing you do,⁵

covering⁶ the altar of the Lord with tears,

with weeping and groaning

in so much that he regarded not the offering anymore

nor receives it with favour from your hands.

14. But you ask, "Why does he not?"

Because the Lord had been witness

---

519. There are several interpretations of the expression עֵר וְעֹנֶה (everyone who awakes and answers) by commentators. Some understood עֵר וְעֹנֶה as "witness" to refer to participants in legal disputes, implying that anyone who was guilty of marrying the daughter of a foreign god would no longer be permitted to participate in legal proceedings within the community. See Wellhausen, *Die Klein Propheten*, 94; Achtemeier, *Nahum–Malachi*, 182, and Fuller, "Text-Critical Problems," 51. Other critical commentators render this expression differently. Driver, *Minor Prophets*, 314, and Baldwin, *Haggai, Zechariah, Malachi*, 238, render it "him that waketh and him that answereth." Other commentators attempt to infuse sexual connotations, translating the words as "the aroused one and the lover." Petersen, *Zechariah, 9–14* and Laalchi, 194–195; Smith, *The Book of the Twelve Prophets*, 50–51, and Glazier-McDonald, *Malachi: The Divine Messenger*, 94–99. Some prefer an emendation to the MT based on LXX and 4QXIIa, supposing that there was a scribal error in the MT in which the word "awake" was mistakenly written for "witness" and so it should be emended to read עֵד וְעֹנֶה (witness). The emendation makes sense in terms of meaning, since the Hebrew term literally means "awake and answering." Smith, *The Book of the Twelve Prophets*, 519. However, Hebrew has many similar idiomatic expressions (1 Kgs 14:10; Mal 4:1), and since this is a Hebrew idiom, Smith claim that it is another way of saying everyone. Smith, *The Book of the Twelve Prophets* 718. The important question is this: What does this pair of words mean? I read "witness and one who answers/respondent by emendation to the Masoretic text on the bases of LXX and 4QXIIa. It is this עֵד and וְעֹנֶה are to be cut off not from the judgement seat but from the dwellings/tents of Jacob – that is anyone who committed the abuse.

5. The textual apparatus suggest that in verse 13– וְזֹאת שֵׁנִית תַּעֲשׂוּ (this second thing you do) – is not original but has probably been added. This study does not agree with this conclusion, and for the reasoning see the section: "Clausal Explanation of Malachi 2:13" in the work on p@@.

6. In verse 13, there is a piel infinitive construct term כַּסּוֹת (covering) used instead of a finite verb. The editors of the BHS noting that the Septuagint (LXX), Syria, and Vulgate read ἐκαλύπτετε (you cover), a second-person masculine plural prefix with a conjunction, suggest a reading that is different from the MT. The problem with this section is that "the Piel infinitive construct כַּסּוֹת (kassot) proves difficult." Hill, *Malachi*, 237. It is also translated as imperfect. Smith, *Micah–Malachi*, 320. However, the verb כָּסָה means "to cover" in the *piel* form. Brown and Briggs, *Hebrew and English Lexicon*, 491. This is also attested to in the Haggai–Zechariah–Malachi corpus in Malachi 2:13 and 2:16. See also. TDOT 7:259-264. This verb is also used figuratively of tears in the form of flooding and drowning (NIV). I interpret "to cover" like Hill, who prefers the usage of the infinitive construct of כַּסּוֹת for two main reasons: (1) it underscores the ongoing activity implied by the nonperfective, and (2) "the form has its compliment in Qal infinitive construct פְּנוֹת (to turn) also in verse 13 and is in keeping with the style of graphic diction employed in the third oracle." Hill, *Malachi*, 237. See also Zehnder, "Fresh Look at Malachi," 231.

between you and the wife of your youth,
to whom you have been faithless,
though she is your companion and your wife by covenant.

15. Did he not make them one,[7] with a portion of the spirit in their union?

And what was the one God seeking? Godly offspring.

So guard yourselves in your spirit[8] and let none of you be faithless to the wife of his youth.

---

7. The BHS editors indicate that וְלֹא־אֶחָד עָשָׂה וּשְׁאָר רוּחַ לוֹ וּמָה הָאֶחָד מְבַקֵּשׁ זֶרַע אֱלֹהִים וְנִשְׁמַרְתֶּם בְּרוּחֲכֶם is doubtful and probably added. Many previous scholars agree with this assertion that the text is difficult and that it is grammatically and syntactically incomplete. Torrey, "Prophecy of 'Malachi,'" 16-20; Hvidberg, *Weeping and Laughter*, 123; Baldwin, *Haggai, Zechariah, Malachi*, 241. Scholars have adopted three approaches to understanding this verse. First, verse 15 is to be understood as a rejoinder by the men whom Malachi accuses on the basis of Abraham's marriage. So these scholars rest their argument on the premise that Abraham sent away one of his two wives – Hagar. This approach connects verse 15 with Abraham as part of the men's argument that if Abraham took a second wife (Hagar), then they cannot be condemned for doing same. The second approach, understands the first אֶחָד to be the object of the sentence, with the second being a reference to God, and revocalizes וּשְׁאָר to be "flesh" in parallelism with spirit to mean "Has He not made them one, with flesh and spirit?" (Zegnder, "Fresh Look at Malachi," 238-9, while the third approach adopts the interpretation that the one who acts in this way loses the vigour to pass on life and, therefore, will not get the offspring he seeks. Glazier-McDonald, "Intermarriage," 611. For a comprehensive explanation on these various approaches, see Zehnder, "Fresh Look at Malachi," 237-241. So, what is the writer saying in verse 15a? Is he saying something about God being one or is he referring to the way Adam and Eve were created as one flesh? The MT is preferable as it stands and makes good sense. The key point Zehnder makes is that there was an "ellipsis at one point in time which omitted זאת which was lost later during the transmission of the text or that it was left out intentionally by a writer who preferred an abbreviated style." Zehnder, "Fresh Look at Malachi," 241.

8. The textual apparatus indicates a difficulty in the interpretation of the Hebrew words אֶחָד (one) and הָאֶחָד (the one). Since the cardinal numeral is grammatically ambiguous, scholars wonder whether they should understand the term אֶחָד, (one) in the first clause as the subject or the object; and if it is the subject, what is to be the understood as the object? Hill, *Malachi*, 246. There are many exegetical and syntactical problems in this text, pointing to the likelihood of textual corruption.

16. "For I hate⁹ divorce," says Yahweh, God of Israel¹⁰

---

9. The Hebrew term שָׂנֵא in verse 16a has proved textually difficult for interpreters. The Masoretes identified this as probably to be read as a third-person perfect masculine singular "he hated divorce." This raises a grammatical problem since God cannot be referring to himself in the third-person singular. Commentators offer various explanations. One translation favours revocalization of the *qal* perfect "he hates" to "hating," with the subject "I" being implied. Rudolph, *Haggai, Sacharja 1–8*, 270. Others emend "he hates" to "I hate." Driver, *The Minor Prophets*, 327; Smith, *Micah–Malachi*, 319. Some emend the Masoretic Text from the perfect form to the imperfect Smith, *Micah–Malachi*, 320, and Wellhausen, *Skizzen und Vorarbeiten*, 199; (This German title is translated "Sketches and Preparatory Work" – translation from German to English mine) or as participle: Keil, *Twelve Minor Prophets*, 454; Rudolph, *Haggai, Sacharja 1–8*, 270. Verhoef concludes that the participle suggests continuity – that is, that the Lord continually hates. Verhoef, *Haggai and Malachi*, 278. Matthews emends the Masoretic text from "he hates" to read "I hate," and he cites the LXX ἀλλὰ ἐὰν μισήσας which translated the verb as a subjunctive aorist "but if having hated" as the basis of his emendation. Matthews, "Haggai, Malachi," 37. Therefore, the text is not clear. The LXX and Targum – along with other commentators – suggest an impersonal subject and translated the directive as "If one sends away out of hate" or "If one hates his wife, let him send away." See Schreiner, "Mischehen-Ehebruch-Ehescheidung," 207–228; Rudolph, *Haggai, Sacharja 1–8*, 270; Fuller, "Text-Critical Problem," 50, 54; Hugenberger, *Marriage as a Covenant*, 70; and Ko, "Be Faithful," 40. All these scholars try to justify divorce in instances where a man hates his wife (permission for divorce). According to Smith, the problem with this text is the shift from the simple third-person masculine perfect to a first-person perfect. Smith, *Micah–Malachi*, 324. Tate, "Questions for Priests," 404, and the NEB translators prefer the reading "for he who hates [his wife] and divorces her covers his garment with violence" because they look for a kind of parallelism in this verse to show that Yahweh hates divorce and hates a man who covers himself with violence or crime. This writer and some other commentators prefer the reading where God is the subject. Schreiner, "Mischehen-Ehebruch-Ehescheidung," 213–214; Verhoef, *Haggai and Malachi*, 278. Verhoef and Hugenberger assert that the subject אֶחָד, (one) is the same as that of verse 15 – the one Yahweh, and that Yahweh is the subject of this verb on other occasions (e.g. Deut 12:31; 16:22; Prov 6:16; Isa 61:8), but the third-person singular with God as subject is contrary to this being the direct speech of Yahweh. In addition, "If he hates, let him divorce" is syntactically awkward in the overall context and not in line with the message of the passage which commands: "do not act faithlessly." This study agrees with scholars who propose the translation "I hate divorce." The reading "I hate divorce" can make sense with a little restoration of accidentally dropped pronoun. We argue that the pronoun אָנֹכִי was accidentally dropped in the process of copying and that with the restoration of that pronoun, the form שָׂנֵא can be taken as a participle and the text translated "for I hate." This makes the translation and meaning significant; it also aligns with the immediate message as well as Malachi's message that supports the idea of Yahweh's judgement against covenant-breaking and his absolute rejection of divorce – see Malachi 2:16 NETtn.

10. The editors of BHS indicate that the Hebrew words אָמַר יְהוָה אֱלֹהֵי יִשְׂרָאֵל in verse 16– which are literally translated "says Yahweh, the God of Israel" – were not there initially but are an addition. What makes the understanding of this section controversial is this basic question: Why would Malachi employ a two-messenger formula? Matthews deletes אָמַר יְהוָה אֱלֹהֵי יִשְׂרָאֵל ("thus says Yahweh, the Lord of Israel"), claiming that this was an expansion. He also argues that "Yahweh, the God of Israel" is inauthentic since it occurs only here in Malachi and regards this as a vertical dittography-repetitive given the presence of "says Yahweh of hosts" in the next line. Matthews, *Haggai, Malachi*, 37. J. M. P. Smith also omits this phrase as a gloss, arguing that there is an intervening divine formula that separates the condition "protasis" from the result "apodosis." Smith, *Micah–Malachi*, 55. But both Verhoef and Hugenberger note that this occurs only here in Malachi and argue that since the MT has the support of 4QXIIa and

It is like a garment that covers wrongdoing, says Yahweh of hosts
Therefore take heed to your spirit, do not act treacherously.[11]

Exegetical Outline of Malachi 2:10–16

This section presents the structure of Malachi 2:10–16. The division of this third oracle, Malachi 2:10–16, follows the basic structure of a prophetic disputation, arranged in a chiastic pattern as demonstrated in the work of Hugenberger:

A God who is one created his people (to be one)
    General sin = infidelity (v.10)
    B Specific sin = infidelity by intermarriage with a pagan (v. 11)
        C Verdict: exclusion, rejection of food offering (v. 12)
        C' Verdict: exclusion, rejection of food offering (v. 13)
    B' Specific sin = infidelity by divorce (v. 14)
A' God who is one made husband and wife to be one
    General sin = infidelity (vv. 15–16a)[12]

---

some other ancient versions, the position of the divine formular is in order and the proposed deletion appears unwarranted. Verhoef, *Haggai and Malachi*, 279, and Hugenberger, *Marriage as a Covenant*, 53.

11. The BHS editors indicate that the Hebrew words וְנִשְׁמַרְתֶּם בְּרוּחֲכֶם וְלֹא תִבְגֹּדוּ in verse 16– translated "Therefore take heed to your spirit, do not act treacherously" – are doubtful and were probably not there initially but added later. The BHS editors suggest that this should be compared with verse 15ba (וְנִשְׁמַרְתֶּם בְּרוּחֲכֶם). Scholarly debates with major possibilities for interpretation of this section emerged. J.M.P. Smith translates this as "take heed to your spirit" and argues that this section is an admonition growing out of verse 14, interpreting spirit as apparently equivalent to "character, purpose or will." Smith, *Micah-Malachi*, 55. Other commentators, observing that guarding one's spirit and abstaining from divorce is in view here, argue that this section is not a disputation but an admonition cautioning the people not to be unfaithful. Baldwin, *Haggai, Zechariah, Malachi*, 241; Hill, *Haggai, Zechariah, and Malachi*, 326; O'Brien, *Priest and Levite*, 73. Hill observes that the verb guard is "to keep watch on your spirit" in such a way as to protect oneself from influences and situations that would compromise the marriage relationship. He concludes that the usage of the term in 16 is in order and that it preserves the best text in this section of verse 16. It is neither doubtful nor added, it fits the context because the prophet is giving a warning to the community: "It is in the best interests of the individual as well as the community that families should not be broken by divorce. Hill, *Haggai, Zechariah, and Malachi*, 254. Compare Zehnder, "Fresh Look at Malachi," 257.

12. Hugenberger, *Marriage as Covenant*, 99.

The writer has called for faithfulness because as Jews they have one father, then verse 16b is a summary exhortation not to commit infidelity of any form.[13]

Text-Critical Problems in Malachi 2:10–16

There are several difficulties with the text of Malachi 2:10–16, particularly because of paradoxical statements, grammar, syntax, and semantic ambiguity. The *BHS* editors note a few examples of these difficulties in verses 10–14.[14] A brief discussion of the text-critical issues in Malachi 2:10–16 is necessary before attempting an exegetical analysis of the passage because of the textual and syntactical difficulties surrounding the Hebrew text, especially in the final two verses (2:15–16). These difficulties not only affect the translation of the passage but also its exegesis.

The *BHQ* attests to the transposition of the two rhetorical questions in verse 10 by the Septuagint (LXX). However, the Masoretic Text (MT) reading is supported by the Vulgate (Vg), the Syriac Peshitta (S), and the Targum (T). The transposition is almost certainly an indication that LXX reads "one father" – referring to the patriarch – and prefers the interpretation as God the Creator over an earthly patriarch, thereby changing the order of the question to reflect this preference.[15] Another textual variant in this verse concerns the vocalization of נבגד which can be pointed either as 3ms Niphal perfect or 1cp Qal imperfect. While the latter reading is contextually more probable and is supported by S, T, and Vg, along with the MT, LXX reads "you abandoned" (ἐγκατελίπετε). The LXX translation is probably an attempt to exclude the prophet from being numbered among the guilty.[16]

There are four textual problems in verse 11. First, the *BHS* proposes that בָּגַד (3ms Qal perfect) should be read instead of the 3fs Qal perfect בָּגְדָה. This suggestion should probably be followed, especially in light of the prevailing masculine context of the passage.

---

13. Hugenberger, *Marriage as a Covenant*, 99. For similar uses of chiasms in OT texts, see Tushima, *Fate of Saul's Progeny*, 167.

14. Elliger and Rudolph, *Biblia Hebraica Stuttgartensia*, 1083.

15. See Verhoef, *Haggai and Malachi*, 265.

16. Smith, *A Critical and Exegetical Commentary on Malachi*, 58. Verhoef appears to concur as he recognizes the possibility of Malachi employing "we" to include himself in the collective guilt. Cf. Verhoef, *Haggai and Malachi*, 266. See also Ko, "Be Faithful," 36.

Second, the *BHS* proposes that בְּיִשְׂרָאֵל and the conjunctive ‍ו be deleted as a variant reading (var lect). There is, however, no textual evidence to regard "in Israel and" as a late addition. Verhoef suggests that Malachi might have strategically employed the phrase to express the totality of all people, in which Judah and Israel are interchangeable terms.[17]

Third, as against MT's בַּת־אֵל נֵכָר ("daughter of a foreign god"), 4QXIIa reads אֵל־נֵכָר בֵּית ("the house of a foreign god"), while LXX reads καὶ ἐπετήδευσεν εἰς θεοὺς ἀλλοτρίους. ("and to pursue another god"). T reads "the daughter of the nations," while S reads "foreign gods." The MT reading – supported by Vg, α' (Aquila in Hexaplaric witness), σ' (Symmachus in Hexaplaric witness), and θ' (Theodotion in Hexaplaric witness) – is to be preferred as the other variants seem to be more exegetical than literal translations. In addition, in light of the reading attested by 4QXIIa, it is more plausible to see *yod* (י) as a scribal interpolation.[18]

Fourth, *BHS* notes that the words from כִּי (verse 11) to the first clause in verse 12 (ending with עֵר) are probably late additions. However, since no manuscript evidence is provided, this suggestion should not be given too much weight.

The first of the three textual problems noted by *BHQ* in verse 12 concerns whether or not the inseparable preposition ל should be prefixed to איש. Both the MT and T read לאיש ("for the man"), while G, S, and Vg provide a reading that does not reflect the prepositional prefix. It seems likely that ל is taken as a direct object marker by these three witnesses, thereby taking "the man" as the object of כרת.[19] Therefore, the reading that reflects the prefix is preferable.

The second problem has to do with ער וענה ("everyone who awakes and answers") as read by the MT. LXX and 4QXIIa read עד וענה ("everyone who witnesses and answers"), while S and T read "son and grandson." Although this problem cannot be resolved text-critically, it is better to emend the MT based on LXX and 4QXIIa so that עד is read instead of ער, with ר taken as a scribal error for ד.

The final textual problem in this verse concerns the reading preserved only by LXX. As against the MT reading ומגיש ("the one who brings"), LXX

---

17. Verhoef, *Haggai and Malachi*, 268.
18. Ko, "Be Faithful," 37; Fuller, "Text-Critical Problems," 51.
19. Ko, 37.

reads ἐκ προσαγόντων ("from bringing"). *BHQ* suggests that LXX might have read מ as a preposition instead of a participial prefix. Therefore, the reading preserved by the MT is to be preferred.

Several textual problems arise in verse 13. First, *BHS* observes that the first clause in the verse (וְזֹאת שֵׁנִית תַּעֲשׂוּ) may be a late addition and that other witnesses only omit שֵׁנִית. However, contextual consideration favour the inclusion of this clause. Second, only LXX differs from the MT in reading ἐμίσουν ("I hate") instead of שֵׁנִית ("second"). As Him Ko suggests, LXX might have been influenced by the verb שׂנא in verse 16, thereby reading the ordinal as a verb.[20] Third, the infinitive כַּסּוֹת ("to cover") read by both the MT and 4QXIIa is translated as ἐκαλύπτετε ("you cover") in LXX, α′, and θ′, with the Vg also supporting this reading. The infinitive is to be preferred on linguistic grounds, especially in light of the threefold infinitive sequence (לקחת, פנות, כסות) in the verse.[21] Finally, MT, Vg, and S read מֵאֵין ("there is no"), while 4QXIIa and LXX read מֵאוֹן ("trouble"). However, it is syntactically more natural to prefer the MT reading.[22]

While there is no significant textual problem in verse 14, scholars generally note the textual corruption in verses 15 and 16.[23] The rather enigmatic opening clause in verse 15 – וְלֹא־אֶחָד עָשָׂה – poses the first difficulty, which concerns the grammatical function of אֶחָד, ("one"), specifically, whether this is the subject or the object. While LXX translates it as the subject, T and S both take it as the object. This is essentially a syntactical problem, and the context must play the major role in resolving the issue.

The second problem relates to the referent of the articular cardinal numeral in the second clause, הָאֶחָד ("the one"). Again, this problem is both syntactical and exegetical and has to be resolved within the context.

The third problem in verse 15 has to do with whether וּמָה הָאֶחָד מְבַקֵּשׁ should be read interrogatively or declaratively ("and what was the one seeking?" or "[when] the one was seeking"). While Vg, S, and T read this

---

20. Ko, 38.
21. Zehnder, "Fresh Look at Malachi," 224–259.
22. Zehnder, 234.
23. Torrey, "Prophecy of 'Malachi,'" 10; Smith, *A Critical and Exegetical Commentary on Malachi*, 54–55; Baldwin, *Haggai, Zechariah, Malachi*, 240.

statement as a question, neither the MT nor 4QXIIa read it explicitly as a question although this is a syntactical possibility.[24]

The final text-critical issue in this verse concerns whether the בגד root should be in the second person (תבגד) or third person (יבגד). LXX, 4QXIIa, T, and Vg read it as the second person ("you act faithlessly"), while the MT reads it as the third person ("he acts faithlessly"). S also probably reads it as the third person but renders it with an indefinite pronoun with the adverb of negation la; ("let none act faithlessly"). This final clause should probably be read as a third-person singular with jussive meaning with the MT and S.

The MT of Malachi 2:16 begins with כִּי־שָׂנֵא שַׁלַּח ("for he hates divorce"). The vocalization presents grammatical difficulties, and there is also a major text-critical issue in verse 16 with reference to the כִּי (for) clause, especially the person of the שׂנא and whether the clause is the protasis of a conditional sentence or the basis of a prohibitive statement. The MT takes the act of divorce as the object of the verb "to hate." 4QXIIa reads שנא שלח בי ים ("except he hates her, to divorce") so that "her" is the object of the verb "to hate." LXX reads ἀλλὰ ἐὰν μισήσας ἐξαποστείλῃς ("but if hating you divorce"), in which "divorce" is taken as a subjunctive aorist second-person singular verb and "hating" as an attendant circumstantial participle.

In addition to these textual problems, there are several syntactical, exegetical, and theological issues in this verse that will be addressed in the exegesis of the passage below. It is clear that scribes have tampered with the text of this verse to reflect their own position on the issue of divorce. As the editors of the NET Bible put it, "It is possible that the first person pronoun אנכי ("I") has been accidentally dropped from the text after כי. If one restores the pronoun, the form שׂנא can be taken as a participle and the text translated "for I hate."

Exegetical Analysis of Malachi 2:10–16 (An Overview)

In this section, an exegetical analysis of Malachi 2:10–16 is presented. The analysis begins with the structural layout of the passage, which is presented

---

24. What further compounds the problem is whether the clause that follows should be taken as the answer or as part of the question. See Clendenen, "Biblical Hebrew Hortatory Texts," 102.

in a poetic manner as revealed in the arrangement of the Hebrew text and the explanation given thereafter. In the preceding section, the writer of Malachi focuses on priestly families and their responsibilities, but here in Malachi 2:10, the direction of his discussion shifts to include all Israelites, as was the case in 1:1–5. The literary form that began in 2:1–9 continues in 2:10–16. It is clear that until verse 9, the dispute has been between the priests and God, but from verse 10 onwards, the scope is enlarged to embrace all people.

The Masoretes divided the text into two sections: the first section consists of verses 10–12, while the second consists of verses 13–16, with the Hebrew sign *parasah petuhah* (פ) serving as the marker that divides the passage. The structural layout begins with a combination of two Hebrew words הֲלוֹא, an interrogative particle, and a negation. This appears in both the first and second clauses and forms a double question that says something about God as the originator of the nation and the people.

The writer begins with a particle in both the first and second clauses. These two Hebrew clauses are very important for understanding this section. The prophet begins with הֲלוֹא אָב אֶחָד לְכֻלָּנוּ ("Have we not all one father?") and הֲלוֹא אֵל אֶחָד בְּרָאָנוּ ("Has not one God created us?"). Both rhetorical questions relate to an ongoing activity or situation that the prophet considers illogical and reprehensible. The rhetorical questions in verses 10a and 10b are similar in their use of the interrogative plus the negative particle הֲלוֹא ("has not?") and presuppose an affirmative response.[25] The first two clauses describe the existing state or situation, while the third provides the reasons for the accusation. These clauses accuse the people of in an illogical and reprehensible manner.

The third Hebrew clause in verse 10, מַדּוּעַ נִבְגַּד אִישׁ בְּאָחִיו, is translated as "Why are we acting treacherously a man to his brother?" In contrast to the first two clauses, which emphasizes the expectation that the people would live as one happy family, the third clause charges Judah with wrongdoing. Verse 10 is a general charge against Judah, accusing the people of unfaithfulness to fellow covenant members and charging them with wrongdoing. The sad truth is revealed in the continuation of the Hebrew phrase לְחַלֵּל בְּרִית אֲבֹתֵינוּ ("to profane the covenant of our fathers") – the people were dealing treacherously with one another by profaning the covenant that God had made with their forefathers (2:10d).

---

25. Van der Merwe, Naude and Kroeze, *Biblical Hebrew Reference Grammar*, 322.

In verse 11, another charge is levelled against the people. In the first clause of verse 11, Judah is openly accused of marrying women who worshipped pagan gods. It is important to remember that God brought these people into existence as a united people who were bound together in a covenant relationship with him. Although they should have acted with faithfulness in their relationships – both with God and with one another – they failed to do so. It is based on the sin of intermarriage that the prophet pronounces God's verdict and judgement on violators in verse 12.

The second division, Malachi 2:13–16, is also divided into two subunits. The first subunit is 2:13–14 and the second is 2:15–16a. These verses form the second indictment, which is centred on another kind of infidelity – divorce – that is the cause of God's displeasure with his people in the area of marital relationships (2:13). In Malachi 2, the people ask the Lord about his displeasure with them (2:14a). Malachi 2:14 answers the question by revealing that there has been a breach of the covenant relationship or a violation of the covenant. The entire passage is unified by the repeated use of the root word from which the Hebrew verb בגד (faithless) is derived. This Hebrew verb – translated "break faith" in Malachi 2:10 – also occurs in verses 11, 14, 15, and 16.

Unfaithfulness among the people leads to the breaking of faith, which in turn profanes or violates Israel's covenant with God, similar to the way the priests had violated the Levitical covenant (Mal 2:8). The text presents two elements of violation or breaking of faith. The first is the violation of the social or horizontal responsibilities of the covenant, which then leads to violations at the religious or vertical level. Verses 10–12 reiterate the vertical aspect of Judah's unfaithfulness, which leads the people to commit detestable acts or abominations. The second element relates to the horizontal dimension of Judah's unfaithfulness, and verses 13–16a focus on this aspect, which involves divorce or the breaking of marital covenants. At the centre of the chiasm is God's verdict and punishment for infidelity (2:12–13). This structural unity argues strongly against those who view this passage as being difficult or as an interpolation.

The immediate context preceding this verse is Malachi 2:1–9, where Malachi exposes the priests' unfaithfulness to the covenantal stipulations. The punishment for their infidelity is introduced by the exclamatory Hebrew particle הִנְנִי (behold), used with a participle. This particle, which has a highly technical meaning within a direct discourse, is an important formula for making a declaration in a covenant lawsuit (see 2 Sam 12:11; 1 Kgs 14:10; Jer 6:19).[26]

The immediate context (Mal 1:6–2:9) plays a significant role in understanding the text. In Malachi 1, two arguments are presented in verses 6a and 6b. In verse 6a, the prophet establishes that Yahweh must be honoured by his people. He then issues a charge against the priests for being disloyal and disrespecting Yahweh's name (1:6b). The priests question this allegation in Malachi 1:6b, but the prophet clearly declares God's word concerning their response. He charges them a second time with unfaithfulness in sacrificing unacceptable animals at Yahweh's altar (1:7a), and once again, these unfaithful priests question this charge (1:7b). In verse 7c, the prophet gives further justification for the allegation of unfaithfulness. The prophet declares that the priests, by their actions, have been unfaithful and have failed to uphold the covenant stipulations.

Exegetical Study of Malachi 2:10–12

Clausal Explanation of Verse 10

The first accusation in this verse begins with two parallel Hebrew clauses, using the Hebrew phrase הֲלוֹא ("Is it not?"). This is a feature of a poetic couplet. In verse 10a, the Hebrew clause הֲלוֹא אָב אֶחָד לְכֻלָּנוּ ("Have we not all one father?") expresses a proverbial reassertion of the exclusive relationship between Yahweh and Israel. Since all Israel has one Father and God created that nation, the people should be united as one big, happy family. However, they were unfaithful in their relationships with one another, thereby profaning the covenant God had made with their fathers.

The second clause, הֲלוֹא אֵל אֶחָד בְּרָאָנוּ ("Has not one God created us?"), is parallel to the first. This clause also begins with הֲלוֹא which describes an existing state or situation.[27] This verse begins with a series of rhetorical questions that invite the people to reflect on their relationship with God as their "one father." Some scholars translate this Hebrew clause הֲלוֹא אָב אֶחָד לְכֻלָּנוּ as "Surely we all have one father?"[28] The literal translation for the BHS text is, "Is there not one father to all of us?" The questions raised here revolve

---

26. For similar use of the Hebrew term הִנְנִי, see Tushima, *Fate of Saul's Progeny*, 231, 253.
27. Brown, Driver, and Briggs, *Hebrew and English Lexicon* 520.
28. Hill, *Malachi*, 221.

around two points: Who are the "we"? and Who is the "one father"? The term "we" in this text is a first-person plural pronoun that refers to more than one person.²⁹ It shows that the addressee is a group of people.

By using "we," the prophet is asserting the familial unity of the people, who share a common parentage and have a dynamic relationship with the "one father" in the clause. The prophet reminds the people of their common parentage by drawing their attention to their familial (covenant) unity through their "one father," who is God.

The second concern in the first clause is the identification of the Hebrew term אָב אֶחָד ("one father"). There has been much debate over the identity of the אָב אֶחָד ("one father") in the text. One commentator suggests that the father here refers to the patriarchs.³⁰ Others interpret the "one father" as Abraham.³¹ However, those who interpret this as referring to Abraham may have missed the point because they see "Creator" and "Father" as two separate concepts. This study, along with other scholars, argues that the "one father" here refers to Yahweh.³² There are two key references to Yahweh as Father in the OT. Deuteronomy 32:6 (NRSV) identifies Yahweh as "your father, who created you." In addition, the prophet himself had earlier referred to God as Father (see Mal 1:6).

If Yahweh is their Father, this implies that the Creator God is also the Father of the people. This dual concept of God as Father and Creator should be understood as complementary (see Isa 64:8). God made himself known and established an exclusive relationship with his people at Sinai (Exod 4:22–23; Isa 44:1–2; 63:16; Hos 11:1). Therefore, the people should worship him as an united family of faith and avoid unfaithfulness that undermines their covenantal unity. The prophet reveals that there is a problem with the people's relationship with Yahweh. They were profaning the covenant by being unfaithful to the stipulations of the covenant God had made with their forefathers (Deut 7:3–4).

---

29. Ogden and Deutsch, *Joel and Malachi*, 94.

30. Baldwin, *Haggai, Zechariah, Malachi*, 237.

31. Calvin, *The Minor Prophets*: The Commentaries on the Twelve Minor Prophets 5 vols. Trans J. Owen; (Edinburgh: Calvin Translation Society, 1848), 539. See Dumbrell, *Faith of Israel*, 238–239; Driver, *Minor Prophets*, 316, and Moore, Haggai and Malachi, 135. Still others interpret the "one father" as "God/Yahweh." Keil, *Twelve Minor Prophets*, 453. See Ogden and Deutsch, *Joel and Malachi*, 94.

32. Van der Woude, "Malachi's Struggle," 110, and Verhoef, *Haggai and Malachi*, 265.

The Hebrew verb לְחַלֵּל is a combination of a preposition and a piel infinitive construct meaning "to profane" or "pollute" or "desecrate."³³ This term is used in the OT to describe the violation of covenant rules (Lev 21:4). The Hebrew verb חָלַל means to make something unholy (Mal 1:12). It paints a picture of someone who vows to the Lord or swears an oath but fails to fulfil it, thereby profaning or breaking their word. The people had disregarded the covenant they had made, treating it with contempt by violating Yahweh's covenantal rules. As mentioned earlier, the basis of their divine paternity was their unity as the people of God, created by him.

Malachi addresses God's special people, warning them not to do anything to dishonour their special covenantal relationship. He then refers to a specific kind of profanation. In the third Hebrew clause of verse 10, he presents this act of treachery as לְחַלֵּל בְּרִית אֲבֹתֵינוּ ("by profaning the covenant of our fathers"). The people addressed in this verse, who are God's special people, profaned the בְּרִית (covenant) of their fathers by acting treacherously towards one another. Malachi 2:10–16 makes it clear that the audience being addressed has now broadened from just the priests to the whole nation. The reference here is not just to the covenant with Levi (Mal 2:4–8) but to the Mosaic covenant, and the charge of covenant unfaithfulness applies not just to the priests but to all Israel.

The next Hebrew verb, נִבְגַּד ("we act faithlessly"), is a qal imperfect first-person common plural form that reveals the kind of profanation expressed in the passage. This root בגד (faithless) appears in its various stems 266 times in the OT³⁴ and 5 times in the book of Malachi (2:10, 11, 14, 15, 16). In OT usage, the term generally describes a violation of the covenant – an act of

---

33. Brown, Driver, and Briggs, *Hebrew and English Lexicon*, 320. Cf. Koehler and Baumgartner, *Hebrew and Aramaic Lexicon*, 319, and Clines, "חָלַל" *DCH* 3:237.

34. These occurrences appear in 227 verses. The term, according to a lemma search using the BibleWorks software, occurs 114 times in the Pentateuch (the bulk of which are found in Leviticus), 55 times in the historical books, 26 times in poetical books, and 71 times in the Prophets (five of which are found in Malachi). A close examination of the semantic range of the term reveals that it denotes unfaithfulness in several different relationships: in Israel's relationship with God (Jer 9:2; Mal 2:11); metaphorically within the marital relationship but depicting Israel's revolt against the Lord (1 Sam 14:33; Ps 78:57; 119:158); in human marriage, where spouses commit act of faithlessness or treachery against one another (Jer 3:20; Mal 2:14); and in general human relationships, denoting unfaithfulness, especially to one's brother (Mal 2:10). The covenant and its obligations forms the background of the biblical usage of the term. See Louis Goldberg, "בגד" *TWOT* 1:89–90; also see *TDOT* 1:470 and Robin Wakely, "בגד" *NIDOTTE* 1:582. See also Clendenen and Taylor, *Haggai– Malachi*, 326.

betrayal or treachery in a relationship that calls for loyalty, kindness, and service. It also connotes acting unfaithfully or treating a woman faithlessly (Exod 21:8; Prov 23:28; Isa 24:16; Jer 3:20; Hos 5:7).³⁵

The people were profaning the בְּרִית (covenant) of their fathers by acting treacherously in relation to the bond that unites all Israel as brothers. This profanation in the form of infidelity involves a violation of their covenant with fellow covenant members, which would attract punishment for infidelity, as seen in various OT texts (Lev 18:29–30; Num 15:30–31; 25:1–9; Josh 23:12–13; Judg 3:6–8).

Scholars have commented on the usage of the term בגד (faithless). Charles D. Isbell says, "Cheating, swindling the gullible, defrauding the poor or helpless members of society, etc – all were called *begeding* or garmenting."³⁶ Isbell may be correct since the original word relates to an improper act within the setting of a community composed of equal partners in a covenant with God (Deut 24:17). The prophet Malachi is thus indicting the people for committing improper acts in the form of unfaithfulness within their covenantal relationship with Yahweh. This term is also used in the context of both covenant and family relationships.³⁷ In other words, the same Hebrew word can be used in relation to covenant faithlessness, marital faithlessness, and faithlessness to Yahweh and his cult.

The writer of Malachi affirms the unity of the people, emphasizing their dynamic social relationship with their Creator and "one father." This theme of the Lord as Israel's Father and Creator runs throughout Malachi's prophecy (Mal 1:6; 2:10; 3:17), but the people addressed are unfaithful to one another (2:10b). In this verse, the prophet raises two major issues related to unfaithfulness: first, the failure to recognize God as God, and second, the resulting unfaithfulness between covenant members. The Hebrew phrase אִישׁ בְּאָחִיו ("with one another") is literally rendered as "a man with his brother." The Bible presents ill-treatment of a brother as a serious crime (Gen 37:27) because they are fellow members of the religious community.

---

35. Holladay, *Hebrew and Aramaic Lexicon*, 33.

36. Isbell, *Malachi*, 50.

37. Brown, Driver, and Briggs, *Hebrew and English Lexicon*, 93, and Botterweck and Ringgren, *Theological Dictionary*, 470–473.

These are the people whom God had brought into existence as a united community in a covenantal relationship with himself. Such a relationship should have produced faithfulness not only to Yahweh but also to one another as members of the covenant community. However, intermarriage with foreigners, which was prohibited on religious grounds, had crept into the community and would lead households – and, by extension, Israel – to adopt the ways of foreign cultures, especially their pagan religious practices (Exod 34:11–16; Num 25:1–2; Deut 7:3–4; Judg 3:5–6; Neh 13:23–27).

Clausal Explanation of Verse 11

The prophet, still in the first section of the structure (2:10–12), challenges the addressees through a general indictment on unfaithfulness. He establishes that there has been unfaithfulness to covenantal obligations, especially in relation to fellow covenant members, as shown in Malachi 2:10. Malachi maintains that the people's relationship with Yahweh has been damaged because they have violated their covenantal obligations to other members of the covenant community. He reiterates that this unfaithfulness violates the bond that unites fellow covenant members.

In verse 11, the prophet continues addressing the people's unfaithfulness to God in specific ways. It is important to note that while in the previous verse (2:10), the prophet began with rhetorical questions, verse 11 is a statement of fact – a direct indictment against Judah. The prophet charges Judah with betrayal in the form of unfaithfulness through intermarriage, using the Hebrew words בָּגְדָה יְהוּדָה ("Judah has acted treacherously").

In this accusation, the prophet shows that Judah's main problem is breaking faith. Judah has acted unfaithfully against the covenantal stipulations. After restating the charge mentioned in verse 10b, the prophet elaborates further in verse 11 with a second accusation, using the Hebrew *waw* conjunctive along with a common feminine singular noun תּוֹעֵבָה (translated "abomination"). This feminine noun, which occurs only here in the Minor Prophets but is found about sixty times in other OT books, means "something abominable," "offensive," or "detestable" (Jer 6:15; 8:12; Ezek 16:50).[38]

The charge in the second clause – וְתוֹעֵבָה נֶעֶשְׂתָה ("and abomination has been committed") – describes the abomination that has been committed.

---

38. Holladay, *Hebrew and Aramaic Lexicon*, 88.

Exegetical Understanding of Malachi 2:10–16

In this verse, the prophet makes a twofold accusation. He describes Judah's offence as an act of breaking faith, which is abominable in the sight of Yahweh, and specifically states where this abomination has been committed – בְּיִשְׂרָאֵל וּבִירוּשָׁלָ͏ִם ("in Israel and in Jerusalem"). This Hebrew word pair בְּיִשְׂרָאֵל וּבִירוּשָׁלָ͏ִם ("in Israel and in Jerusalem") is problematic because at the time, the northern kingdom of Israel had not existed for over three hundred years. The BHS editors suggest deleting "in Israel."[39] Some commentators also suggest deleting "in Israel,"[40] while other suggest deleting "in Jerusalem."[41] But the question remains: Why is "in Israel" mentioned here? Verhoef argues that the term "in Israel and in Jerusalem" reveals the universality and totality of the offence of unfaithfulness, and thus should be retained.[42] Stuart observes that Malachi understands God's people as the Israel of the patriarchal promises, the Israel of the Pentateuch, the true Israel, even though in Malachi's day all that was left of political Israel was in fact Judah yet even so the remnant of God's people was truly called "Israel."[43]

After presenting his charge, the prophet continues his discussion in the next Hebrew clause, כִּי חִלֵּל יְהוּדָה קֹדֶשׁ יְהוָה אֲשֶׁר אָהֵב ("for Judah has desecrated the sanctuary of the Lord, which he loves"). In this clause, he maintains that Judah's unfaithfulness has led to abomination – specifically, intermarriage with Gentiles – which resulted in the profanation and desecration of Yahweh's sanctuary (2:11). A similar concern about mixed marriages and other relationships that undermine the spiritual purity of the covenant people is a recurring theme in the OT (Exod 34:15–16; Lev 20:2–5; Deut 7:3–4).

In verse 11, the offender and the offence are clearly identified. The offender is Judah, and the offence involves unfaithfulness in marriage – specifically, intermarriage with pagans. The question arises: How widespread was such religious intermarriage at that time? This question can only be answered from the historical record of the Ezra-Nehemiah corpus. The problem was so serious during this period after the exile that the leaders, prompted by pastoral concern, led the nation in repentance and covenant renewal (Nehemiah 9–10;

---

39. Elliger and Rudolph, *Biblia Hebraica Stuttgartensia*, 1083.
40. Kittel, *Biblia Hebraica*, 974; and Wellhausen, *Die Klein Propheten*, 240.
41. Jones, *Haggai, Zechariah and Malachi*, 45, and van der Woude, "Malachi's Struggle," 100.
42. Verhoef, *Haggai and Malachi*, 268.
43. Stuart, "Malachi," 1297.

13:23–27; Ezra 9:2) and even went to the extent of compelling those with non-believing wives to divorce them (Ezra 10:2–3).

Contrary to those who do not see this text as addressing marital unfaithfulness, there is ample evidence that the term בגד has three nuances, with the primary focus being on marital unfaithfulness in the form of deserting one's lawful marriage partner to enter an unlawful marriage with another woman (Exod 21:8; Jer 3:20; Mal 2:14).[44] The charge of betrayal, in terms of unfaithfulness, which was introduced in verse 10, is further developed in verse 11. Several ancient versions (LXX, *Vetus Latima*, and Peshitta) render the verses in a way that shows Judah going after other gods, deliberately avoiding any mention of mixed marriages and focusing attention on the phrase "daughter of a foreign god."[45] This writer, along with several other commentators, prefers the rendering of the Hebrew word בָּעַל (own, rule over, master) that conveys the idea of taking possession of a woman as one's wife, which fits the context of Malachi.[46] The men of Judah were unfaithful in their physical marriage relationships, and it is their marital unfaithfulness that is referred to as detestable and abominable. It is important to remember the language of the book of Deuteronomy, where divine instructions were given to God's people (Deut 7:1–4; 24:1–4).[47] As the people of God, bound by specific covenantal obligations under the Mosaic covenant, they were prohibited from marrying foreign wives (Deut 7:1–6);[48] however, as discussed earlier, Judah had violated these covenantal stipulations.

The prophet is dynamic in presenting his message. He begins with Judah, who is the guilty party. The people of Judah were unfaithful to the Lord whom they loved. The prophet then shows that this act of תּוֹעֵבָה of ("an abomination") is practised throughout the land by stressing that this abomination was committed both בְּיִשְׂרָאֵל וּבִירוּשָׁלָם ("in Israel and in Jerusalem"). Previously, the Israelites had been addressed as God's covenant people; but for a period,

---

44. Glazier-McDonald, *Malachi: The Divine Messenger*, 85. See also Holladay, *Hebrew and Aramaic Lexicon*, 33, and Botterweck and Ringgren, *Theological Dictionary*, 1:470–473.

45. Torrey, "Prophecy of 'Malachi,'" 6–7; Isaksson, *Marriage and Ministry*, 32–33.

46. Verhoef, *The Books of Haggai and Malachi*, 269; Glazier-McDonald, *Malachi: The Divine Messenger*, 92–93.

47. Verhoef, *Haggai and Malachi*, 270.

48. Jones, *Haggai, Zechariah and Malachi*, 45.

the nation was divided into two separate kingdoms. Based on their covenant relationship with God, Malachi addresses the remnant as "Israel."

In the final Hebrew clause in verse 11 – וּבָעַל בַּת־אֵל נֵכָר ("and has married the daughter of a foreign god") – the prophet reveals Judah's unfaithful actions. As a nation, Judah had married foreign woman (2:11d), as denoted in the construct-genitive phrase בַּת־אֵל נֵכָר ("daughter of a foreign god").[49] When the men of Judah returned from captivity many of them sent their covenanted wives away and married foreign women who served other gods,[50] thereby bringing idolatry into the nation.[51]

Walter C. Kaiser observes that "Israel was openly indulging in marrying women who worshipped pagan gods,"[52] ignoring the warnings against marrying foreign women set out in the Mosaic covenant (Deut 7:–4). Markus Zehnder also captures Judah's problem in his comment: "Malachi's main accusation consists in the argument that the men of Judah desecrated the קֹדֶשׁ יְהוָה (holy place of Yahweh) and married the בַּת־אֵל נֵכָר 'daughter of a foreign god' (Verse 11)."[53] Zehnder emphasizes that the main concern here is not the sanctuary but marital unfaithfulness "between men belonging to the YHWH-congregation and women whose families are of foreign religious background."[54] The prophet's concern is pastoral because the focus of Malachi is not ethnic but religious intermarriage of Jews with the "daughters of foreign gods."

The prophet's focus is the marital relationships between members of Yahweh's congregation and women of foreign faiths who worship other gods. The phrase בַּת־אֵל נֵכָר ("daughter of a foreign god") shows that there is a relationship between God's people and a specific category of women. The act of unfaithfulness resulting in intermarriage is evident in the fact that the men of Judah were no longer satisfied with the wives of their youth, as v14 makes

---

49. Holladay, *Hebrew and Aramaic Lexicon*, 51.
50. Dentan, "Malachi," 1135.
51. Throughout the OT, there are warnings concerning marital unfaithfulness and jeopardizing the spiritual purity of the community in Israel (Gen 6:1–7; Exod 34:11–16); Deut 13:6–11; 31:19–20. See also Josh 23:7, 12–13; Judg 2:1–3; 3:5–7). This problem continued in the postexilic community among the priests, who were the leaders of the people (Ezra 9:2; Neh 13:23–30).
52. Kaiser, "Divorce in Malachi 2:10–16," 74, 76.
53. Zehnder, "Fresh Look at Malachi," 225.
54. Zehnder, 228. Clendenen and Taylor, *Haggai–Malachi*, 336.

clear בֵּינְךָ וּבֵין | אֵשֶׁת נְעוּרֶיךָ אֲשֶׁר אַתָּה בָּגַדְתָּה בָּהּ ("between you and the wife of early life who you acted faithlessly with").

The one accused of wrongdoing in verse 14 had married a wife and then divorced this covenantal wife and married another woman in her place. The new wife in this case is clearly identified by Malachi as בַּת־אֵל נֵכָר ("daughter of a foreign god"). The question arises: Who are the "daughter[s] of a foreign god"? Other OT passages explain that the daughter of a foreign god is a woman from a tribe or nation outside Israel (Exod 34:15–16; Deut. 7:3–4; Num 25:1–2 Josh 22: 16; Ezra 9:2 and 1 Kgs 11:1–4).

The result of this abomination was the profanation of the Lord's sanctuary. Although the desecration of the sanctuary is not the actual issue raised here, it is one of the consequences of marital unfaithfulness in Judah. It is such marriages to the daughters of foreign gods that caused Judah to profane the holy place (Exod 34:15–16; Mal 2:11). The prophet's use of the Hebrew particle כִּי (ki) explains why Judah's behaviour has become an abomination in the sight of the Lord.[55]

Clausal Explanation of Verse 12

The *BHS* editors point out that from כִּי in v11 to the end of verse 12 is uncertain, and it is difficult to determine the object of "cut off." This section would be clear if "the tents of" is seen as an indirect object while witness or respondent is syntactically seen as the direct object. Note that the offence committed as a result of Judah's unfaithfulness in marriage led to the abomination described in Malachi 2:11.

Here in verse 12, the prophet begins with a *hiphil* jussive form of the third-person masculine singular verb יַכְרֵת ("may he cut off"). This Hebrew verb – כָּרַת "cut off" – which appears in all its stems about 289 times in 281 verses in the OT.[56] Of these occurrences, it appears 69 times in the Pentateuch, 97 times in the historical books, 21 times in the poetical books, and 102 times in the Prophets – but it occurs only once in Malachi (2:12). It is noteworthy that this term is used in relation to ברית (covenant), either referring to God's

---

55. Brown, Driver, and Briggs, *Hebrew and English Lexicon*, 475.

56. Brown, Driver, and Briggs, 503–504. See also Shoshan, *New Concordance*, 563–565; Stamm, *Hebrew and Aramaic Lexicon*, 500; Lisowsky, *Konkordanz Zum Hebräischen*, 700–702, and Koehler and Baumgartner, *Hebrew and Aramaic Lexicon*, 889.

covenant with the patriarchs and, through them, with the nation of Israel (Gen 9:11; 15:18; Exod 24:8; 34:10; Isa 55:3; Hos 2:18) or in relation to covenants between humans (Gen 21:27, 32; 26:28; 31:44; Exod 23:32).

When used in relation to covenants between humans, this term sometimes appears in prohibitory contexts, where God warns his people not to make covenants with the inhabitants of the land (Exod 34:12). When used in relation to inanimate objects, the term means "to destroy" or "perish" (Gen 41:36; Isa 10:7; 22:25).[57] When used with animate objects, it consistently means to kill ("put to death") or destroy (Gen 17:14).[58] The term may also refer to cutting down trees (Deut 19:5; Isa 14:8; 37:24), extermination or killing (Jer 44:11), covenant-making (Gen 15:18), or divorce (Isa 50:1).[59]

In the context of covenant violations, the question arises: How did the Israelites "cut" a covenant? The covenant began by cutting an animal into pieces, which symbolizes that the party that broke the covenant should face death (Gen 15:9–18). The term originated in the Torah, where Pentateuchal laws discuss this concept of being cut off. In the Torah, the penalty for sin is death, and Yahweh is the only one who can do this cutting off (Lev 17:10; 20:3). In the Torah, the term "cut off" means death.

In this context, what is intended is not the banishment of a guilty party in the form of social or religious excommunication. The verb used here is

---

57. Another significant use is in relation to Levitical offerings, where it connotes cessation or removal (as in Joel 1:9).

58. It must be noted that some scholars argue for excommunication. See Achtemeier, *Nahum–Malachi*, 182, and Smith, *Critical and Exegetical Commentary of Malachi*, 50. Smith prefers the reading "blotting out or destroying the evildoers and his descendants over the milder banish or excommunicate."

Verhoef claims that it has to do with "excommunication of the guilty members from the communion of the people of God." Verhoef, *Haggai and Malachi*, 290. (i.e., banishment from the faith community) as a viable connotation when used with animate objects (BDB, *The Brown-Driver-Briggs Hebrew and English Lexicon*, 503. E.S. Kalland, "כרת" in *Theological Wordbook of the Old Testament*, vol. 1, ed Harris, Archer and Waltke [Chicago: Moody Press, 1980], 456–467. See also R. K. Harrison, *Introduction to the Old Testament* (London: Tyndale, 1969), 476–479). However, the context of usage does not support this connotation. For instance, Exodus 31:14 includes a parallel clause where the infinitive *twm* ("to kill") is used for both the offence and the punishment for that offence. Also relevant is the use of the term as a punishment for idolatry – an offence that clearly warrants capital punishment (Hos 8:4). See Koehler and Baumgartner, *Hebrew and Aramaic Lexicon*, 889. See also Kellard, "כרת," *TWOT* 1: 456–457. See also Holladay, *Hebrew and Aramaic Lexicon*, 165.

59. Brown, Driver, and Briggs, *Hebrew and English Lexicon*, 503. See also Koehler and Baumgartner, *Hebrew and Aramaic Lexicon*, 500, Stamm, *Hebrew and Aramaic Lexicon*, 500, and Hill, *Malachi*, 235.

a hiphil jussive – may he [God] cut off [put to death] the guilty man who violates the intimate relationship of the covenant people. The sinner must be "cut off" from his people. This concept of putting to death is also found in several OT passages (Lev 18:29–30; 19:8; Num 15:30–31; 25:6–18), which describe punishment for infidelity.

The concept of punishment through death provides a better understanding of the "cutting off" in this verse. Some sins are so severe that they require elimination of the offender from the community of faith. The prophet teaches that anyone who is guilty of the sin of religious intermarriage must not remain within the community of Judah. Malachi, as an insider, understands the concept of "cutting" in terms of death as a punishment for unfaithfulness. With this understanding, he applies this concept of punishment to covenant-breakers.

The New Revised Standard Version (NRSV) translates this Hebrew term לְאִישׁ as "anyone."[60] But this writer and other commentators argue that the Hebrew word used here is not generic but gender-specific. The prophet is specific about the offender – "the man," "that man," or even a "husband"[61] who is guilty of such an act. Any man who marries a foreign woman and is thus guilty of religious intermarriage commits a treacherous act among the people in that community.[62] Such a man is excluded from the communion of God's people, and his food offering is also rejected.

Malachi emphasizes that the Lord who made a covenant with his people is not only a witness to the covenant-making (cutting) but is also ready to act as a witness in bringing to trial anyone who fails in their covenantal obligations. Hill argues that "Malachi is a prophet of the post-exilic era best associated with the reforms of Ezra and Nehemiah."[63] Since Malachi was familiar with the history of the covenant in the Pentateuch, he was conversant with the term he uses, especially in relation to "cutting" and punishing covenant violators through death.

The cutting begins with the covenant, and that same Hebrew word is used here for judgement on any covenant violator. The prophet's pastoral concern

---

60. Malachi 2:12 (NRSV).
61. Koehler and Baumgartner, *Hebrew and Aramaic Lexicon*, 1:43.
62. Hill, *Malachi*, 234.
63. Hill, 80–81.

for the people of the faith community is expressed in his statement that the sinner who breaks faith with the wife of his youth should be punished. The offender in verse 12 is described literally as "the man who does this" (לְאִישׁ אֲשֶׁר יַעֲשֶׂנָּה). The Hebrew term אֲשֶׁר יַעֲשֶׂנָּה ("who does it") refers to any man in Judah who acted treacherously by intermarrying with the daughter of foreign god. It is לְאִישׁ אֲשֶׁר יַעֲשֶׂנָּה ("to a man who does it"), the guilty man or any member of the covenant community who has acted in an unfaithful manner in marital relationship, that יַכְרֵת יְהוָה (Yahweh will cut off), while he is still presenting an offering to him. He would be removed from among the faith community as punishment for his infidelity because if he remained in their midst, he would pollute the people.

The prophet then moves to the second segment of verse 12. Although translating the second part of this verse is difficult, the literal rendering provides a clue: "May Yahweh cut off the man who does it, witnessing and answering, from the tents of Jacob" (Mal 2:12). The divine author uses Malachi, his servant, to remind the people of the punishment for infidelity in the marriage relationship. Anyone who "does it, witnessing and answering" would be cut off from the tents of Jacob. Anyone living in Jacob's tent and acting unfaithfully in their covenant marriage relationship would be punished, even to the extent of having their food offerings rejected (2:12b). This would discourage others from engaging in religious intermarriage.

Summary of Malachi 2:10–12

The prophet begins with the theme of unity in verse 10, exposing infidelity among the addressees in general terms. In verse 11, he continues with the theme of unfaithfulness to covenantal relationships among the people in Yahweh's community, focusing specifically on Judah's sin of infidelity. Verse 12 presents the verdict, stating Yahweh's punishment for infidelity.

Exegetical Study of Malachi 2:13–16a

Clausal Explanation of Malachi 2:13

In the chiastic structural pattern discussed earlier in this work, the second pivot of this pattern is found in verse 13, which, like verse 12, is also centred on God's verdict. Note that verses 10–12 introduce infidelity in the form of religious intermarriage with pagans and the verdict on covenant violators. The prophet then develops the theme of unfaithfulness in the second section

(13–16a). In this section, he does not immediately move to the accusation but prefaces his argument in verse 13 with vivid imagery depicting the result of Yahweh's rejection of the men's worship due to their infidelity to both their God and their wives.

In the previous section (2:11–12), the prophet discussed a specific indictment of Judah's unfaithfulness and condemned it. In verse 13, the prophet begins with the Hebrew clause וְזֹאת שֵׁנִית תַּעֲשׂוּ which literally translates as "and this second thing you do," or perhaps more smoothly "another thing you do."[64] The textual apparatus suggest that in verse 13– וְזֹאת שֵׁנִית תַּעֲשׂוּ (this second thing you do) – is not original but has probably been added. The LXX interprets שֵׁנִית as ἃ ἐμίσουν "which I hate." With others this study notes that the LXX has missed a straightforward use of the word שֵׁנִית to introduce further revelations in the prophetic books (see: Jer 1:13; Ezek 4:6; Hag 2:20; Zech 4:12).[65] Hill concurs on the use of שֵׁנִית and argues that the feminine singular ordinal extends the indictment of verse 11.[66]

Due to the poor quality of the text, several commentators claim that verses 11, 12, and the beginning of verse 13 are later additions.[67] Van der Woude suggests deleting שֵׁנִית,[68] but Hugenberger notes that if the LXX reading were original, we would expect to find אֲשֶׁר ("which"), since this word occurs eleven times in Malachi.[69] The meaning of שֵׁנִית here is not chronological but logical; it specifies another example of unfaithfulness in the context of intermarriage.

As demonstrated by other scholars, this paragraph is united and coherent as it stands.[70] Clendenen concludes that the charge of marital unfaithfulness is introduced by the clause literally translated "and this [is] a second [thing] you do."[71] Zehnder's claim that MT's usage is correct and aligns with what the prophet was saying about the unfaithfulness of the addressees seems to

---

64. Hill, 221.
65. Clendenen and Taylor, *Haggai–Malachi*, 342; Stuart, "Malachi," 1334
66. Hill, *Malachi*, 236.
67. Torrey, "Prophecy of 'Malachi,'" 9; Isaksson, *Marriage and Ministry*, 30; and Van der Woude, "Malachi's Struggle," 66.
68. Van der Woude, "Malachi's Struggle," 68.
69. Hugenberger, *Marriage as a Covenant*, 33, and Verhoef, *Haggai and Malachi*, 262.
70. Rudolph, *Haggai, Sacharja 1–8*, 272–273, and Verhoef, *Haggai and Malachi*, 264.
71. Clendenen and Taylor, *Haggai–Malachi*, 342.

make most sense of the text.⁷² The Hebrew phrase וְזֹאת שֵׁנִית תַּעֲשׂוּ ("and this second thing you do") points to a relationship with what was discussed in the second part of verse 12. Verses 11 and 12 focus on religious infidelity, but the writer moves beyond that in verse 13, where he mentions another specific example of unfaithfulness – divorce. The prophet addresses this case of divorce or physical infidelity in verse 14. But before mentioning the offence, he quickly comments on the impact of the people's transgression on their religious activities.

In this verse, the prophet continues to address the same dispute but also introduces another problem, using a Hebrew numeral. The Hebrew numeral שֵׁנִית in verse 13 shows that there are other acts of marital unfaithfulness that were not mentioned in 2:10–12. There has been some confusion over the proper understanding of this numeral and the syntax in these translations requires further clarification. The Hebrew term שֵׁנִית is used in different ways in the OT and could mean "another."⁷³ The second feminine adjective plural of numeral ordinals⁷⁴ has the idea of "second"⁷⁵ as it was used in some other passages in the Scriptures (Exod 2:13; Num 2:16). This usage fits the context here because the *qal* imperfect תַּעֲשׂוּ – from עשה – which is translated "you do" or "you are doing," conveys the idea of an ongoing, progressive action.⁷⁶ Therefore, this study, along with other commentators, translates this term as "second thing."⁷⁷

The entire clause could be translated as "This is a second thing that you do," "This is another thing you do," "This is another thing you are doing," or "another thing you do."⁷⁸ The implication is that while similar to the issue of unfaithfulness discussed in verses 10–12, this clause is not identical and also refers to wrongdoing revealed in the clause כַּסּוֹת דִּמְעָה אֶת־מִזְבַּח יְהוָה בְּכִי וַאֲנָקָה ("you cover the Lord's altar with tears, with weeping and wailing").

---

72. Zehnder, "Fresh Look at Malachi," 231, 233. See also Hill, *Malachi*, 236; Verhoef, *Haggai and Malachi*, 272.

73. Clendenen and Taylor, *Haggai–Malachi*, 342.

74. Kelley, *Biblical Hebrew*, 97.

75. Brown, Driver, and Briggs, *Hebrew and English Lexicon*, 1041.

76. Brown, Driver, and Briggs, 793; Harris, Archer, and Waltke, *Theological Wordbook*, 1708.

77. Brown, Driver, and Briggs, *Hebrew and English Lexicon*, 1041. See also Holladay, *Hebrew and Aramaic Lexicon*, 379, and Hill, *Malachi*, 237.

78. Verhoef, *Haggai and Malachi*, 272.

In this verse, the prophet does not immediately address another sin committed by the people but comments on the effect the transgression mentioned earlier in the text has had on their religious activities. He points out that not only do the men intermarry, they also brings the cultic rites of their wives to Yahweh's altar, covering it with דִּמְעָה ("tears") בְּכִי ("weeping"), and אֲנָקָה ("groaning"). The people wept because God no longer listened to their prayers or paid attention to their offerings. Since they were practising formal religion at the Lord's altar, their sacrifices were rejected and would no longer be accepted (2:13). The prophet reiterates that no matter how good the offering might be, Yahweh would turn away from it, and it would no longer receive God's favour. Yahweh would no longer turn his face towards their offering or receive, with favour, anything from their hands.

Here, the prophet expresses God's displeasure and reveals God's attitude towards the people's offerings (Mal 2:13b; 1 Kgs 8:22, 28–30). Malachi observes that Yahweh's turning away from their offerings is as a result of their unfaithfulness. However, he does not mention the specific offence in verse 13, reserving this for verse 14. We observe that the intermarriage of the men of Judah with the daughters of foreign gods and the sending away of their legitimate wives, which was discussed earlier, had caused Yahweh to reject their offerings. In verse 14, Malachi addresses another specific sin of infidelity – divorce.

Clausal Explanation of Verse 14

The previous verses have established that the people's unfaithfulness to their fellow covenant members and their specific sins of marital unfaithfulness have resulted in Yahweh turning away from them and rejecting their offerings. The question-and-answer format used elsewhere in the text continues here, with verse 14 providing the grounds for the statement made in verse 13.

Malachi cites the people's question in the first clause of verse 14: עַל־מָה ("Why does he not?") or literally, "Upon what basis?"[79] This refers back to God's earlier statement that he would no longer accept their offerings. There are more complaints as the people want to know on what grounds Yahweh refuses their sacrifices (2:14a). The prophet's reply says nothing about ritual weeping. Instead, he answers their question with three Hebrew clauses that

---

79. Clendenen and Taylor, *Haggai–Malachi*, 346.

centre on both cultic unfaithfulness and marital unfaithfulness in the postexilic community of Judah. It is important to note that both the cultic problem and the issue of physical marital unfaithfulness are addressed.

The prophet partially answers the question by stating that the people try to serve Yahweh with an offering that he does not accept (2:13a). However, he answers the question more fully in verse 14, where he explains the issue of infidelity to wives by using three Hebrew clauses. He begins with כִּי־יְהוָה הֵעִיד בֵּינְךָ וּבֵין אֵשֶׁת נְעוּרֶיךָ ("because the Lord served as the witness between you and the wife of your youth"). This clause is causal in nature. The prophet provides an answer by explaining Yahweh's rejection of the worship offered by the people of Judah, using a construction that introduces a causal clause by a clausal adverb. The Lord had rejected their offerings because they had betrayed the wives of their youth. The Hebrew phrase אֵשֶׁת נְעוּרֶיךָ, translated as "wife of your youth," is a construct-genitive. This phrase occurs four times in the OT (Prov 5:18; Isa 54:6; Mal 2:14–15).

The concept of treaty and covenant was central in ancient Near Eastern contexts.[80] These agreements could take the form of a suzerainty or parity treaty[81] and ranged from business agreements concerning loans to national treaties with foreign powers or gods, or between a male and a female.[82] Edwin Yamauchi explains further by referring to the Code of Hammurabi (§128) which states that "a woman is not a wife without a *riskatu* (contract)."[83] Similarly, the Egyptians also had contractual agreements in marriage.[84] Such contractual agreements were present in the laws of surrounding nations before the time of the Jews.

In the ANE, such marriage contracts contained stipulations and sanctions. These stipulations were agreed to by both parties, and sanctions were

---

80. Moshe Weinfeld, "Berith," *TDOT* 2:253–265. See also Weinfeld, "Covenant of Grant," 90, 184–203, and McCarthy, *Treaty and Covenant*, 21–29.

81. MacCulloh, "Covenant," 206; Mendenhall, "Covenant," 714. See also McCarthy, *Treaty and Covenant*, 2–3, 21–27, 28–48, and Ogedegbe, "Concept of Love," 120.

82. Instone-Brewer, *Divorce and Remarriage*, 3. See also Verhoef, *Haggai and Malachi*, 180–184.

83. Yamauchi, "Cultural Aspects of Marriage," 245. See also Westbrook, "Old Babylonian Marriage Law," 58–60, and Matthews, "Marriage and Family," 8.

84. Yamauchi, "Cultural Aspects of Marriage," 8.

enforced in the presence of witnesses when stipulations were broken.[85] There were penalties for parties who failed to honour these contractual agreements, which were documented through a legally witnessed ceremony or written document.[86] In this ancient context, there was a type of contractual agreement similarly to treaty-making that governed both marriage and the dissolution of marriage.[87]

For the Jews, however, the bond that held them together was much stronger because it was not merely contractual but a covenant. The primary meaning of covenant was an agreement made between two parties, in the presence of witnesses, and such a covenant could be kept or broken.[88] There are similarities between the covenants described in the Bible and the ancient Near Eastern treaties, with the Hittite vassal treaties providing a helpful basis for understanding biblical covenants.

The use of the term "wife of your youth" reveals a cultural context that helps readers understand the culture of the original audience. Understanding this cultural context is vital for the proper interpretation and application of Malachi 2:14. Consideration of the broader cultural context of Malachi 2:10–16 is important because the people addressed in this text had their origins in the ancient Near East. Understanding the cultural setting as it relates to marriageable age is important for interpreting this passage. In Jewish culture, boys became marriageable at the age of thirteen, with the bar mitzvah ceremony marking their personal commitment to Yahweh and his covenant.[89] This was the age at which parents would begin negotiating marriage arrangements for their children.[90] Such marriages were usually arranged long before the wife finally moved in to the husband's family home.[91] The Jews viewed

---

85. Weinfeld, "Covenant of Grant," 253–265. See also Yamauchi, "Cultural Aspects of Marriage," 241–252, and Verhoef, *Haggai and Malachi*, 183.

86. Instone-Brewer, *Divorce and Remarriage*, 4. See also Wittee and Nichols, "Covenant Marriage," 16–17.

87. Matthews, "Marriage and Family," 1.

88. Matthews, 1. See also Thompson, "Ancient Near Eastern Treaty," 6.

89. Yamauchi, "Cultural Aspects of Marriage," 241–243. See also Achtemeier, *Nahum-Malachi*, 182.

90. Yamauchi, 241–243. See also Stienstra, *YHWH Is the Husband*, 93, Matthews, "Marriage and Family," 7, and Stuart, "Malachi," 1340.

91. Yamauchi, "Cultural Aspects of Marriage," 241–243. See also Matthews, "Marriage and Family," 7.

the husband's covenant obligations as part of his bar mitzvah education and his commitment to Yahweh. Thus, in Jewish culture, marriage was not just a civil agreement but a religious covenant.[92] This covenant was binding because agreements and promises made in God's name were binding, and God himself bore witness to the union between the man and the woman.

The concept of covenant is central in the Torah and played a crucial role in the relationship between the Jewish people and God. Once a covenant was cut, any breach of the covenant relationship constituted an offence that required punishment. Divorce was another important issue for the people of the ancient Near East. Since marriage was viewed as a legally binding contract, attested to by a ceremony with witnesses, divorce also required a formal procedure. In the ancient Near East, not every marriage lasted a lifetime, and the law provided various grounds for divorce. When it came to termination of a marriage or putting away a spouse, it was necessary to present a bill of divorcement.[93] Any man wishing to divorce his wife was required to provide her with a "get." A "get" was a legal document also known as a "bill of divorcement" or a "book of cutting off."[94]

In the cultural environment of the time, if a man wanted to divorce his wife, he was required to follow the ancient Near Eastern divorce procedure of providing a bill of divorcement.[95] In addition, the marriage contract included penalty clauses that would apply if a man divorced his wife without legitimate grounds.[96] In Jewish culture, divorce was recognized as a valid means of ending a marriage, and the custom of writing a bill of divorcement was included in their legislation.[97] This document may have originated from an ancient ceremony practised by ancient Near Eastern people of the surrounding nations during the biblical period. At that time, a man who was

---

92. Hugenberger, *Marriage as a Covenant*, 172. See also Block, "Marriage and Family," 44.

93. Smith, "Commentary on Malachi," 56. See also Matthews, "Marriage and Family," 25; Sprinkle, "Old Testament Perspectives," 530, and Stuart, "Malachi," 1342.

94. Danby, "Gittin, 81a-b," 307–329. Cf. Stienstra, *Yahweh Is the Husband*, 89. See also Novak, "Jewish Marriage," 49, and Broyde, "Covenant-Contract Dialectic," 56.

95. Instone-Brewer, *Divorce and Remarriage*, 3. See also Yamauchi, "Cultural Aspects of Marriage," 241–252; Matthews, "Marriage and Family," 25–26; and Broyde, "Covenant-Contract Dialectic," 49, 56.

96. Matthews, "Marriage and Family," 25, 27.

97. "Gittin, 1a-b," in *The Mishnah*, Translated into English, De Sola and Raphall, London, 1843. See also Stienstra, *YHWH Is the Husband*, 89.

divorcing his wife would cut off the edge of his garment as a symbol of the finality of their separation and divorce.[98] This practice is also mentioned in the Bible (Isa 50:1; Jer 3:8). According to Matthews, some of these verses are referenced in Jewish documents written in Aramaic, which were discovered at Elephantine, in the southern part of Egypt, in the fifth century BCE.[99]

One of the negative aspects of Israelites marriage was the authority given to men to divorce their wives with ease. While the law envisaged the possibility of divorce (Deut 24:1–4), scholars argue that this law was included to prevent hasty decisions being taken.[100] In other words, the aim of these provisions was to ensure that the marriage relationship could not be terminated hastily or impulsively and that Jewish men would not rashly choose divorce in a moment of anger or confusion. In keeping with the practice in other neighbouring cultures, the provision of a certificate of divorce was required to begin a formal public process of divorce, which was carried out only after serious reflection.[101] These proceedings took place in the presence of witnesses and required adherence to strict rules regarding documentation.[102]

The certificate of divorce was issued so that the woman would be able to prove her divorce and be free to remarry (Deut 24:1–4). This understanding of the divorce process in the ancient Near East helps the reader to understand both the practice of marriage (to "the wife of your youth") and the guidelines that discouraged hasty or frivolous divorce.

Although the answer to the people's question is not found in the main initial clause, we see the answer in the relative clause introduced by אֲשֶׁר ("who," "what," or "that"). The prophet claims that the men of Judah – who are addressed in the collective singular אַתָּה ("you") – are guilty of acting treacherously against their wives. The prophet describes the woman אֲשֶׁר אַתָּה בָּגַדְתָּה בָּהּ ("against whom you have dealt treacherously") in three ways: in the first clause, as אֵשֶׁת נְעוּרֶיךָ ("wife of your youth"); in the second clause, as וְהִיא חֲבֶרְתְּךָ ("your companion"); and finally, also in the second clause, as וְאֵשֶׁת בְּרִיתֶךָ ("your wife by covenant"). This threefold description of the woman

---

98. Matthews, "Marriage and Family," 25.
99. Matthews, 7.
100. Stienstra, *YHWH Is the Husband*, 88.
101. Stuart, "Malachi," 1342.
102. Kaiser, "Divorce in Malachi 2:10–16," 80.

emphasizes the closeness and intimacy of the marriage partners, which makes the treacherous behaviour of the spouse all the more detestable.

In essence, the prophet is emphasizing that Yahweh had witnessed the covenant between "you and the wife of your youth" (Mal 2:14 NIV). Zehnder says that "the formulation [of the first clause] יְהוָה הֵעִיד בֵּינְךָ וּבֵין | אֵשֶׁת נְעוּרֶיךָ (lit. – Yahweh, he is the witness between you and between the wives of your youth) makes clear that the relations between the addressed men and the 'wives of their youth' are legal marital relations."[103] He asserts, "It is rather legal marriages between members of the Yahweh congregation and Israelite women that the prophet is speaking about."[104] It is these women that the men of Judah have acted treacherously against, that the prophet describes as: "to whom you have been faithless."[105]

In this clause, the prophet reveals that the sinful unfaithfulness of the men of Judah – in sending away their covenanted wives and considering this a private affair – is known to God. Such an action is a serious offence that violates the marriage covenant and also dishonours God, who had acted as the witness to their covenant. (cf. Exod 20:14; Prov 2:17; Ezek 16:8–14).

The prophet then moves on to the last clause. The Hebrew phrase וְהִיא חֲבֶרְתְּךָ וְאֵשֶׁת בְּרִיתֶךָ is an adverbial clause – translated as "though she is your companion and your wife by covenant" – which elaborates on the second clause. The reason the behaviour of the men of Judah is called treachery is that their wives had entered into a covenant with them but the men had violated this covenant. It is made clear here that the Lord was displeased with his people "because of the broken marriage vows which God was a party to since marriage is a covenant to which He is a witness."[106] This final clause makes clear that the marriage has been dissolved, the covenantal wife has been divorced, and the man has married the daughter of foreign god (Mal 2:11).

Clausal Explanation of Verses 15–16

In the previous section (2:10–12), the prophet addressed the first offence, which is infidelity through intermarriage with a pagan (2:11). In verse 14,

---

103. Zehnder, "Fresh Look at Malachi," 235.
104. Zehnder, 235.
105. Verhoef, *Haggai and Malachi*, 275.
106. Kaiser, "Divorce in Malachi 2:10–16," 75. Hill, *Malachi*, 240.

the prophet revealed the second offence of the men of Judah: infidelity by divorce or the sending away of their lawful wives. The prophet emphasizes that God is deeply concerned about such acts of marital unfaithfulness by his people. This section serves as a concluding admonition that also presents a way forward for the addressees. The prophet begins this final section with advice and warning against marital unfaithfulness, observing that such actions – especially the sending away of their lawful Jewish wives – would have religious consequences.

First, the prophet points out that the one who marries the daughter of a foreign god is also guilty of following the gods of this unlawful wife.[107] In addition, the one who marries the daughter of a foreign god is seeking a visible fulfilment of his marriage in terms of offspring. The prophet has already noted that Yahweh's punishment for any act of marital unfaithfulness involves the offender being cut off from participating in religious fellowship. Now, in the next clause, he describes the punishment for anyone who sends away or divorces his legal wife and marries the daughter of a foreign god. Such a union with a foreign woman will never bear godly offspring because the man has violated the marriage union, which is a part of the covenant with the fathers, and a divine institution.

In the structural layout of the Hebrew text of verse 15 there are four clauses. The verse can be divided into two sections: verse 15a and 15b. The interpretation of this verse as a whole is challenging.

Explanation of Verse 15a

Earlier, in verse 14, the prophet identifies the second sin as unfaithfulness, resulting in injustice against the covenant wives by sending them away. He shows that God is deeply concerned about such acts of marital unfaithfulness among his people. In verse 15, the first clause begins with a coordinating Hebrew word וְלֹא which is a *waw* + the negative particle. This is followed by אֶחָד ("one"), and the interpretation of this word is the first challenge. The word is translated as "one" in the first clause of verse 15 – and a decision has to be made as to whether it is a subject, an object, or a predicate adjective of "did he make?" Or is this אֶחָד ("one") referring to the term אֶחָד ("one") as it is

---

107. Similar cases from the OT were mentioned earlier in this work. For further discussion on how the religious practices of the new spouse contaminate commitment to Yahweh, see Glazier-McDonald, *Malachi: The Divine Messenger*, 109.

used in verse 10? Another syntactical problem is whether אֶחָד ("one") refers to God, to Adam, to Abraham, or to the guilty person discussed earlier in verse 12. Scholars acknowledge that interpreting this verse is difficult and observe that this section poses numerous grammatical and syntactical challenges.[108] Both Verhoef and Baldwin claim that the text is difficult and unintelligible. Verhoef says that "it is impossible to make any good sense of the Hebrew as it stands."[109] However, Verhoef differs from Baldwin in his belief that even with the limited materials in the verse, a meaningful interpretation is still possible.[110]

Earlier in this work, the study explored the text-critical issues in Malachi and discovered that the difficulty in verse 15 centres on the syntax of the verse, and in particular whether we should regard the subject as divine or human. Several commentators propose that the word אֶחָד ("one") in the first clause refers to the Pentateuchal ancestry of Israel, such as Abraham,[111] while others link this section with the similar usage of the term אֶחָד in Malachi 2:10, where it refers to Yahweh.[112] Others, however, believe that the term רוּחַ refers to spirit, life force, or the spirit of God.[113] Verhoef asserts that although the MT is problematic because the text is grammatically and syntactically incomplete,[114] it is preferable to follow this reading if sense can be made of it. He translates this verse as, "Did he not make you one with your wives and a remnant of that spirit-created unity still belongs to the relationship?" (Mal 2:15).

In essence, despite the fact that the men of Judah were continuing in their treachery, there was still a remnant of the spiritual bond between God and Israel. The text is intelligible because the treachery and faithlessness of divorce as practised in postexilic Judah stand diametrically opposed to the legacy of covenantal oneness and faithfulness that Israel received from Yahweh. In

---

108. Torrey, "Prophecy of 'Malachi,'" 10; Hvidberg, *Weeping and Laughter*, 123; Welch, *Postexilic Judaism*, 120. See also: Dentan, "Malachi," 1136; Baldwin, *Haggai, Zechariah, Malachi*, 240. See also Shields, "Syncretism and Divorce," 79, and O'Brien, *Priest and Levite*, 72.

109. Verhoef, *Haggai and Malachi*, 275.

110. Verhoef, 275–277.

111. Keil and Delitzsch, The Twelve Minor Prophets, 453; Driver, *Minor Prophets*, 316; Baldwin, *Haggai, Zechariah, Malachi*, 237; McKenzie, "Covenant Themes in Malachi," 552, and Dumbrell, *Faith of Israel*, 202. All these scholars identify the "one father" here as Abraham.

112. Glazier-McDonald, *Malachi: The Divine Messenger*, 83; Smith, *Micah–Malachi*, 321; Verhoef, *Haggai and Malachi*, 265; Kaiser, "Divorce in Malachi 2:10–16," 75.

113. Kaiser, "Divorce in Malachi 2:10–16," 76; Verhoef, *Haggai and Malachi*, 276, and Clendenen and Taylor, *Haggai–Malachi*, 354.

114. Verhoef, *Haggai and Malachi*, 275

addition, marrying the daughter of a foreign god was certainly not the way the people were to seek godly offspring.

The multiple issues with this verse have led some scholars to suggest emending[115] the entire verse because they consider that, starting from the first clause, it is unclear whether the Hebrew words are used as a question or a statement. The Vulgate and Peshitta render this term as a question;[116] some scholars see it as a negative statement.[117] Verhoef and I observe that the text does not give any indication that this is a question.[118]

Contrary to the view that the text is unintelligible or corrupt, this study and other commentators argue that the text is intelligible and does make sense. They suggest that this assumption can be tested by a re-translation of the verse. Hugenberger translates the verse as follows: "Did he not make them one, with a remnant of the Spirit [in their union?] belonging to it? And what was the one [God] seeking? A godly offspring."[119] We agree with Hugenberger for several reasons. To begin with, while the first clause does not begin with a question because there is no sign of a question in the Masoretic text but instead begins with a Hebrew negative particle, which could be used as a declarative negation, it seems to make more sense in the context to take it is a question (as do many English versions).[120] In addition, given Malachi's concern with the issue of marital unfaithfulness, the "he" is to be understood as referring to God (the subject) and the "one" as referring to the one-flesh union (the object of "make") that God instituted from the beginning, with himself as a witness (Gen 2:23–24).[121]

In light of this observation, the text is closely connected to the preceding discussion on unfaithfulness in the covenant relationship. It reveals a violation of the one-flesh principle (see 2:10) and highlights the sending away of the covenant wife, which is both a violation of the cleaving principle and an act

---

115. Meyers and Meyers, *Haggai, Zechariah 1–8*, 52. Petersen, *Zechariah 9–14 and Malachi*, 194. Smith, *Critical and Exegetical Commentary on Haggai, Zechariah, Malachi and Jonah* , 54.

116. See Hugenberger, *Marriage as a Covenant*, 136.

117. Rudolph, "Zu Mal 2:10–16," 88.

118. Verhoef, *Haggai and Malachi*, 276.

119. Hugenberger, *Marriage as a Covenant*, 133.

120. Holladay, *Hebrew and Aramaic Lexicon*, 170; Brown, Driver, and Briggs, *Hebrew and English Lexicon*, 520.

121. Smith, *Micah–Malachi*, 324; Hugenberger, *Marriage as a Covenant*, 133.

of covenant unfaithfulness and disloyalty to God. Contrary to those who view unfaithfulness as relating solely to the cult, the prophet sees this kind of sending away "as an act of betrayal against the marriage partner, probably because the way the accused were divorcing their wives is contrary to the stipulations of the laws of the Mosaic covenant (Exod 20:14; Deut 5:18; 24:1–4)."[122]

The key issue in this passage is marital unfaithfulness that resulted in profanation of the covenant. This profanation was the direct result of their unfaithfulness in marital relationships.

Explanation of 15b

The writer moves to the 'B' part of verse 15. The textual apparatus suggests that עָשָׂה וּשְׁאָר רוּחַ לוֹ וּמָה הָאֶחָד was possibly not original but was added later. The difficulties in this verse suggest the possibility of textual corruption. Only the last clause – "do not be unfaithful to your childhood wife" – is clear. As it stands, there are syntactical and exegetical problems with this verse. The first issue is whether to understand the term אֶחָד in the first clause as the subject or the object. If it is the subject, then what is the object? Another problem is the identity of the "one father" – should this be understood as a divine subject or as a human subject? Yet another issue is whether the verb עָשָׂה means "do" or "make."

In the second clause, we encounter a problem of identity: Is the spirit here human or divine? To this day, there are numerous interpretations, resulting from various proposals for emending the verse.[123] There are two major, widely held interpretations of verse 15: first, considering אֶחָד as the pronominal subject of its clause, and second, considering it as a predicate that refers to the divinely intended marriage relationship. Despite the fact that the text is problematic and sometimes difficult to understand it is advisable to follow the Masoretic text because other ancient versions are no clearer. Based on the limited material available and the clear intention of Malachi – as revealed in the final part of the verse, which encourages husbands to remain faithful to their first wives – this interpretation aligns with the overall context.[124]

---

122. Hill, *Malachi*, 226.

123. Hugenberger, *Marriage as a Covenant*, 125–172, offers a complete coverage of various options.

124. Baldwin, *Haggai, Zechariah, Malachi*, 240.

This work translates verse 15b as "Did he not make you one with your wives? A remnant of that spirit-created unity still belongs to the relationship." In essence, despite the continuing treachery of the men of Judah, there was still a remnant of the spiritual bond. The text is intelligible because the treachery and faithlessness of divorce as practised in postexilic Yehud is diametrically opposed to the covenantal legacy of "oneness and faithfulness" that Israel received from Yahweh.

The third Hebrew clause וְנִשְׁמַרְתֶּם בְּרוּחֲכֶם ("so guard yourselves in your spirit") begins with a conjunctive-sequential Hebrew *waw*. The admonition in this clause flows from verse 15a. The *niphal* conjugation of the Hebrew word וְנִשְׁמַרְתֶּם is reflexive and is translated "so guard yourselves." This could also be translated as "and you (each one) take care to yourselves (each other)"[125] or "so you shall be on guard in your spirit."[126]

This 'B' part of verse 15 aligns with the prophet's message from verse 10b onwards, where he speaks of not breaking faith. This part of the verse has two clauses: the first, וְנִשְׁמַרְתֶּם בְּרוּחֲכֶם is translated as "so guard yourself in your spirit," while the second, וּבְאֵשֶׁת נְעוּרֶיךָ אַל־יִבְגֹּד: is translated as "and with the wife of your youth let him not act faithlessly."[127]

The Hebrew construction here is dynamic, revealing the urgency of a change in behaviour. The community was guilty of wrongdoing, and the writer uses the Hebrew phrases וּבְאֵשֶׁת נְעוּרֶיךָ ("and with the wife of your youth") and אַל־יִבְגֹּד ("let him not act treacherously") to show that the covenantal unfaithfulness in the community should stop. The Hebrew phrase אַל־יִבְגֹּד ("let him not act treacherously") is intelligible in the context even though there is a shift in the person. This is acceptable when there is no change in subject (see the Hebrew of Isa 1:29).

The act of marital unfaithfulness – sending away the covenant Jewish wives – has religious consequences.[128] The prophet goes on to describe the punishment for anyone who commits the offence of sending away (divorcing) their covenant wife and marrying the daughter of a foreign god. He

---

125. Glazier-McDonald, *Malachi: The Divine Messenger*, 108.
126. Clendenen and Taylor, *Haggai–Malachi*, 357.
127. Clendenen and Taylor, 357.
128. Similar cases from the OT were mentioned earlier in this work. For further discussion on how the religious practices of the new spouse contaminate commitment to Yahweh, see Glazier-McDonald, *Malachi: The Divine Messenger*, 109.

concludes verse 15 with a warning not to intermarry and not to be faithless or deal treacherously with the wife of one's youth (2:15b), which aligns with the warnings of the book of Deuteronomy against disobeying Yahweh's word (Deut 4:9, 15).

Although the exact meaning of the text may be uncertain, it seems clear that the prophet is addressing the treachery and unfaithfulness of divorce that was being practised in postexilic Judah. This act is diametrically opposed to the legacy of covenantal oneness and faithfulness that Israel received from Yahweh (Jer 32:39; Ezek 37:17). The prophet concludes this section with a warning not to be faithless, which serves as the antidote to the frivolous divorces taking place in postexilic Judah. In order not to frustrate the singular purpose of the divine institution of marriage, the men of Judah were not to divorce the wives of their youth in favour of the daughters of foreign gods.

In summary, the prophet proposes a solution – from the author of marriage himself – to the problem of marital unfaithfulness in the community. He emphasizes upholding the marriage covenant and raising religiously pure children, rather than children from mixed marriages that violate covenant stipulations. This could also be the solution to similar problems in the Nigerian church

Clausal Explanation of Malachi 2:16

Part "A" of verse 16 begins with the Hebrew particle conjunction כִּי. There are different readings of this term in the OT (Gen 3:14, 19; Ps 6:3; Isa 5:7).[129] It could be translated differently, as either "for" or "because."[130] The term is polyvalent in nature and may serve as an admonition, a conditional statement, or as introducing a non-conditional causal sense.[131] There are several rendering of the term "כִּי" that are translated "for" in the OT. This word can also be used in temporal clauses ("while"), conditional clauses ("if"),[132] or causal clauses ("because," "for," and "since.")[133] Some interpreters prefer the

---

129. John O. Oswalt, "כִּי" *TWOT* 1:437–438.

130. Brown, Driver, and Briggs, *Hebrew and English Lexicon*, 475. See also Holladay, *Hebrew and Aramaic Lexicon*, 156.

131. Brown, Driver, and Briggs, *Hebrew and English Lexicon*, 475. See also Westbrook, "Prohibition," 403.

132. Harris, Archer, and Waltke, *Theological Wordbook*, 0976.

133. Harris, Archer, and Waltke, 0976. Cf. Deuteronomy 4:29, 28:2, and 28:9, as well as the admonition in Genesis 26:22.

admonition,[134] others prefer the conditional,[135] while still others prefer the causal interpretation of the term.[136] This study does not favour either the admonition reading – "if he hates divorce, says Yahweh God of Israel" – or the temporal usage of the word כִּי translated as "if" but favours the explanatory translation "for" because the Hebrew text contains a divine quotation formula אָמַר יְהוָה ("says Yahweh"). Given the context, this rendering could be viewed as explanatory.

In Malachi 2:16, there are three Hebrew clauses. The first Hebrew clause is כִּי־שָׂנֵא שַׁלַּח אָמַר יְהוָה אֱלֹהֵי יִשְׂרָאֵל ("For he hates divorce, says Yahweh, the God of Israel"). The Hebrew verb שָׂנֵא ("hate") appears awkward syntactically because of its use in the third-person masculine form of the *qal* here. This has generated scholarly debate over the translation of the related verb. Some emend the verb to the second person, translating this as "but if you hate her send her away,"[137] others see this verb as a verbal adjective,[138] and still others re-point the Masoretic Text and render שָׂנֵא as a *qal* participle ("the one hating").[139]

This first clause raises some questions: Who hates divorce? Is it Yahweh? If it is Yahweh, why is the statement made in the third person? This is the final verse in the second structural layout of Malachi 2:10–16. In the previous verse (15), the prophet discussed what God desires: godly offspring for a community that belongs to God in postexilic Judah. He also emphasized the urgency of change, urging them to cease wrongdoing and insisting that unfaithfulness to covenant wives must end. In the previous section, the prophet discussed the punishment that would come upon offenders, especially those who divorced the wives of their youth and married the daughters of foreign gods.

Verse 16a has proved textually difficult for interpreters. The textual apparatus suggests that שָׂנֵא "he hates divorce" was probably *legendum* (read) שנאתי "I hate divorce." That would resolve the major problem with this section,

---

134. Holladay, *Hebrew and Aramaic Lexicon*, 156.

135. Waltke and O'Connor, *Biblical Hebrew Syntax*, 38.2d.

136. R. L. Smith, *Micah–Malachi*, 1984, 319. See also: Rudolph, *Haggai, Sacharja 1–8*, 261, and Glazier-McDonald, *Malachi: The Divine Messenger*, 82. For a detailed discussion on the various readings of this term, see Hugenberger, *Marriage as a Covenant*, 67–69.

137. The Vulgate, Targum, and some manuscripts of the LXX. See Fuller, "Text-Critical Problems," 54–55, and Smith, *Micah–Malachi*, 320.

138. Fuller, "Text-Critical Problems," 54–56, and Rudolph, *Haggai, Sacharja 1–8*, 270.

139. Glazier-McDonald, *Malachi: The Divine Messenger*, 110–111.

that the first verb appears in the third person rather than in the first person. The third-person form appears awkward if Yahweh, through his prophet, is the speaker, which is implied by the messenger formula.[140] It is difficult to reconcile such a translation with the third person. The problem arises from the Masoretic pointing of the Hebrew word since the Masoretes pointed it as a perfect third-person masculine singular, translating it as "he hates."[141]

The question that arises is this: If Yahweh is the subject here, why is this verb stated in the third person? The LXX and Targum even suggest an impersonal subject, translating it as "If one sends away out of hate" or "If one hates, let him send away,"[142] thereby justifying hatred for divorce. Translating the form as a third-person singular verb with God as the subject seems contrary to the direct speech in v16 but presumes that the subject הָאֶחָד, the one Yahweh of the verb can be taken from verse 15. As indicated earlier, the Hebrew phrase כִּי־שָׂנֵא שַׁלַּח is translated as "for he [Yahweh] hates [such] putting away." The translators of the New English Translation (NET) Bible note that this form "makes little sense in the context unless one emends the following word to a third person verb as well,"[143] as Shields also points out.[144] Hugenberger translate this as "if he hates and divorces."[145]

In resolving this problem, scholars have proposed two main interpretations of the terms "hate" and "sending away." Some scholars argue that an interpretation relating the one who hates divorce to Yahweh is untenable[146] because they believe that the MT's usage of these terms does not make sense. Hugenberger describes nine major interpretative approaches to understanding these terms, dividing these into four categories.

The first approach denies any reference to divorce in Malachi 2:16 due to grammatical and lexical problems associated with the verse.[147] These scholars

---

140. Hill, *Malachi*, 249.

141. Malachi 2:16 (NETtn10). (New English Translation textnote 10).

142. The Targum renders the term כִּי (if) in a conditional form, the Vulgate reads "cum odio habueris dimittee" (but if you hate her, send her away), and the Septuagint reads ἀλλὰ ἐὰν μισήσας ἐξαποστείλῃς, (but if you hate her send her away). For a further explanation, see Shields, "Syncretism and Divorce," 80–81.

143. Malachi 2:16 (NET).

144. Shields, "Syncretism and Divorce," 81–85.

145. Hugenberger, *Marriage as a Covenant*, 72–73.

146. Baldwin, *Haggai, Zechariah, Malachi*, 241, and O'Brien, "Judah as Wife," 244.

147. Hugenberger, *Marriage as a Covenant*, 51–57.

observe that if the subject of שָׂנֵא is Yahweh, then the third-person form used in the text is awkward.[148]

The second approach interprets the text as requiring or permitting divorce.[149] While this group of scholars agree that Malachi refers to divorce, they adopt a wide variety of views on his precise attitude towards divorce. They claim that ancient versions such as the LXX eliminate the awkward shift in person that is found in the MT. This group teaches that Malachi recommends divorce in 2:16 as the lesser of two evils in instances where the wife does not find favour in the eyes of the husband.

The third category consists of scholars who interpret Malachi 2:10–16 as an absolute prohibition of divorce.[150] This interpretation is based on the consideration of the primary interpretative question concerning the determination of the subject of שָׂנֵא.

The final category is scholars who limit the kind of divorce prohibited in the verse.[151] These scholars teach that Malachi prohibits divorce only when the offended woman initiates divorce and, therefore, conclude that Malachi condemns only unjustified divorce. The reason for this interpretation is their understanding of כִּי as being conditional.

The problem with the majority of interpreters is that they assume that Deuteronomy 24:1–4 should be the general rule governing divorce.[152] I agree with the translators of the NET Bible who translate this term as, "'For I hate divorce,' says the Lord" and assert that it is possible that the first-person pronoun אָנֹכִי – translated as "I" – has accidentally been dropped from the text after כִּי. If this pronoun is restored, then שָׂנֵא can be taken as a participle with the meaning "I hate."[153] The second reason for taking this position is that in part 'a' of verse 16, the prophet uses the term כִּי ("for"). The use of this word in this context shows that the prophet is not introducing a new problem but merely explaining to readers the reason for the problems mentioned earlier and responding to their question about why God is no longer accepting their

---

148. Isaksson, *Marriage and Ministry*, 32; Smith, *Micah–Malachi*, 323.
149. Hugenberger, *Marriage as a Covenant*, 57–62
150. Hugenberger, 62–65.
151. Hugenberger, 65.
152. For an elaborate discussion on this idea, see McKenzie, "Covenant Themes in Malachi," 552–553.
153. Malachi 2:16 (NETtn).

offerings. In this verse (Mal 2:16a), the prophet introduces the real problem he wants to discuss – שַׁלַּח ("sending away"). The writer of Malachi uses the Hebrew term כִּי ("for") to connect the previous discussion with the message he intends to convey to his readers in verse 16.

The question that arises is this: Was Moses instituting divorce in Deuteronomy 24:1–4, or was he attempting to resolve an existing problem? Kaiser observes that Moses was addressing an existing problem.[154] That was what led Moses to make provision for a bill of divorce. Moses was not acting in contradiction to what was stated in Genesis 2:24–25. Moses would only have had the authority to set aside Genesis 2 if he had been the one who instituted marriage. But Moses was not the author of marriage; he was merely responding to the existing problem of rampant divorce and attempting to protect women who were being set aside in this manner.

The second Hebrew clause – וְכִסָּה חָמָס עַל־לְבוּשׁוֹ אָמַר יְהוָה צְבָאוֹת ("'and the one covering his garment with violence,' says the Lord of hosts") – shows that the sin of marrying the daughter of a foreign god (intermarriage) is not the only issue causing Yahweh's displeasure with his people. In verse 16 the prophet reveals that Yahweh hates divorce, as well as וְכִסָּה חָמָס עַל־לְבוּשׁוֹ ("the one covering his garment with violence").[155]

Andrew Olu Igenoza observes that the statement "I hate divorce" is a forceful one.[156] He points out that from the beginning of the text, the prophet has been addressing the issue of unfaithfulness (2:10) and that this theme is clarified further in verse 11–12.[157] Igenoza says that this becomes even clearer in verses 13–15 and notes that the earlier accusation of breaking faith with the wife of one's youth is specifically identified as divorce by the prophet in verse 16.[158]

Yahweh evaluates the moral behaviour of the addressees and condemns as morally wrong the expulsion of their wives in order to marry women of foreign faiths. He regards divorce as a severe wrong and likens a person

---

154. Kaiser, "Divorce in Malachi," 81.
155. Igenoza, *Polygamy*, 187.
156. Igenoza, 186.
157. Igenoza, 186.
158. Igenoza, 186.

who does this to a garment stained and soiled by an act of sinful violence or extreme wickedness.[159]

In light of the issue of unfaithfulness addressed in the text, the prophet affirms the general truth that God is opposed to divorce, especially divorce of a lawfully covenanted and faithful wife.[160] The divorce referred to here is the sending away of the wife married in one's youth and marrying the daughter of a foreign god. Such unfaithfulness through divorce and intermarriage violates the covenant relationship with both God and the wife. This then makes sense of the final part of 2:16 "Guard yourself in your spirit and do not break faith."

Distinctive Use of Marriage and Kinship Imagery in Malachi 2:10–16

The purpose of this section is to present evidence, based on literary analysis, that the style of Malachi in this text is both beautiful and forceful. The text contains a rich diversity of literary artistry in communicating Malachi's indictment of marital unfaithfulness. In this section, the focus will be on Malachi's artistic portrayal of the commitment of Yahweh to his people. The prophet demonstrates that the terms used to describe this relationship – which will be discussed in three phases in this work – are very important in understanding how God relates to his people.

In this text, there are three relational word pairs used to express God's relationship with his people. These are "love-hate," "father-son," and "husband-wife". I believe that explaining these relational concepts is crucial for understanding Malachi 2:10–16.

The First Pair: Love and Hate (אָהֵב and שָׂנֵא)

The Hebrew term אָהֵב – translated as "love" – and the word שָׂנֵא – translated as "hate" – are two contrasting terms used by the prophet to express the relationship between Yahweh and the people addressed in the text. From the beginning of the book, the prophet reveals that God's attitude is one of unchanging and continuous love for his people (Mal 1:2–3). God has loved Israel and continues to love them, both in the history of their relationship

---

159. Zehnder, "Fresh Look at Malachi," 256.
160. Hill, *Malachi*, 288.

and in the present. The term "love" is emphasized to convey the essential relationship between God and his people.

In contrast to אָהֵב ("love"), the prophet uses the term שָׂנֵא ("hate"). The Hebrew verb שָׂנֵא, which is translated as "to hate," is a *qal* perfect third-person masculine singular, usually translated as "he hated." Contrary to those who see this verse as unintelligible, this translation is appropriate when used in relation to Yahweh. In verse 16, the subject is God which requires only a slight change in the pointing of the Masoretic version to read a participle with a suppressed personal pronoun translated as a continuous tense – "I am hating." In other words, Yahweh hates anyone who sends away the wife of his youth.

In this situation, the addressees, who are divorcing the beloved wives of their youth, are doing the opposite of loving – they are hating. The term שָׂנֵא ("hate") is not new, either in the book of Malachi or in the entire OT. It describes Yahweh's hostility in response to a broken covenant relationship in Malachi 1:3. The term is used when God abhors or is displeased with something in the life of his people. In other sections of Scripture, too, this term has similar connotations. Malachi 2:16 reveals that Yahweh specifically hates two things: (1) divorce or sending away and (2) the man who covers himself with violence.

The prophet uses the love-hate language of relationship to reveal God's reaction to injustices arising from both physical and legal marital unfaithfulness. In other words, God hates marital unfaithfulness that results from the distortion of the legal marriage between covenant members. The prophet uses the love-hate imagery to express Yahweh's displeasure over the social misbehaviour that results in marital unfaithfulness among the people of God in that community.

The Second Pair: Father-Son Imagery (אָב and בֵּן)

The language of God's fatherhood can be traced back to creation. The filial relationship is related to the context of the book of Deuteronomy, where fathers are commanded to instruct their sons in their religious heritage. This kind of relationship, which existed since long ago, is now made manifest in Malachi (Mal 1:6; see also Exod 20:12). The prophet, using the language of a father-son relationship, argues for the oneness of the Jewish people. He observes that God is the "one father" of all Israel (2:10) and describes how they should respond to him (1:6).

The prophet maintains that God, the Creator, is their father and that the people are his son. He reiterates that the two are connected by covenant and that the people are expected to remain faithful to God's covenant stipulations. Since they are family, their love relationship should mirror the father-son relationship. Any form of marital unfaithfulness profanes such a relationship. A son must honour the name of the father he bears and maintain the good name of his parents. In this situation, however, the loyalty due to God has been undermined by unworthy people, whose unfaithful behaviour destabilizes the father-son relationship. As sons of God, the addressees should not act unfaithfully in any way. Just as earthly fathers discipline unfaithful sons, the Lord, in his righteous judgement, will not allow disrespectful sons to escape the punishment due to any violator of the father-son covenant.

The Third Pair: Husband-Wife Imagery (בָּעַל and אִשָּׁה)

The rhetoric that Judah בָּעַל ("marry") is a familial love language of relationship. The Hebrew term בָּעַל is translated as "to own," "to rule over," "be lord," or "marry."[161] The term is used in various ways in the OT. It is used to mean husband of a woman in many places in the OT (see Gen 20:3, Exod 21:3, Deut 22:2 and Isa 62:5), as well as used by the preceding prophets in which they identified God as the husband and the people of God as wife in Hosea 2:16.

In Malachi's context, Judah is seen as the one בָּעַל (marrying and taking possession) of the daughter of a foreign god. The prophet claims that the people of God – in this instance, the Judahites – had left the covenanted wives of their youth and taken foreign women as brides or wives. The prophet's use of the husband-wife relationship in his rhetoric is well-constructed. Judah is the one who is acting unfaithfully against the wife of his youth, who is described in Malachi 2:14 as a covenant wife. The rhetoric using the husband-wife relationship reveals an ongoing problem between Judah and her spouse – that is, God – and it is clear that marital unfaithfulness is the prophet's key concern.

This section (Mal 2:10–16) is structured into two parts. In the first part (2:10–12), the prophet challenges the people with a broad indictment of unfaithfulness and establishes that there is general unfaithfulness to covenantal obligations. In verse 10, he addresses the act of dealing treacherously

---

161. Koehler, and Baumgartner, *Hebrew and Aramaic Lexicon*, 142–143; See also Block, "Marriage and Family," 62, and Manus, "Biblical Foundations for Ecofeminism," 11.

against fellow covenant members. He then reiterates that the people's relationship with Yahweh is affected by their violations of covenantal obligations to other members of the religious community (2:11). Their unfaithfulness involves a violation of the bond that unites fellow covenant members.

The prophet then moves from verses 10–12 to verses 13–15a, which is a specific indictment of marital unfaithfulness. In Malachi 2:11–12 and 2:13–15a, the prophet states the cause of God's displeasure with the people. The prophet concludes with an exhortation against unfaithfulness in marriage (2:15b–16). He emphasizes that God hates divorce and warns against marital unfaithfulness among God's people.

Insights from the Exegetical Study of Malachi 2:10–16

In this work several prominent themes that are theologically relevant for contemporary Christians and especially Christian couples are identified. These themes are discussed below.

God as Creator and Father

The theme of God as Creator and Father is crucial to Malachi's understanding of Yahweh's covenant and his faithfulness (Mal 2:10). The knowledge of God as both Creator and Father in the context of his covenantal love relationship, particularly as it relates to marriage, is fundamental to Israel's well-being. It was this relationship that made God confront his people with their unfaithfulness, which led to disobedience within the covenantal marriage union described in Malachi 2:10–16. Since each person bears personal responsibility, the Creator and Father will hold each one responsible for upholding the covenantal relationship.

The theological theme of God as Creator is prominent in the text. The prophet emphasizes that the same God who created Israel as his children is also the one Father who created all people, making them male and female (2:10 and see: Gen 1:27). In this text, God's fatherhood is understood in terms of his role as Creator of the people of Israel (Mal 1:6; 2:10). Unlike pagan gods, God is the Creator who made a covenant with his people. The theme of

God as Creator is central to the prophet's argument.[162] God is their Creator, and the people are God's covenant people.

Since God is their Creator and they share a common origin, the implication is that such an intimate relationship with God should prevent members of the covenant community from breaking faith with one another. Therefore, any kind of marital unfaithfulness is unacceptable to the Creator, and any such violation disrupts the relationship between God and the Israelites. This passage presents a balanced theology of the concept of God as both Father and Creator, the one who is highly exalted over all yet also deeply concerned for his people.

Judgement for Covenantal Unfaithfulness

Another important theme that runs through the text is judgement for covenantal unfaithfulness. The prophet introduces this theme of judgement early in the book. Initially, he accuses the priests of unfaithfulness, but later broadens the scope to include individuals among the people of the land. Earlier, he foretold judgement for unfaithful priests, warning that they would receive humiliating treatment (2:3–6). Similarly, there would be judgement for covenant violators, particularly in relation to marital unfaithfulness.

In this text, Yahweh, through the prophet, highlights the moral failure among the people in relation to marriage. As a result of their unfaithfulness, there would be judgement for those who were unfaithful to fellow covenant members, as well as for those guilty of marital unfaithfulness. Yahweh would not accept their offerings or worship. The prophet warns the people that God would punish those who violated the covenant, either by being unfaithful to their fellow covenant members or through unfaithfulness in the marriage union.

The One-Flesh Relationship of Marriage

Another key theme that runs throughout the text is the one-flesh relationship in marriage. The prophet refers back to the original creation of humanity in Genesis. He observes that God's ideal for marriage is one man and one woman for life. The prophet refers to the foundational passage that sets forth

---

162. Wendland, "Linear and Concentric Patterns," 108–121. See also Wendland, "Rhetorical Style and Structure," 35.

the biblical standard for the institution of marriage, a passage that Jesus himself quoted: "Have you not read that he who made them from the beginning made them male and female, and said, 'For this reason a man shall leave his father and mother and be joined to his wife, and the two shall become one flesh?' So, they are no longer two but one flesh" (Matt 19:4–6 RSV; see also Gen 2:24; Mark 10:6–9).

In this passage, the prophet refers to Genesis, where God created humanity male and female and brought together man and woman as one flesh. The prophet reiterates the one-flesh nature of marriage, which was instituted by God to be a lifelong companionship. He maintains that this union must be preserved and that marrying the daughters of foreign gods and divorce (sending away covenant wives) violate the principles of this one-flesh relationship. The one-flesh relationship is designed to produce godly offspring, which is something that no other relationship can do. As noted earlier, the prophet emphasizes God's ideal of the permanence of marriage as a lifelong union so that nothing destroys the bond that originally made husband and wife one flesh.

Chapter Summary

Malachi 2:10–16 has been the subject of ongoing debate, and scholars disagree on whether this passage should be interpreted literally or figuratively. However, the problem goes beyond this debate. The exegesis of Malachi 2:10–16 reveals that the real issue in this passage is unfaithfulness in covenantal relationships. There are two kinds of unfaithfulness: a violation of the one-flesh principle in the covenant relationship and a violation of the cleaving principle within the postexilic community. Both these violations have social and religious consequences. Unfaithfulness breaks the bond of unity between fellow covenant members in Yahweh's congregation (Mal 2:10), while marrying the daughters of foreign gods shows that intermarriage with heathen women was being tolerated (Mal 2:11).

The divorce of the covenant wife in Malachi 2:10–16 had religious implications, especially the introduction of syncretism into the worship of Yahweh (2:13–16; see also Ezra 9–10; Neh 13:23–27). Malachi makes the theological argument that marriage is a covenant grounded in the providential design of creation and the covenant with Yahweh. Therefore, anyone entering into this covenant should be faithful to its covenantal ideals. This is why the prophet begins by addressing the nation of Israel as a family and pointing out the problem of disunity resulting from unfaithfulness. He then proceeds to show that the nation, as a spiritual family with a shared parentage, has turned to acts of unfaithfulness and that such unfaithfulness is not only taking place within the nation but in individual lives.

The prophet then makes it clear that the people have committed marital unfaithfulness, pointing out that just as the worship of foreign gods is a breach of the covenant with Yahweh (idolatry), the breach of the covenant with one's spouse is also disloyalty (adultery) and that both these actions have fatal consequences. The prophet uses relational language to rebuke the leading families of Judah, pointing out that this issue brings about instability in society. The prophet concludes his message with a strong admonition to Jewish husbands not to commit infidelity but to remain faithful to their covenant wives. Anyone who does otherwise will be judged for violating the terms of the covenant and undermining family solidarity.

CHAPTER SIX

Malachi 2:10–16 and Its Implications for Pastoral Ministry in Africa

Introduction

The exegesis of Malachi 2:10–16 in the previous chapter revealed that the prophet Malachi's focus in this passage, as well as in the broader context of the entire book, presents many challenges to scholarship. These challenges concern unfaithfulness in covenantal marital unions, separation within marital unions, the sending away of the wife of one's youth, divorce, and intermarriage. In this chapter, I identify and discuss three key issues arising from the historical-cultural context of Malachi 2:10–16 and draws implications from these issues for the African church.

Exegesis of Malachi 2:10–16: Issues Related to Marriage

Unfaithfulness in Covenantal Marriage

The first issue highlighted in the exegesis of Malachi 2:10–16 is unfaithfulness within the covenantal marriage relationship. This unfaithfulness is expressed by the Hebrew verb בגד ("faithless"). In the OT, this word is used in various ways to mean cheating or deceit (Jer 9:2), breaking one's promise (Hos 5:7), or betrayal or breach of a covenant or treaty in human agreements.[1] It could

---

1. Botterweck and Ringgren, *Theological Dictionary*, 1:470–473.

also refer to a betrayal or violation of a promise made to a man's legal wife by establishing a relationship with another woman.[2] This verb expresses unfaithfulness or treacherous behaviour in the covenantal marriage relationship of God's people.[3] In essence, within the historical and cultural context of Malachi, בגד ("faithless") is an act of unfaithfulness committed against one's partner in the covenantal marriage union.

Separation in the Marriage Union

Another major issue arising from the exegetical and theological analysis of Malachi 2:10–16 is that unfaithfulness – which was discussed earlier – now leads the men of Judah to separate from their lawful covenantal wives and marry foreign women.[4] This marriage to foreign women by the men of Judah resulted in the separation of Jewish wives from their lawful husbands and the husbands from the wives of their youth. This left the woman in a state of abandonment andor desolation, which was a tragic consequences of faithless behaviour in Judah's society.

Since God's ideal for marriage is oneness, with a man and a woman coming together as one entity, this must also be the standard for marriage within the faith community. Therefore, this practice of the men of Judah separating from their covenantal wives to marry the daughters of foreign gods was sinful. It violated the covenant that God established at creation. Separating from one's covenantal wife and marrying the daughter of a foreign god is an act of violence that violates God's ideal of an indissoluble union.

Divorce or Sending Away of the Wife of One's Youth

Another issue raised in the exegesis of Malachi 2:10–16 is the issue of divorce or the sending away of the wife of one's youth. The "wives" referred to here are those bound by a solemn marriage covenant. According to Achtemeier, these wives are the women whom the men of Judah had married when they were younger.[5] These women – whom Malachi refers to as "the wife of your youth" and "your companion" (Mal 2:14 NRSV) – are the wives whom the

---

2. Botterweck and Ringgren, 1:470.

3. Koehler and Baumgartner, *Hebrew and Aramaic Lexicon*, 108, and Holladay, *Hebrew and Aramaic Lexicon*, 261–263. See also Robin Wakely, "בגד" *NIDOTTE* 1:582–595.

4. Uppsala Seth Erlandsson, "בגד," (to act faithlessly) *TDOT* 1:470.

5. Achtemeier, *Nahum–Malachi*, 182.

men of Judah are now sending away in order to marry other foreign women. Their actions violate the covenant promises made to their legal spouses.[6]

Divorce and Intermarriage

Another issue raised by the exegetical and theological analysis of the text is intermarriage after the divorce or sending away of the Jewish wives. The issue here is not just intermarriage but the fact that it takes place after these Jewish men send away their legally covenanted Jewish wives. This practice undermined the people's loyalty to Yahweh because it permitted foreign cults to infiltrate Israel through the daughters of foreign nations.[7] Intermarriage with foreign women by the people of Judah posed a serious threat to the unity of God's people – not on the basis of ethnicity but on theological grounds. In light of this understanding of the text, remarriage after divorce is a difficult issue – not because of ethnic hatred but because intermarriage contradicts the purpose of Jewish marriage, which was primarily to maintain and perpetuate the covenant community.

Malachi 2:10–16: Implications of Marital Unfaithfulness for the African Church and Society

The family is the bedrock of society. However, society is experiencing moral decay due to problems within marriage and the growing instability of marriage. Unfaithfulness in covenantal marriage relationships continues to be an undeniable reality in human existence. As a result of such unfaithfulness, marriages are failing. Although this problem is increasing in contemporary society, it seems that scholars in Africa have not taught sufficiently or clearly enough about the nature of the marriage covenant as taught by the prophet Malachi.

The issue of unfaithfulness leading to divorce, which was raised in the historical-cultural context of Malachi 2:10–16, remains an issue for the

---

6. Botterweck and Ringgreen, *Theological Dictionary of the Old Testament*, I: 470. See also David Novak, "Jewish Marriage: Nature, Covenant, and Contract," in *Covenant Marriage in Comparative Perspective* (eds. John Witte, Jr., and Eliza Ellison, Grand Rapids: Wm. B. Erdmanns Publishing Company, 2005), 40.

7. Botterweck and Ringgren, *Theological Dictionary*, 2:337. Hill, *Malachi*, 233, and Glazier-McDonald, *Malachi: The Divine Messenger*, 92–93.

contemporary African church and society. Unfaithfulness in marital relationships is increasingly common in contemporary African society. Some older men are no longer satisfied with the wives of their youth, and some African leaders in high positions abandon their legal wives – whom they married in their youth – in favour of younger or more attractive women, who then become first ladies or wives of governors.

This is similar to the situation addressed in the book of Malachi, where some Jewish men divorced their legal wives in favour of foreign women. Such unfaithfulness in relationships has wreaked havoc in society. Given the extent of marital infidelity in contemporary society, there is an urgent need to remind both the faith community and society at large of God's order as presented in Malachi 2:10–16.

There is a need for pastors to understand the biblical measures revealed in Malachi for curbing marital unfaithfulness in Yahweh's congregation of the postexilic community in order to seriously consider possible application in contemporary faith communities. These measures can be contextualized for the contemporary African church and society. In other words, the message of Malachi 2:10–16 provides valuable insights that can be helpfully applied in Africa. Malachi's teachings on how to live faithfully within a marriage are significant for all married couples – those within the believing community as well as those in contemporary society.

In this chapter, we examine the implications of Malachi's theology related to the issue of marital unfaithfulness and discusses how the covenant for personal family piety could be honoured within both the faith community and society at large.

God's Standard for Marriage: A New Order for the Church in Africa

The issue of unfaithfulness discussed in Malachi 2:10–16 is a significant concern in the African church, and calls for an upholding of the biblical standards seen in this passage for the covenantal marriage of his people. The implications of such a theology of covenant faithfulness in marriage for the contemporary African church and society are discussed below.

The Permanence of Marriage as an Unbroken Covenant

It was noted earlier that marriage is an institution ordained by God. This institution is not just a family affair but also serves social and religious purposes. One important pastoral concern for the community is to recognize that God, as the creator and founder of the institution of marriage, is concerned about its permanence.[8] However, in modern times, many people treat marriage lightly, assuming that they can easily divorce their spouses and marry others at will. In other words, people who have entered into covenant marriages are violating their covenant by sending away their covenantal partners, not realizing that this also violates the unity of the community.[9]

Israel's history shows that the community's existence was founded on their covenant with Yahweh, the one who created them as one flesh. Malachi presents the word of God – who is the divine initiator of the marriage institution – as a pointer to the unbroken nature of the covenant.

Marriage: A High and Holy Calling

A new insight that Malachi offers regarding the institution of marriage is that it is a covenant, not a contract. Malachi maintains that marriage is an institution ordained and protected by God and that anything contrary to this elevated view of marriage as a covenant should be avoided. This pastoral concern has also been expressed by some African Christian scholars.[10] Both Igenoza and Ogunkunle reiterate that the one-flesh union of a man and wife among members of Yahweh's congregation is very important in underpinning families where the couple produce godly offspring to who they pass on true faith and trust in God.[11] Any kind of unfaithfulness that undermines such a marriage union would adversely impact the well-being of others in the community. This assertion is supported by Yahweh's categorical statement that he hates divorce (Mal 2:16), a statement that affirms the high and holy calling of marriage.[12]

---

8. Mbiti, *African Religions and Philosophy*, 140; Oppong, *Middle Class African Marriage*, 31. See also Kore, *Promoting Healthy Marriage*, 21.
9. Akao, "Concept of Sexuality," 41.
10. Ogunkunle, "Biblical Injunction," 49.
11. Igenoza, *Polygamy*, 186, and Ogunkunle, "Biblical Injunction," 49.
12. Achtemeier, *Nahum-Malachi* , 183. See also: Hill, *Malachi*, 241.

Faithfulness within the Marriage Union

The covenant relationship between God and his chosen people, as presented in Malachi 2:10–16, is characterized by faithfulness. It is clear that unfaithfulness within the marriage union undermines the organic unity of Judah as God's elect, just as it adversely affects the people of God in contemporary society. Therefore, faithfulness in marriage becomes even more imperative for those acting treacherously against their covenant partners in contemporary society. The prophet urges Yahweh's congregation, specifically Jewish husbands, to uphold the biblical ideal of lifelong companionship and the permanence of marriage by remaining loyal and faithful to the wives of their youth (Mal 2:14–15).

Faithfulness: Crucial for Family Unity in the African Church

Since the bond of unity between marriage partners and covenant members had been broken by separation (Mal 2:10), the prophet stresses the importance of family unity within Yahweh's congregation in Judah as part of the intended new order in the postexilic community. He teaches the people that God, who is their Creator and Father, wants them to be one spiritual family. He also emphasizes that, as a spiritual family of shared parentage, the people of God should not allow unfaithfulness of any kind to undermine their unity.

To drive home his point, the prophet draws the attention of the leaders back to the creation story (Gen 1:27). He observes that the same God who made the Jewish husband also made the Jewish wife, with whom the husband is now breaking faith.[13] The prophet concludes that such an act of marital unfaithfulness is contrary to the broader commitment to faithfulness in covenant agreements as set out in the covenant stipulations of the Torah, which were discussed earlier in this work. It is clear that infidelity in marriage is displeasing to God.

Just as frivolous and impulsive decisions regarding marriage were made in Malachi's time – for instance, marrying the daughters of foreign gods and treating divorce and violence lightly – a similar attitude of frivolity and impulsiveness exists in relation to marriage unions in contemporary society. Marital unfaithfulness is all too evident within the African church, too.

---

13. Ogunkunle, "Biblical Injunction," 51.

Intermarriage: Prohibited on a Theological Basis

Malachi is against intermarriage not on the basis of ethnic or racist sentiment but on theological grounds. Although there are instances in the OT where God works outside the Israelites' tradition – for example, the story of Ruth – the prophet strictly forbids marriage with persons outside this tradition, insisting that marriage partners should belong to the same religious and national group.[14] Therefore, contrary to those who argue that because God sometimes works outside Israel's tradition, Christians may abandon the biblical tradition of monogamous marriage within the Christian faith in favour of mixed marriages, Christians must rather uphold biblical principles when making decisions about marriage, and marry only those who are also Christians.

Although the prophet addresses faithlessness within the covenant marriage relationship, he also presents a theological concern, using the relationship of husband and wife as a reminder of the covenant relationship God had established with Israel (Exod 24:1–11).

Malachi's Theology of Marital Faithfulness: Implications for Personal Family Piety in the African Church

The immediate implication of Malachi's theology in relation to marital unfaithfulness is centred on the faith community. For both Jews and Africans, the family is the bedrock of society. Just as Christianity involves brotherhood, Israel is seen as a unified whole.[15] Like the Israelites, Christianity fosters brotherhood and couples in African churches – like God's people in postexilic Judah – view God as both Creator and Father. Today, however, marriage is not viewed in the way that it was originally established by God as a divine covenantal institution.

As in Malachi's day, scholars in recent times also observe that marital unfaithfulness is prevalent within covenantal marriage unions in contemporary society. This unfaithfulness among Christians in Africa, especially in

---

14. Folarin, *Old Testament Prophecy*, 121.
15. McConville, "Law and Theology," 19.

the Nigerian church, remains a serious problem.[16] In contemporary society, unfaithfulness is a cause for great concern, often prompting spouses to resort to divorce.[17] The phenomenon of men sending away the wives of their youth and marrying the daughters of foreign gods, as seen in Malachi's day, is also prevalent in today's society with continued damaging consequences.[18]

The academic community must respond to the challenges posed by the marital crisis within both the faith community and society at large. African scholars need to present sound biblical teachings on marital faithfulness, helping people to understand God's purposes for marriage and showing how the teachings of Malachi can help to safeguard the institution of marriage. These issues must be thoughtfully addressed to reduce cases of marital unfaithfulness and the miuses of divorce.

The family of faith in the African church, like in Malachi's time, is experiencing a crisis of faithlessness, which requires a fresh presentation of the biblical ideal for marriage. In our rapidly changing world, it is important that the Christian faith and the Christian family remain intact. God's word on the indissolubility of the covenantal marriage union has not changed. This is evident in the way the prophet traces the shared parentage of the people of Israel to their family roots.

The challenge for the church in Africa is taking the oneness of people in the faith community seriously. There is also a need to rediscover sound biblical teaching on marital unfaithfulness, which will help families to grasp God's purpose for marriage and understand how to safeguard family togetherness in marriage and protect the institution of marriage from marital unfaithfulness. The coming together of husband and wife in a one-flesh union demands a commitment to making the marriage work. If either party breaks faith, they are ignoring this aspect of oneness and the fact that they both belong to the same Father. When a couple comes together in marriage, they make vows. If these marriage vows are kept, the union has great potential to fulfil God's plan, which includes bearing godly children who will follow God's ways and worship him.

---

16. Kato, *Christian Home*, 13. See also Kore, *Culture and the Christian Home*, 3. See also Abe, "Berith."

17. Igenoza, *Polygamy*, 186. See also Kore, *Truths for Healthy Churches*, and Kunhiyop, *African Christian Ethics*, 227–234.

18. Ayandokun, *Counseling Made Easy*, 100. See also Igenoza, *Polygamy*, 186.

Just as the prophet emphasizes the importance of oneness and harmony in the family so that such couples and families might be a model for those around them, this is also God's desire for families in the African church. He wants families who come together in a covenant love relationship to remain as one spiritual family in order to produce godly offspring. Yahweh's displeasure with the frivolous sending away of covenant wives by the Jews of Malachi's time is also relevant to the faith community today. However, this is not on an ethnic or racial basis but on theological grounds.

Therefore the church, through the ministry of its leaders, must not wait until marital unfaithfulness destroys homes. Biblical counselling measures should be implemented to help strengthen Christian homes, as well as homes in contemporary society. Theologians and Christian counsellors in Africa should follow the preventive actions discussed in this work. God, who created humanity both male and female, established the institution of marriage and provided guidelines to prevent marital instability. Therefore, these guidelines, including those presented in the book of Malachi, should be taught clearly to church leaders in Africa, and they, in turn, should teach these in their own churches and homes in order to bring about stability in marriages.

CHAPTER SEVEN

Conclusion and Recommendations

As stated previously, the primary aim of this work is not to continue the previous scholarly debate over whether the issue of marriage and divorce addressed in the text is literal or figurative. Instead, I attempted to demonstrate how the prophet Malachi deals with the issue of marital unfaithfulness and to show how his teachings serve as a guide for resolving marital problems within the faith community and contemporary society.

Therefore, I examined various previous discussions and interpretative views. I observed that the majority of scholarly engagement with this text is still centred on the debate over whether marital unfaithfulness should be understood literally or figuratively. While some scholars focus solely on idolatry, others also see marital unfaithfulness as an important issue in the text. In contrast, I argued that the theology of Malachi in relation to the issue of marital unfaithfulness is a central aspect of the passage, pointing out that Yahweh expects marriage among couples in his congregation to be based on a covenantal love relationship.

I have shown that there is a profound theological understanding of the issue of marital unfaithfulness in this text by tracing the divine institution of marriage to the covenant Yahweh made with Israel's forefathers in the Pentateuch and pointing to Israel's covenantal election as the one people of God.

Therefore, the covenant is the basis of Israel's relationship with God. In Malachi 2:10–16, this covenant is seen as requiring the trust and loyalty of God's people as a necessary prerequisite for a stable marriage union, godly offspring, and a harmonious family life. The passage clearly states that the people share a common parentage and are bound together by the covenant relationship between them and Yahweh. In view here is the Mosaic covenant in the context of the Torah. This study also examines other OT examples of God's teaching on marriage in both the prophetic books and the Ketubim. These form the background for understanding the issue of unfaithfulness that is addressed in Malachi 2:10–16. This text fits well within the overall structure of the book of Malachi and also aligns with the postexilic prophetic literature.

In my exegesis of the text, I pointed out that marital unfaithfulness is a prominent issue, contrary to scholars who do not view this as a central concern. I argued that the people addressed in the text share a common parentage and are expected to sustain the bond of unity in their covenantal relationships within the community of faith – both in ordinary relationships as citizens and in the marriage union. However, the text reveals that the people were unfaithful to both their fellow covenant members and their marriage partners, which was contrary to the ideal of the divine institution of marriage instituted by Yahweh.

I also argued that the people addressed in the text were compromising their relationship with Yahweh by acting treacherously in two ways: first, towards God, by failing to keep the bond of unity with fellow covenant members (Mal 2:10), and second, by failing to keep the bond of unity with their wives who were their covenantal partners. The prophet Malachi presents various arguments against the separation of Jewish men from their covenantal marriage partners, explaining to readers that these men were divorcing themselves from their lawful wives for the purpose of marrying foreign women. Malachi gives four major reasons why these men should not separate from their lawful Jewish wives:

1. The bond of unity is a covenant relationship initiated by Yahweh, who is the Creator, Father, and witness to the marriage covenant.
2. The intimate and emotional connection these men share with their Jewish wives, whom Malachi refers to as "the wife of your youth" and "your companion" (Mal 2:14 NRSV).
3. The bond of shared faith between these men and their Jewish wives, who are described as "your wife by covenant" (Mal 2:14 NRSV).
4. The one-flesh relationship, considered from the perspective of the creational unity between a man (male) and woman (female) as partners.

The prophet concludes with an admonition for the addressees to avoid marital unfaithfulness and remain faithful to their covenantal wives of their youth.

Malachi understands God to have declared that the covenantal marriage union is permanent and that divorce is prohibited. Malachi sets out the concept of mutual relationship in the form of keeping faith, contrary to the unfaithfulness in marriage union that was found among the people. God's view on marital unfaithfulness is clearly expressed in the declaration, "I hate divorce" (Mal 2:16 NRSV). This is also affirmed in the words of Jesus Christ: "It was because you were so hard-hearted that Moses allowed you to divorce your wives, but from the beginning it was not so." (Matt 19:8 NRSV).

The sound biblical teaching found in Malachi 2:10–16, with its prohibition of marital unfaithfulness and divorce, encourages the permanence of the marriage relationship as a one-flesh union for couples in the church across the world. Today, many people are troubled and confused as a result of marital unfaithfulness and need God's direction for their marriages.

Malachi offers a prophetic model of God's counsel for addressing marital problems and stabilizing homes in order to ease the agony of heart and emotional distress experienced by many married couples and their families. In addition, God has high expectations for his people – both in the postexilic faith community and in modern society – and expects them to live according to his values and principles.

Although some of the issues discussed in Malachi do not concern us directly, general principles on marital unfaithfulness may be applied to a variety of situations in our lives. Therefore, Malachi's theology in relation to marital unfaithfulness is relevant for personal family piety within both the faith community (the church) and contemporary society.

The Contributions of This Research

This work to make significant contributions to scholarship in several ways.

First, in an age where some people see biblical truth as relative and believe that no single law can be applied universally, this research notes that God was displeased with the marital unfaithfulness of his covenant community in postexilic Judah, an issue that is even more prevalent in modern times. It is hoped that this work will contribute significantly to the field of prophetic studies by offering readers a deeper theological understanding of marriage as a covenant and divorce as covenant-breaking.

Second, this study presents the ethical demands of the Bible, emphasizing the need for spiritual transformation of readers and their responsibility to live in accordance with the teachings of Scripture. This research aims to advance the contemporary understanding of marital unfaithfulness and to demonstrate, using literary and exegetical methods, how Malachi serves as a guide for the contemporary faith community. The study uses historical-grammatical exegesis, which other scholars can apply in their own engagement with the text.

Third, since biblical values are true for every age and originate from an eternal, uncreated, and unchanging God, in Malachi, the concept of marriage as a covenant is rooted in the very unity of God, while divorce is seen as a covenant-breaking action that displeases him. This is because, from the beginning, the bond between God and Israel was uniquely based on Yahweh's covenantal relationship with his people. Therefore, a breakdown in the marriage bond not only violates the marriage covenant but also breaches the bond of unity between Yahweh and his people.

Fourth, God's goal in Malachi 2:10–16 is to restore the original, glorious, and eternal institution of marriage as a reflection of God's covenant relationship with his people. This relationship has a Christological origin, a soteriological basis, and, as its climax, an eschatological goal. This research contributes significantly to building biblical ethical values related to marriage as a covenant and divorce as covenant-breaking, using the prophetic model. This has implications for pastoral ministry in Africa and for today's believing community of God's people.

Fifth, it is hoped that future research will validate the findings of this study and extend this approach to other genres of biblical literature. As such, this work serves as a resource for subsequent researchers.

Finally, this research aim to help both academic and church communities to develop a deeper theological understanding of the issue of marital unfaithfulness and provide insights that may reduce marital problems within homes.

Areas for Further Research

Although the oracular unit of Malachi 2:10–16, especially the theme of marital unfaithfulness within the marriage union, has been examined, it is recommended that further exegetical study be carried out on other related passages from other parts of the Bible. Since the entire book of Malachi could not be covered, some areas of the book remain unexplored. One such area is the unfaithfulness of the priests in their failure to honour God and their unfaithfulness in despising the Lord's covenant and neglecting their responsibilities to teach the people.

Since this research did not include an exegesis of every OT passage on marital unfaithfulness, further study is needed on marriage as a covenant and divorce as covenant-breaking – especially the aspect of marital unfaithfulness – in other OT and NT books. In addition, another area that remains unexplored is the concept of God seeking reconciliation with and restoration of Israel as an faithless wife, as seen in other parts of the Hebrew Bible, including the prophetic corpus and the Writings. The NT – especially the Gospels, the Epistles of Paul, and the book of Revelation – also remains unexplored, especially with regard to the metaphor of divine marriage and the consequences of marital unfaithfulness.

Bibliography

Aalders, G. C. *Genesis: Volume 1: Biblical Student's Commentary*. Translated by William Heynen. Grand Rapids: Zondervan, 1981.

Abe, Gabriel O. "Berith: Its Impact on Israel and Its Relevance to the Nigerian Society." In African Journal of Biblical Studies, Vol. 1 (1986): 66–73.

Achtemeier, Elizabeth Rice. *Nahum–Malachi*. Interpretation: A Bible Commentary for Teaching and Preaching. Atlanta: John Knox, 1986.

Ackroyd, Peter S. "The Book of Haggai and Zexhariah 1-VIII," Journal of Jewish Studies 3 (1952): 151–156.

Ackroyd, Peter. *Exile and Restoration*. Philadelphia: Westminster John Knox, 1968.

Adams, Jay E. *Marriage, Divorce, and Remarriage in the Bible*. Grand Rapids: Zondervan, 1980.

———. *Christian Living in the Home*. Phillipsburg: Presbyterian & Reformed, 1972.

Ahlström, G. W. *Joel and the Temple Cult of Jerusalem*. VTSup 21. Leiden: Brill, 1971.

Akao, J. O. "The Old Testament Concept of Sexuality." In *Biblical View of Sex and Sexuality from African Perspective*, edited by Samuel O. Abogunrin, 15–47. Ibadan: Nigerian Association for Biblical Studies, 2006.

Albertz, Rainer. *A History of Israelite Religion in the Old Testament Period*. 2 vols. Translated by John Bowden. OTL. Louisville: Westminster John Knox, 1994.

Albright, W. F. *The Biblical Period from Abraham to Ezra: An Historical Survey*. New York: Harper & Row, 1963.

Albright, W. F. *Archeology, Historical Analogy and Early Biblical History*. Baton Rouge: Louisiana State University, 1966.

Alden, Robert L. "Malachi." In *The Expositor's Bible Commentary, Vol. 7: Daniel and the Minor Prophets*, edited by Frank E. Gaebelein, 699–725. Grand Rapids: Zondervan, 1985

Alexander, Denis. "The Scientific Community and the Practice of Science." In *Can We Be Sure About Anything? Science, Faith and Postmodernism*, edited by Denis Alexander, 127–40. Leicester: Apollos, 2005.

Alter, Robert. *The Art of Biblical Poetry*. New York: Basic Books, 1985.

Apple, Raymond. "Marriage." *Encyclopedia Judaica CD*.

Archer, Gleason. "Daniel." In *The Expositor's Bible Commentary, Vol. 7*, edited by Frank E. Gaebelein, 3–157. Grand Rapids: Zondervan, 1985.

———. *A Survey of Old Testament Introduction*. Chicago: Moody, 1994.

Avery-Peck, Alma J. "Covenant." In *The Encyclopedia of Judaism*, vol. 1: A–I, edited by Jacob Neusner, Alman J. Avery-Peck, and William Scott Green, 136–51. Leiden: Brill, 2000.

Ayandokun, E. A. *Counseling Made Easy: Vital Hints on Caring for People with Marriage Spices*. Lagos: Gloryline Christian Publications, 2010.

Baker, David W. "Israelite Prophets and Prophecy." In *The Face of Old Testament Studies: A Survey of Contemporary Approaches*, edited by David W. Baker and Bill T. Arnold, 266–94. Grand Rapids: Baker Academic, 1999.

Baker, David W., and Bill T. Arnold, eds. *Face of Old Testament Studies*. Grand Rapids: Baker Academic, 1999.

Baldwin, Joyce G. *Haggai, Zechariah, Malachi: An Introduction and Commentary*. TOTC. London: Tyndale, 1972.

Barrett, C. K., ed. The New Testament Background: Writings from Ancient Greece and the Roman Empire That Illuminate Christian Origins. Rev. ed. New York: Harper & Row, 1989.

Bartholomew, Craig G., and Ryan P. O'Dowd. *Old Testament Wisdom Literature*. Downers Grove: IVP Academic, 2011.

Barton, John. *Reading the Old Testament*. Philadelphia: Westminster, 1984.

Bechtel, Lyn M. "Shame as a Sanction of Social Control in Biblical Israel: Judicial, Political, and Social Shaming." *JSOT* 16, no. 49 (1991): 47–76.

Berlin, Adele. *Poetics and Interpretation of Biblical Narrative*. Winona Lake: Eisenbrauns, 1994.

Blenkinsopp, Joseph. *A History of Prophecy in Israel*. Philadelphia: Westminster, 1983.

Block, Daniel I. "Marriage and Family in Ancient Israel." In *Marriage and Family in the Biblical World*, edited by Ken M. Campbell, 33–102. Downers Grove: IVP Academic, 2003.

Blomberg, Craig L. "Marriage, Divorce, Remarriage, and Celibacy: An Exegesis of Mathew 19:3–12." *Trinity Journal* 11, no. 2 (1990):162–96.

Bock, Darrell L. "Lexical Analysis: Studies in Words." In *Interpreting the New Testament Text: Introduction to the Art and Science of Exegesis*, edited by Darrell L. Bock and Buist M. Fanning, 135–53. Wheaton: Crossway, 2006.

Bock, Darrell L., and Buist M. Fanning, eds. *Interpreting the New Testament Text: Introduction to the Art and Science of Exegesis*. Wheaton: Crossway, 2006.

Botterweck, G. J., H. Ringgren, and Heinz Josef-Fabry, (eds.) *Theological Dictionary of the Old Testament*. Vol. 7. Translated by David E. Green. Grand Rapids: Eerdmans, 1974.

Brenner-Idan, Athalya. *The Israelite Woman: Social Role and Literary Type in Biblical Narrative*. Sheffield: JSOT Press, 1985.

Bright, John. *A History of Israel*. 2nd ed. Philadelphia: Westminster; London: SCM, 1972.

———. *A History of Israel*. 3rd ed. London: SCM, 1981.

Brockington, L. H. *Ezra, Nehemiah and Esther*. NCB. London: Nelson, 1969.

Bromiley, G. W. *God and Marriage*. Grand Rapids: Eerdmans, 1980.

Brown, Colin, ed. *The New International Dictionary of New Testament Theology*. Carlisle: Paternoster, 1986.

Brown, F., S. Driver, and C. Briggs. *The Brown-Driver-Briggs Hebrew and English Lexicon*. Peabody: Hendrickson, 1996.

Broyde, Michael J. "The Covenant-Contract Dialectic in Jewish Marriage and Divorce Law." In *Covenant Marriage in Comparative Perspective*, edited by John Witte Jr. and Eliza Ellison, 53–69. Grand Rapids: Eerdmans, 2005.

Bruce, F. F. *Israel and the Nations: From the Exodus to the Fall of the Second Temple*. Exeter: Paternoster, 1987.

Bullinger, E. W. *Figures of Speech Used in the Bible*. Grand Rapids: Baker Books, 1968.

Bullock, C. Hassell. *An Introduction to the Old Testament Prophetic Books*. Chicago: Moody, 1986.

Bulmerincq, von Alexancer. *Der Prophet Maleachi*, Bond 2: Kommetar zum Buche des propheten *Maleachi*. Tartu: Kommisisonsverlag von J. G. Kruger, 1932.

Burton, Ernest De Wit. "The Biblical Teaching Concerning Divorce." *The Biblical World* 29, no. 2 (February 1907): 121–127.

Calvin, John. *Commentaries on the Twelve Minor Prophets*. Vol. 15. Translated by J. Owen. Repr. Grand Rapids: Baker Book, 1979.

Carcopino, Jerome. *Daily Life in Ancient Rome*. London: Penguin Books, 1962.

Cary, M., and T. J. Haarhoff. *Life and Thought in the Greek and Roman World*. London: Methuen, 1961.

Cathcart, Kevin J., and Robert P. Gordon, trans. *The Targum of the Minor Prophets*. The Aramaic Bible 14. Edinburgh: T&T Clark, 1989.

Chary, Théophane. *Les Prophètes et le culte á partir de l'exil*. Tournai: Desclée, 1855.

Childs, Brevard S. *Biblical Theology in Crisis*. Philadelphia: Westminster, 1970.

———. *Biblical Theology of the Old and New Testaments*. London: SCM, 1992.

———. "Interpretation in Faith: The Theological Responsibility of an Old Testament Community." *Int* 18 (1964): 432–449.

———. *Introduction to the Old Testament as Scripture*. Philadelphia: Fortress, 1979.

Clendenen, E. Ray. "The Interpretation of Biblical Hebrew Hortatory Texts: A Textlinguistic Approach to the Book of Malachi." PhD diss., University of Texas, 1989.

———. "The Structure of Malachi: A Textlinguistic Study." *CTR* 2 (1987): 3–17.

Clendenen, E. Ray, and Richard A. Taylor. *Haggai–Malachi: An Exegetical and Theological Exposition of Holy Scripture*. NAC. Nashville: Broadman & Holman, 2004.

Clines, David J., ed. *The Dictionary of Classical Hebrew*. Vol. 3. Sheffield: Sheffield Academic Press, 1996.

Coggins, R. J. *Haggai, Zechariah, Malachi: Old Testament Guides*. Sheffield: JSOT Press, 1977.

Collins, C. J. "The (Intelligible) Masoretic Text of Malachi 2:16." *Presb* 20 (1989): 36–40.

Collins, John J. "The Message of Malachi." *TBT* 22 (1984): 209–215.

Corley, Bruce, Steve W. Lemke, and Grant I. Lovejoy, eds. *Biblical Hermeneutics: A Comprehensive Introduction to Interpreting Scripture*. 2nd ed. Nashville: Broadman & Holman, 2002.

Cornes, Andrew. *Divorce and Remarriage: Biblical Principles and Pastoral Practice*. London: Hodder & Stoughton, 1993.

Craigie, Peter C. *The Book of Deuteronomy*. NICOT. Grand Rapids: Eerdmans, 1985.

Craigie, Peter C., Page H. Kelly, and Joel F. Drinkard, Jr. *Jeremiah 1–25* WBC 26. Nashville: Thomas Nelson, 1991.

Crispin, Ken. *Divorce: The Forgivable Sin?* London: Hodder & Stoughton, 1989.

Danby, Herbert, trans. "Gittin, 81a-b." In *The Mishnah*, 307–21. London: Oxford University Press, 1933.

Daniel-Rops, Henri. *Daily Life in the Time of Jesus*. Ann Arbor: Servant Books, 1980.

Davidson, Benjamin. *The Analytical Hebrew and Chaldee Lexicon*. Lynn: Hendrickson, 1981.

Davis, John Jefferson. *Evangelical Ethics: Issues Facing the Church Today*. 2nd ed. Phillipsburg: Presbyterian & Reformed Publishing, 1993.

———. *Moses and the Gods of Egypt*. Grand Rapids: Baker, 1986.

DeCanio, Frank T. *Analysis and Synthesis of the Books of the Bible*. Ilorin: Great Ajibaye Industries, Nigeria Limited, 2003.

Delitzsch, Friedrich. *Babel and Bible*. New York: G. P. Putman's Sons, 1903.

Dentan, R. C. "Malachi." In *The Interpreter's Bible, vol. 6*, edited by G. A. Buttrick, 1116–44. New York: Abingdon, 1956.

Di Marco, A. "Der Chiasmus in der Bibel." *LB* 36 (1979), 3–70.

Dockery, David S., and George H. Guthrie. *The Holman Guide to Interpreting the Bible*. Nashville: Broadman & Holman, 2004.

Drinkard, Joel F. "The Socio-historical Setting of Malachi." *RevExp* 84 (1987): 383–90.

Driver, R. S., ed. *The Minor Prophets*. The Century Bible. Edinburgh: T&T Clark; New York: Oxford University Press, 1906.

Duhm, Bernhard. *Die Theologie der Propheten*. Bonn: Marcus, 1875.

Dumbrell, W. J. *The Faith of Israel: A Theological Survey of the Old Testament*. 2nd ed. Grand Rapids: Baker Academic, 2002.

———. "Malachi and the Ezra-Nehemiah Reforms." *Reformed Theological Review* 35 (1976): 45–52.

Eichrodt, Walther. *Theology of the Old Testament*. Vol. 1. London: SCM, 1961.

Eissfeldt, Otto. *The Old Testament: An Introduction*. New York: Harper & Row, 1965.

Elliger, K. *Das Buch der Zwölf Kleinen Propheten II*. Das Alte Testament Deustsch. Göttingen: Vandenhoeck & Ruprecht, 1951.

Elliger, K., and W. Rudolph, eds. *Biblia Hebraica Stuttgartensia*. Stuttgart: Deutsche Bibelgesellschaft, 1967.

Eliot, Thomas Stearns. *On Poetry and Poets*, 1st ed. London: Faber & Faber, 1957,

Enuwosa, Joseph. "Africentric Hermeneutics: The Divorce Option in Matthew 5:32 in Urhobo Cultural Context." *AJBS* 23, no. 1 (April 2006): 49–72.

Epistein, I. and Maurice S. trans. Babylonian Talmud: Tractate Gittin 9:3. Online: http://www.comeandhear.com/gittin/gittin_2.html#chapter_i.

Estes, Daniel J. *Handbook on the Wisdom Books and Psalms*. Grand Rapids: Baker Academic, 2005.

Evans, Tony. *Tony Evans Speaks out on Divorce and Remarriage*. Chicago: Moody, 1995.

Even-Shoshan, A., ed. *A New Concordance of the Old Testament*. Jerusalem: Kiryat Sepher, 1983.

Ewald, H. *Die Propheten des Alten Bundes*. 2nd ed. Göttingen: Vandenhoeck & Ruprecht, 1867.

Fadipe, N. A. *The Sociology of the Yoruba*. Ibadan: Ibadan University Press, 1970.

Fausset, A. R. "Malachi." In *A Commentary, Critical and Explanatory on the Old and New Testaments, vol. 1*, edited by R. Jamieson, A. R. Fausset, and D. Brown. Hartford: S. S. Scranton, 1878.

Fee, Gordon D., and Douglas Stuart. *How to Read the Bible for All Its Worth*. Grand Rapids: Zondervan, 1993.

Feinberg, Charles L. *The Minor Prophets*. Chicago: Moody, 1976.

Feinberg, John S, and Paul D. Feinberg, eds. *Tradition and Testament: Essays in Honor of Charles Lee Feinberg*. Chicago: Moody, 1981.

Ferguson, Everett. *Backgrounds of Early Christianity*. 2nd ed. Grand Rapids: Eerdmans, 1993.

Filbeck, David. *Yes, God of the Gentiles, Too: The Missionary Message of the Old Testament*. Wheaton: Billy Graham Center, 1994.

Fischer, James A. "Notes on the Literary Form and Message of Malachi." *CBQ* 34 (1972): 315–320.

Fishbane, M. *Biblical Interpretation in Ancient Israel*. Oxford: Clarendon, 1985.

Floyd, Michael H. *Minor Prophets: Part 2*. Grand Rapids: Eerdmans, 2000.

Folarin, George O. *Studies in Old Testament Prophecy*. Bukuru: African Christian Textbooks, 2004.

Friedman, N. "Imagery." In *The New Princeton Encyclopedia of Poetry and Poetics*, edited by A. Preminger. Princeton: Princeton University Press, (1965): 350–368.

Fuller, Russell. "Text-Critical Problems in Malachi 2:10–16." *JBL* 110, no. 1 (Spring 1991): 47–57.

Gaebelein, Frank E. *The Expositor's Bible Commentary*. Vol. 7. Grand Rapids: Zondervan, 1985.

Galambusch, Julie. *Jerusalem in the Book of Ezekiel: The City as Yahweh's Wife*. SBL Dissertation Series 130. Atlanta: Scholars Press, 1992.

Garland, David E. "A Biblical View of Divorce." *RevExp* 84 (1987): 419–432.

Gelston, Anthony, ed. *The Peshitta of the Twelve Prophets*. Oxford: Clarendon, 2011.

———. *The Twelve Minor Prophets*. BHQ 13. Stuttgart: Deutsche Bibelgesellschaft, 2011.

Gerham, Henry S. "The Burden of the Prophets." *Jewish Quarterly Review* 31 (1940): 50–66.

Gesenius, Wilhelm. *Gesenius' Hebrew Grammar*. Edited by E. Kautzsch. Translated by A. E. Cowley. Mineola: Dover, 2006.

Glazier-McDonald, Beth. "Intermarriage, Divorce, and the *Bat-'ēl Nēkār*: Insights into Malachi 2:10–16." *JBL* 106 (1987): 603–611.

———. "Mal'ak Habberit: The Messenger of the Covenant in Mal 3:1." *Hebrew Annual Review* (1987): 93–104.

———. "Malachi." In *The Women's Bible Commentary*, edited by Carol A. Newsom and Sharon H. Ringe, 227–31. London: SPCK, 1992.

———. "Malachi 2:12: 'ēr wĕ'ōneh Another Look." *JBL* 105 (1986): 295–298.

———. *Malachi: The Divine Messenger*. SBL Dissertation Series 98. Atlanta: Scholars Press, 1987.

Gordon, C. H. "Biblical Customs and The Nuzi Tablets." *Biblical Archeologists* 3 (1940): 1–12.

———. "Hebrew Origins in the Light of Recent Discoveries." In *Biblical and Other Studies*, edited by A. Altmann, 238–43. Cambridge: Harvard University Press, 1963.

Gordon, R. P. "Review of A Prophet Confronts His People: The Disputation Speech in the Prophets, by A. Graffy." VT 35, no. 1 (1985): 125–126.

Gorman, Michael. "Divorce and Remarriage from Augustine to Zwingli." https://www.christianitytoday.com/2000/08/divorce-and-remarriage-from-augustine-to-zwingli/.

Gowan, Donald E. *Theology of the Prophetic Books: The Death and Resurrection of Israel.* Louisville: Westminster John Knox, 1998.

Gower, Ralph. *The New Manners and Customs of Bible Times.* Chicago: Moody, 1987.

Gunkel, Hermann. "Die Isrealitische Literatur." In *Die Kulter der Gegenwart*, I. 7, reprint. Darmstadt: Wissenschaftliche Bauchgeseltschaft, (1963): 51–102.

———. "Fundamental Problems of Hebrew Literary History." In *What Remains of the Old Testament*, 59–60. New York: Macmillan, 1928.

———. *What Remains of the Old Testament and Other Essays.* Translated by A. K. Dallas. New York: Macmillan, 1928.

Gunkel, Herman et al., eds. "Die Propheten als Schrifsteller und Dichter." In *Die Schriften des Alten Testaments.* Vol. 2. 2nd ed. Gottingen: Vandenhoeck& Ruprecht, 1923.

Hailey, Homer. *A Commentary on the Minor Prophets.* Grand Rapids: Baker Books, 1972.

Halévy, J. "Le Prophète Malachie." *Revue Sémitique* 17 (1909): 1–44.

Hallo, W. H., and K. L. Younger, eds. *The Context of Scripture.* Vol. 1. Leiden: Brill, 1997.

———. *The Context of Scripture.* Vol. 2. Leiden: Brill, 1997.

Hamilton, Victor P. *The Book of Genesis: Chapters 1–17.* NICOT. Grand Rapids: Eerdmans, 1990.

Harris, R. Laird, Gleason Archer Jr., and Bruce K. Waltke. *Theological Wordbook of the Old Testament.* Vol. 1. Chicago: Moody, 1980.

Harrison, George W. "Covenant Unfaithfulness in Malachi 2:1–16." *CTR* 2 (1987): 63–72.

Harrison, R. K. *Introduction to the Old Testament.* Grand Rapids: Eerdmans, 1975.

Harrisville, Roy A., and Water Sundberg. *The Bible in Modern Culture: Baruch Spinoza to Brevard Childs.* 2nd ed. Grand Rapids: Eerdmans, 2002.

Harvey, Julien. *La Pledoyer Prophétique Contre Israël après la Rupture de l'alliance Scholasticat de l'Immaculée-Conception. Etude d'une formulae litteraire de l'Ancien Testament.* Paris: Desclee de Brouwer, 1967.

Hendrix, J. D. "'You Say': Confrontation Dialogue in Malachi." *Rev Exp* 84 (1987): 465–477.

Herion, Gary A. "The Impact of Modern and Social Science Assumptions on the Reconstruction of Israelite History." *JSOT* 11, no. 34 (1986): 3–33.

Heron, Jr. Robert W. "Mark's Jesus on Divorce: Mark 10:1–12 Reconsidered." *JETS* 25, no. 3 (1982): 273–294.

Hill, Andrew E. *Haggai, Zechariah, and Malachi*: TOTC. Downers Grove: IVP Academic, 2012.

———. *Malachi: A New Translation with Introduction and Commentary*. The Anchor Bible Commentary. New York: Doubleday, 1998.

Hillers, D. R. *Treaty-Curses and the Old Testament Prophets*. BibOr 16. Rome: Pontifical Biblical Institute, 1964.

Hinson, David F. *The Books of the Old Testament*. London: SPCK, 1992.

Hirsch, E. D. *Validity in Interpretation*. New Haven; London: Yale University Press, 1967.

Holladay, William L. *A Concise Hebrew and Aramaic Lexicon of the Old Testament*. Grand Rapids: Eerdmans; Leiden: Brill, 1971.

Hölscher, G. *Die Profeten*. Leipzig: Hinrichs, 1914.

Hoonacker, A. van. *Les Douze Petits Prophètes*. Paris: Gabalda, 1908.

Horst, Friedrich. *Die Zwölf Kleinen Propheten*, Handbuch Zum Alten Testament, no. 14. Tübingen: Mohr Siebeck, 1938.

Hugenberger, Gordon Paul. *Marriage as a Covenant: A Study of Biblical Law and Ethics Governing Marriage, Developed from the Perspective of Malachi*. VTSup 52. Leiden: Brill, 1994.

Hurley, James B. *Man and Woman in Biblical Perspective*. Leicester: Inter-Varsity Press, 1981.

Hvidberg, Flemming Friis. *Weeping and Laughter in the Old Testament: A Study of Canaanite-Israelite Religion*. Leiden: Brill, 1962.

Igenoza, Andrew Olu. *Polygamy and the African Churches: A Biblical Appraisal of an African Marriage System*. Ibadan: Oluben, 2003.

Instone-Brewer, David. *Divorce and Remarriage in the Bible: The Social and Literary Context*. Grand Rapids: Eerdmans, 2002.

———. *Divorce and Remarriage in the Church: Biblical Solutions for Pastoral Realities*. Bletchley: Paternoster, 2003.

———. "Three Weddings and a Divorce: God's Covenant with Israel, Judah and the Church." *TynBul* 47 (1996): 1–25.

Isaksson, Abel. *Marriage and Ministry in the New Temple*. Lund: Gleerup; Copenhagen: Ejnar Munksgaard, 1965.

Isbell, C. D. *Malachi*. Grand Rapids: Zondervan, 1980.

Isiugo Abanihe, Uche C. "Stability of Marital Unions and Fertility in Nigeria." *Journal of Biosocial Science* 30 (1998): 33–41.

Itapson, E. I., and George E. Janvier. *A Study of the Major and Minor Prophets of the Old Testament: A Textbook for Africa*. Kaduna: Baraka, 2005.

Jacobs, R. Mignon. "Malachi, Book of." In *Dictionary for Theological Interpretation of the Bible*, edited by Kevin J. Vanhoozer, 474–77. Grand Rapids: Baker Academic, (2005).

Jensen, Irving L. *Haggai, Zechariah and Malachi*. Chicago: Moody, 1976.

Johnston, P. S. "Malachi." In *New Dictionary of Biblical Theology*, edited by T. Desmond Alexander, Brian S. Rosner, D. A. Carson, and Graeme Goldsworthy, 260–62. Downers Grove: IVP Academic, 2000.

Jones, David Clyde. "Malachi on Divorce." *Presbyterian* 15 (1989): 16–22.

———. "A Note on the LXX of Malachi 2:16." *JBL* 109 (1990): 683–685.

Jones, D. R. *Haggai, Zechariah and Malachi*. TBC. London: SCM, 1962.

Josephus, Flavius. *Josephus: The Complete Works*. Translated by William Whiston. Nashville: Nelson, 1998.

Joüon, Paul. *A Grammar of Biblical Hebrew*. Translated and revised by T. Muraoka. 2 vols. Rome: Pontifical Biblical Institute, 1991.

Kafang, Zamani Buki. *An Introduction to the Intertestamental Period*. Kaduna: Baraka, 2001.

Kaiser, Walter C. *The Christian and the Old Testament*. Pasadena: William Carey Library, 1998.

———. "Divorce in Malachi 2:10–16." *CTR* 2, no.1 (1987): 73–84.

———. *Malachi: God's Unchanging Love*. Grand Rapids: Baker Books, 1984.

———. "New Approaches to Old Testament Ethics." *JETS* 35 (September 1992): 289–297.

———. *The Old Testament Documents: Are They Reliable?* Downers Grove: InterVarsity Press, 2001.

———. "The Promise of the Arrival of Elijah in Malachi and the Gospels." *Grace Theological Journal* 3 (1982): 221–233.

———. *Toward an Exegetical Theology*. Grand Rapids: Baker Books, 1981.

———. *Toward Old Testament Ethics*. Grand Rapids: Zondervan, 1983.

Kato, Byang H. *The Christian Home*. Jos: Challenge Press, 1979.

Katzenstein, H. J. "'Before Pharaoh Conquered Gaza' (Jeremiah XLVII 1)." *VT* 33 (1983): 249–251.

Kaufmann, Yehezkel. *History of the Religion of Israel: From the Babylonian Captivity to the End of Prophecy*. Vol. 4. New York: KTAV, 1977.

Keck, Leander E., ed. *The New Interpreter's Bible*. Vol. 7. Nashville: Abingdon, 1996.

Keener, Craig S. *. . . And Marries Another: Divorce and Remarriage in the Teaching of the New Testament*. Peabody: Hendrickson, 1991.

Keil, Carl Friedrich and F. Delitzsch. *The Twelve Minor Prophets: Commentary on the Old Testament*, vol. 1. Translated by James Martin. Grand Rapids: Eerdmans, 1868.

———. *The Twelve Minor Prophets: Commentary on the Old Testament*. Vol. 2. Translated by James Martin. Grand Rapids: Eerdmans, 1949.

Kelley, P. H. *Biblical Hebrew: An Introductory Grammar*. Grand Rapids: Eerdmans, 1992.

Kenkel, W. F. "Divorce." In *The New Catholic Encyclopedia*, 2nd. Ed., vol. 4, edited by J. McDonald, James A. Magner and R. P. Marin. New York: McRoaw-Hill (edited by . New York: McGraw-Hill, (1976):928–930.

Kessler, John A. "The Shaking of the Nations: An Eschatological View." *JETS* 30 (1987): 159–166.

Kitchen, Kenneth, A. "The Patriarchal Age: Myth or History?" *BAR* 21 no. 2 (March/April 1995): 48–94.

Kittel, R and P. Kahle, ed. *Biblia Hebraica*. 3rd ed. Stuttgart: Deutsche Bibelgesellschaft, 1937.

Elliger, Karl and Wilhelm Rudolph, eds. *Biblia Hebraica Stuttgartensia*. Stuttgart: Deutsche Bibelgesellschaft, 1997.

Klein, George L. "An Introduction to Malachi." *CTR* 2, no. 1 (1987): 19–35.

Knight, Douglas A., and Gene M. Tucker. *The Hebrew Bible and Its Modern Interpreters*. Chico: Scholars Press, 1985.

Ko, Ming Him. "Be Faithful to the Covenant: A Technical Translation of and Commentary on Malachi 210–16." *BT* 65, no. 1 (2014): 34–48.

Koehler, Ludwig, and Walter Baumgartner, eds. *The Hebrew and Aramaic Lexicon of the Old Testament*. Vol. 1. 3rd ed. Leiden: Brill, 1996.

Kore, Danfulani. *Culture and the Christian Home*. Lagos: Integrated Press, 1997.

———. *Promoting Healthy Marriage and Family Life*. Kaduna: Baraka, 2004.

———. *Truths for Healthy Churches*. Bukuru: African Christian Textbooks, 2006.

Kostenberger, Andreas J. *God, Marriage, Family: Rebuilding the Biblical Foundation*. Wheaton: Crossway, 2004.

Kugel, James L. *The Idea of Biblical Poetry: Parallelism and Its History*. New Haven: Yale University Press, 1981.

Kunhiyop, Samuel Waje. *African Christian Ethics*. Nairobi: WordAlive, 2008.

———. *African Christian Ethics*. Kaduna: Baraka, 2004.

Kynes, William L. "The Marriage Debate: A Public Theology of Marriage." *TJ* NS 28, no. 2 (Fall 2007): 187–203.

Lamsa, George M. *The Holy Bible from Ancient Eastern Manuscripts*. Philadelphia: Holman, 1957.

Laney, Carl J. "Deuteronomy 24:1–4 and the Issue of Divorce." *BSac* 149 (January–March 1992): 3–15.

Lange, John Peter. *Minor Prophets*. Grand Rapids: Zondervan, n.d.

LaSor, William Sanford. *Old Testament Survey: The Message, Form, and Background of the Old Testament*. 2nd ed. Grand Rapids: Eerdmans, 1996.

Lisowsky, G. *Konkordanz Zum Hebräischen Alten Testament*. Germany, Stuttgart: Deutsche Bibelgesellschaft, 1993.

Lloyd, Peter C. "Divorce among the Yoruba." *American Psychologist*, New Series, 70, no. 1. (February 1968): 67–81.

Longman, Tremper, III. "Literary Approaches and Interpretation." In *New International Dictionary of Old Testament Theology and Exegesis*, edited by Willem A. VanGemeren, 103–24. Grand Rapids: Zondervan, 1996.

———. *Literary Approaches to Biblical Interpretation*. Grand Rapids: Zondervan, (1987): 25–55.

———. "What I Mean By Historical-Grammatical Exegesis: Why I Am Not a Literalist." *Grace Theological Journal* 11, no. 2 (1990): 137–153.

Lowery, David K. "Validation: Exegetical Problem Solving." In *Interpreting the New Testament Text: Introduction to the Art and Science of Exegesis*, ed. Darrell L. Bock and Buist M. Fanning, 155–66. Wheaton: Crossway Books, 2006.

Lund, N. W. "The Presence of Chiasmus in the Old Testament," *The American Journal of Semitic Languages and Literature* 46 (1930): 104–126.

MacCulloch, J. A. "Covenant." In *Encyclopedia of Religion and Ethics*. Vol. 4. Edited by J. Hastings, 203–7. Edinburgh: T&T Clark, 1959.

Malamat, A. "The Last Kings of Judah and the Fall of Jerusalem: An Historical-Chronological Study." *IEJ* 18 (1968): 137–156.

———. "The Twilight of Judah: In the Egyptians-Babylonian Maelstrom." *VTS* 28 (1975): 123–145.

Manus, C. "Biblical Foundations for Ecofeminism and Its Challenges in the Nigerian Context." *Ife Journal of Religions* 6, nos. 1 & 2 (2010): 1–19.

March, W. Eugene. "Prophecy." In *Old Testament Form Criticism*, edited by John H. Hayes, . San Antonio: Trinity University Press, 1977): 141–77.

Margoliouth, D. S. "Christ's Answer to the Question about Divorce." *ExpTim* 39 (1927–28): 272–5.

Mason, Rex. *The Books of Haggai, Zechariah and Malachi*. CBC. New York: Cambridge University Press, 1977.

Matthews, I. G. "Haggai, Malachi," in *An American Commentary on the Old Testament*, The Minor Prophets, 2. Philadelphia: American Baptist Publication Society, 1935.

Matthews, J. G. "Tammuz Worship in the Book of Malachi." *JPOS* 11 (1931): 42–50.

Matthews, Victor H. "Marriage and Family in the Ancient Near East." In *Marriage and Family in the Biblical World*, edited by Ken M. Campbell, 1–32. Downers Grove: InterVarsity Press, 2003.

Mbiti, John S. *African Religions and Philosophy*. New York: Praeger, 1969.

McCarthy, D. J. *Treaty and Covenant: A Study in Form in the Ancient Oriental Documents and in the Old Testament*. AnBib 21. Rome: Pontifical Biblical Institute, 1963.

McComiskey, Thomas Edward. "Hosea." In *The Minor Prophets*. Volume 1 of *An Exegetical and Expository Commentary*, edited by Thomas Edward McComiskey, 1–237. Grand Rapids: Baker Academics, 1993.

McConville, J. Gordon. *Exploring the Old Testament: A Guide to the Prophets*. Vol. 4. London: SPCK, 2002.

———. *Law and Theology in Deuteronomy*. JSOTSup 33 Sheffield: University of Sheffield Press, 1984.

———. "Malachi" in *Exploring the Old Testament: A Guide to the Prophets*, vol. 4, 259–269. Downers Grove: InterVarsity Press, 2002.

McKenzie, Steven L., and Howard N. Wallace. "Covenant Themes in Malachi." *CBQ* 45 (1983): 549–563.

Meek, Theophile J., trans. "The Code of Hammurabi." In *Ancient Near Eastern Texts Relating to the Old Testament*, edited by James B. Pritchard, 163–80. 2nd ed. Princeton: Princeton University Press, 1969.

Mendenhall, G. E. "Covenant." In *The Interpreter's Dictionary of the Bible, vol 3*, edited by G. A Buttrick. New York: Abingdon, 1962: 1:714–723.

Merrill, Eugene H. *Haggai, Zechariah, Malachi: An Exegetical Commentary*. Chicago: Moody, 1994.

Meyers, E. M. "Priestly Language in the Book of Malachi." *Hebrew Annual Review* 10 (1986): 225–37.

Meyers, E. M., and C. L. Meyers. *Haggai, Zechariah 1–8: A New Translation, with Introduction and Commentary*. Anchor Yale Bible 25B. New York: Doubleday, 1987.

Milgrom, Jacob. *Cult and Conscience: The Asham and the Priestly Doctrine of Repentance*. SJLA 18. Leiden: Brill, 1976.

Minor, M. *Literary-Critical Approaches to the Bible: An Annotated Bibliography*. West Cornwall: Locust Hill, 1992.

Moore, Thomas V. *Haggai and Malachi*. London: Banner of Truth, 1968.

Moran, W. L. "The Ancient Near Eastern Background of the Love of God in Deuteronomy." *CBQ* 25 (1963): 77–87.

Mowinckel, Sigmund. *Prophecy and Tradition: The Prophetic Books in the Light of the Study of the Growth and History of the Tradition*. Oslo: Kommission Hos J Dybwad, 1946.

Muilenburg, James. "Form Criticism and Beyond." *JBL* 88 (March 1969): 1–18.

Murphy, C. Nancy. *Reasoning and Rhetoric in Religion*. Valley Forge: Trinity, 1994.

Murray, D. F. "The Rhetoric of Disputation: Re-examination of a Prophetic Genre." *JSOT* 38 (1987): 95–121.

Murray, John. *Divorce*. Philadelphia: P&R, 1976.

Novak, David. "Jewish Marriage: Nature, Covenant and Contract." In *Covenant Marriage in Comparative Perspective*, edited by John Witte Jr. and Eliza Ellison, 26–52. Grand Rapids: Eerdmans, 2005.

Nürnberger, Klaus. *Biblical Theology in Outline*. Pietermaritzburg: Cluster, 2004.

O'Brien, Julia M. "Historical Criticism as Liberator and Master: Malachi as a Post-exilic Document." In *The Yahweh/Baal Confrontation and Other Biblical Literature and Archaeology: Essays in Honour of Emmett Willard Hamrick*, edited by Julia M. O' Brien and Fred J. Horton, 57–79. Studies in Bible and Early Christians 35. Macon: Mellon Biblical Press, 1995.

———. "Judah as Wife and Husband: Deconstructing Gender in Malachi." *JBL* 115, no. 2 (1996): 241–250.

———. "Malachi in Recent Research." *CurBS* 3 (1995): 81–94.

———. "On Saying No to a Prophet." *Semeia* 72 (1997): 111–24.

———. *Priest and Levite in Malachi*. SBL Dissertation Series 121. Atlanta: Scholars Press, 1990.

Obilom, J. O. C. *Prophetism and the Minor Prophets*. Jos: Afab Educational Books, 2005.

O'Connor, M., and Carol L. Meyers, eds. *The Word of the Lord Shall Go Forth: Essays in Honour of David Noel Freedman in Celebration of His Sixtieth Birthday*. Winona Lake: Eisenbrauns, 1983.

Ogden, Graham S. "The Use of Figurative Language in Malachi 2:10–16." *BT* 39 (1988): 223–230.

Ogden, Graham S., and Richard. R. Deutsch. *Joel and Malachi: A Promise of Hope, a Call to Obedience*. ITC. Grand Rapids: Eerdmans, 1987.

Ogedengbe, B. G. "The Concept of Love in the Old Testament." In *Biblical View of Sex and Sexuality from African Perspective*, edited by S. O. Abogunrin, 112–24. Ibadan: NABIS, 2006.

Ogunkunle, C. "Biblical Injunction on Marriage and Sexual Union in the Context of Christian Marriage in Nigeria." In *Biblical View of Sex and Sexuality from African Perspective*, edited by S. O. Abogunrin, 48–60. Ibadan: NABIS, 2006.

Olusanya, P .O. "A Note on Some Factors Affecting the Stability of Marriage among the Yoruba of Western Nigeria." *Journal of Marriage and the Family* 32, no.1 (February 1970): 150–155.

Oppong, Christine. *Middle Class African Marriage*. London: Allen & Unwin, 1981.

Osborne, Grant R. *The Hermeneutical Spiral: A Comprehensive Introduction to Biblical Interpretation*. Downers Grove: InterVarsity Press, 1991.

Otto, Randall E. "The Prophets and Their Perspective." *CBQ* 63, no. 2 (April 2001): 219–240.

Paterson, John. "Divorce and Desertion in the Old Testament." *JBL* 51, no. 2 (June 1932): 161–170.

Perkin, Hazel W. "Divorce." In *New International Bible Dictionary*, edited by J. D. Douglas and Merrill C. Tenney, 279–80. Grand Rapids: Zondervan, 1987.

Perrin, N. *What Is Redaction Criticism?* London: SPCK, 1970.

Petersen, David Lee. *Late Israelite Prophecy*. Missoula: Scholars Press, 1977.

———. "Malachi and the Language of Divorce: Mal 2:10–16." Paper Presented at the Annual Meeting of the Society of Biblical Literature, 6 December 1987.

———. *Zechariah 9–14 and Malachi*. OTL. Louisville: Westminster John Knox, 1995.

Pfeiffer, Egon. "Die Disputationsworte im Buche Maleachi: Ein Beitrag zur Formgeschichtlichen Struktur." *EvT* 19 (1959): 548–568.

Popenoe, David, and Barbara Dafoe Whitehead. "The Personal and Social Costs of Divorce." In *Marriage, Health, and the Professions*, edited by John Wall, Don Browning, William Doherty and Stephen Post, 33–48. Grand Rapids: Eerdmans, 2002.

Pritchard, James B., ed. *Ancient Near Eastern Texts Relating to the Old Testament*. 2nd ed. Princeton: Princeton University Press, 1955.

Purdue, Leo G. "The Israelite and Early Jewish Family." In *Families in Ancient Israel*, edited by Leo G. Purdue, Joseph Blenkinsopp, John J. Collins, and Carol Meyers, 163–222. Louisville: Westminster John Knox, 1997.

Pusey, E. B. *The Minor Prophets: A Commentary*. Grand Rapids: Baker Books, 1979.

Rad, Gerhard von. *Deuteronomy*. The Old Testament Library. London: SCM, 1966.

———. *Old Testament Theology*. Vol. 2. London: SCM, 1965.

Rahlfs, Alfred and Robert Hanhart, eds. *Septuaginta*. Stuttgart: Deutsche Bibelgesellschaft, 1979, 2006.

Ratner, Jeffrey Robert. "Gender Agreement in Biblical Hebrew." PhD diss, Hebrew Union College, 1983.

Redditt, P. L. "The Book of Malachi in Its Social Setting." *CBQ* 56 (1994): 240–55.

———. *Haggai, Zechariah, Malachi*. NCB. Grand Rapids: Eerdmans, 1994.

Reeder, Caryn A. "Malachi 3:24 and the Eschatological Restoration of the Family." *CBQ* 69, no. 4 (October 2007): 695–709.

Retief, Frank. *Divorce: Hope for the Hurting*. Cape Town: Struik Christian Books, 1990.

Rosberg, Gary, and Barbara Rosberg. *Divorce-Proof Your Marriage*. Wheaton: Tyndale, 2002.

Routledge, Robin. *Old Testament Theology: A Thematic Approach*. Nottingham: Apollos, 2008.

Rudolph, Wilhelm. *Haggai, Sacharja 1–8, Sacharja 9–14, Maleachi*. KAT 13.4. Gütersloh: Mohn, 1976.

———. "Zu Mal 2:10–16." *ZAW* 93 (1981): 85–90.

Schereschewsky, B. Z. "Marriage." In *Encyclopedia Judaica*, vol. 11: Lek–Mil. Jerusalem: Keter, 1971.

Schereschewsky, B. Z. "Divorce and the Jews." In *Encyclopedia Judaica*, vol. 6 DI-FO, 122–35, Jerusalem: Keter, 1971.

Schrage, Wolfgang. *The Ethics of the New Testament*. Translated by David E. Green. Philadelphia: Fortress, 1988.

Schreiner, Stefan. "Mischehen-Ehebruch-Ehescheidung: Betrachtunges zu Malachi 2:10–16," *Zeitschrift fur die altestamentliche Wissenschaft*, 91 (1979): 207–228.

Schultz, Samuel. *Deuteronomy: The Gospel of Love*. Chicago: Moody, 1971.

Shields, Martin A. "Syncretism and Divorce in Malachi 2:10–16." *ZAW* 3 (1999): 68–86.

Shields, Norman. *Christian Ethics*. Bukuru: Africa Christian Textbooks, 2004.

Silva, Moises, ed. *Foundations of Contemporary Interpretation*. Grand Rapids: Zondervan, 1996.

Smith, G. A. *The Book of the Twelve Prophets*. Vol. 2. In *The Expositor's Bible*, edited by W. Robertson Nicoll. 3rd ed. New York: Armstrong & Son, 1899.

Smith, J. M. P. *A Critical and Exegetical Commentary on Haggai, Zechariah, Malachi and Jonah*: ICC, Book 2, 1–88. Edinburgh: T&T Clark, 1912.

Smith, Ralph L. *Micah–Malachi*. Word Biblical Commentary 32. Waco: Word Books, 1984.

Smith, Mark. "'Your People Shall Be My People': Family and Covenant in Ruth 1:16–17." *CBQ* 69, no. 2 (April 2007): 242–258.

Smith, R. L. *Micah–Malachi*. WBC 32. Waco: Word, 1984.

Smoke, Jim. *Growing through Divorce*. Eugene: Harvest House, 1995.

Snuth, David L. "Divorce and Remarriage from the Early Church to John Wesley." *TJ* 11, no. 2 (1990): 131–142.

Soden, Wolfram von. *The Ancient Orient: An Introduction to the Study of the Ancient Near East*. Grand Rapids: Eerdmans, 1994.

Soulen, Richard N., and R. Kendall Soulen. *Handbook of Biblical Criticism*. 3rd ed. Louisville: Westminster John Knox, 2001.

Sparks, Kenton L. *Ancient Texts for the Study of the Hebrew Bible: A Guide to the Background Literature*. Peabody: Hendrickson, 2005.

Speiser, Ephraim A. *Genesis*. ABC. Garden City: Doubleday, 1965.

Sprinkle, Joe M. "Old Testament Perspectives on Divorce and Remarriage." *JETS* 40 (1997): 529–550.

Stamm, J. J. *The Hebrew and Aramaic Lexicon of the Old Testament*. Translated and edited by M. E. J. Richardson. 4 vols. Leiden: Brill, 1994–1999.

Stein, R. H. "Divorce." In *Dictionary of Jesus and the Gospels*, edited by Joel B. Green, Scot McKnight, and I. Howard Marshall, 192–200. Downers Grove: InterVarsity Press, 1992.

———. "Is It Lawful for a Man to Divorce His Wife." *JETS* 22, no. 2 (June 1979): 115–121.

Stienstra, Nelly. *YHWH Is the Husband of His People*. Kampen: Kok Pharos, 1993.

Stott, John. *Divorce*. Downers Grove: InterVarsity Press, 1973.

———. *Involvement: Social and Sexual Relationships in the Modern World.* Old Tappan: Revell, 1985.

Stuart, Douglas. "Malachi." In *The Minor Prophets: A Commentary on Zephaniah, Hagia, Zachariah, Malachi.* Volume 3 of *An Exegetical and Expository Commentary*, edited by Thomas Edward McComiskey, 1245–396. Grand Rapids: Baker Academic, 1998.

Sweeney, Marvin A. *The Twelve Prophets.* Berit Olam. Collegeville: Liturgical Press, 2000.

Tate, M. E. "Questions for Priests and People in Malachi 1:2–2:16." *RevExp* 84 (1987): 391–401.

Tate, W. Randolph. *Interpreting the Bible: A Handbook of Terms and Methods.* Peabody: Hendrickson, 2006.

Terry, Milton S. *Biblical Hermeneutics.* Phillips & Hunt: New York, 1883.

Thomas, D. Winton, ed. *Documents from Old Testament Times.* New York: Harper & Brothers, 1961.

Thompson, J. A. *Deuteronomy: An Introduction and Commentary.* TOTC. Leicester: Inter-Varsity Press, 1976.

———. "The Significance of the Ancient Near Eastern Treaty Pattern." *TynBul* 13 (1963): 1–6.

Thompson, Thomas L. *The Historicity of the Patriarchal Narratives.* Berlin: de Gruyter, 1974.

Torrey, Charles Cutler. "The Prophecy of 'Malachi.'" *JBL* 17 (1898): 1–15.

Tucker, Gene M. "Covenant Forms and Contract Forms." *VT* 15 (1965): 487–503.

———. *Form Criticism of the Old Testament.* Philadelphia: Fortress, 1971.

Tushima, C. T. A. *The Fate of Saul's Progeny in the Reign of David.* Eugene: Pickwick, 2011.

Van der Merwe, Christo H. J., Jacobus A. Naude and J. H. Kroeze. *A Biblical Hebrew Reference Grammar.* Sheffield: Sheffield Academic, 1999.

VanGemeren, Willem A. *Interpreting the Prophetic Word: An Introduction to the Prophetic Literature of the Old Testament.* Grand Rapids: Zondervan, 1990.

———, ed. *New International Dictionary of Old Testament Theology and Exegesis.* Vol. 1. Grand Rapids: Zondervan, 1997.

Van Seters, John. *Abraham in History and Tradition.* New Haven: Yale University Press, 1975.

Vaux, Roland de. *Ancient Israel: Its Life and Institutions.* London: Darton, Longman & Todd, 1968.

———. *Social Institutions.* Volume 1 of *Ancient Israel.* New York: McGraw-Hill, 1965.

———. *The Bible and the Ancient Near East.* Translated by Damian McHugh. London: Darton, Longman & Todd, 1966.

Vawter, Bruce. "The Biblical Theology of Divorce." *Proceedings of the Catholic Theological Society of America* 22 (1967): 223–243.

Verhoef, Pieter A. *The Books of Haggai and Malachi:* NICOT. Grand Rapids: Eerdmans, 1987.

Waltke, Bruce K. *An Old Testament Theology*. Grand Rapids: Zondervan, 2007.

Waltke, Bruce K., and M. O'Connor. *An Introduction to Biblical Hebrew Syntax*. Winona Lake: Eisenbrauns, 1990.

Walton, John H. *Ancient Near Eastern Thought and the Old Testament: Introducing the Conceptual World of the Hebrew Bible*. Grand Rapids: Baker Academic, 2006.

Weber, Robert and Bonifatius Fischer. *Biblia Sacra: Iuxtra Vulgatam Versionem*. Stuttgart: Deutsche Bibelgesellschaft, 1994.

Weinfeld, Moshe. "The Covenant of Grant in the Old Testament and the Ancient Near East." *JAOS* 90 (1970): 185–200.

———. *Deuteronomy 1–11*. ABC 5. London: Doubleday, 1991.

Weiser, Artur. *The Old Testament: Its Formation and Development*. New York: Association Press, 1966.

Welch, Adam C. *Post-Exilic Judaism*. London; Edinburgh: Blackwood, 1935.

Wellhausen, Julius. *Die kleinen Propheten: Übersetzt und Erklärt*. Berlin: de Gruyter, 1892.

———. *Prolegomena to the History of Ancient Israel*. London: Adam & Charles Black, 1885.

———. *Prolegomena Zur Geschichte Israels*. 6th ed. Berlin: de Gruyter, 1927. Reprinted as *Prolegomena to the History of Ancient Israel*. New York: Meridian, 1957.

———. *Skizzen und Bvorarbeiten*. 2nd ed. Charleston: Nabu, 1985.

Wendland, Ernst.R. "Linear and Concentric Patterns in Malachi." *BT* 36 (1985): 108–121.

———. "Linear and Concentric Patterns in the Rhetorical Style and Structure of Malachi." https://translation.bible/wp-content/uploads/2024/06/wendland-1985-linear-and-concentric-patterns-in-malachi.pdf.

Wenham, Gordon J. *Genesis 1–15*. WBC 1. Waco: Word, 1987.

Wenham, J. Gordon, and William E. Heth. *Jesus and Divorce*. London: Hodder & Stoughton, 1984.

West, Gerald. *Contextual Bible Study*. Pietermaritzburg: Cluster, 2003.

Westbrook, Raymond. "Old Babylonian Marriage Law." *AfOB* 23 (1988): 148–208.

———. "The Prohibition on Restoration of Marriage in Deuteronomy 24:1–4." In *Studies in Bible: Scripta Hierosolymitana* 31, edited by S. Japhet. Jerusalem: Magnes, 1986.

Westermann, Claus. *Basic Forms of Prophetic Speech*. Translated by H. C. White. London: Lutterworth; Philadelphia: Westminster, 1967.

Wight, Fred. *Manners and Customs of Bible Lands*. Chicago: Moody, 1953.
Wilson, R. R. *Form Critical Investigation of the Prophetic Literature: The Present Situation*. SBLSP, 1973.
Wimsatt, W. K. *The Verbal Icon: Studies in the Meaning of Poetry*. Kentucky: University Press of Kentucky, 1954.
Wimsatt, W. K., and M. Beardsley. "The Intentional Fallacy." In *The Verbal Icon: Studies in the Meaning of Poetry*, 3–20. Kentucky: University Press of Kentucky, 1954.
Wiseman, D. J. *Chronicles of Chaldean Kings (626–556 BC) in the British Museum*. London: British Museum, 1956.
Witte, John, Jr., and Eliza Ellison, eds. *Covenant Marriage in Comparative Perspective*. Grand Rapids: Eerdmans, 2005.
Witte, John, Jr., and Joel A. Nichols. "Introduction: Covenant Marriage v. Contract Marriage." In *Covenant Marriage in Comparative Perspective*, edited by John Witte and Eliza Ellison, 1–25. Grand Rapids: Eerdmans, 2005.
Wolff, Herbert M. *Haggai and Malachi*. Chicago: Moody, 1976.
Wolff, Hans Walter. *Anthropology of the Old Testament*. Philadelphia: Fortress, 1974.
Woude van der, A. S. "Malachi's Struggle for a Pure Community: Reflections on Malachi 2:10–16." In *Tradition and Re-interpretation in Jewish and Early Christian Literature: Essays in Honour of Jürgen C. H. Lebram*, edited by J.W. van Henten, H.J. de Jonge, P.T. van Rooden and J.W. Wesselius, 65–71. Leiden: Brill, 1986.
Woudstra, M. "The Everlasting Covenant in Ezekiel 16:59–63." *CTJ* 6, no. 1 (1971): 22–48.
Wright, C. J. H. *Walking in the Ways of the Lord: The Ethical Authority of the Old Testament*. Downers Grove: InterVarsity Press, 1995.
Wright, H. Norman. *The Secrets of a Lasting Marriage*. Ventura: Regal Books, 1995.
Yamauchi, Edwin M. "Cultural Aspects of Marriage in the Ancient World." *BSac* 135 (July–September 1978): 234–52.
———. *Persia and the Bible*. Grand Rapids: Baker Books, 1990.
———. *The World of the First Christians*. Tring: Lion, 1981.
Yamsat, Pandang. *A Study of Marriage and Divorce and The Single Life in 1 Corinthians 7*. Jos: Crossroads Communications, 2000.
Yilpet, Yoilah. "Canon Criticism and Its Significance for Evangelical Theology." *TCNN Research Bulletin* 44 (2005): 30–40.
Zehnder, Markus. "A Fresh Look at Malachi 2:13–16." *VT* 53, no. 2 (2003): 224–259.
Zuck, R. B., ed. *A Biblical Theology of the Old Testament*. Chicago: Moody, 1991.

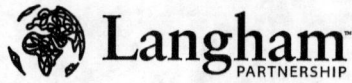

Langham Literature, with its publishing work, is a ministry of Langham Partnership.

Langham Partnership is a global fellowship working in pursuit of the vision God entrusted to its founder John Stott –

> *to facilitate the growth of the church in maturity and Christ-likeness through raising the standards of biblical preaching and teaching.*

Our vision is to see churches in the Majority World equipped for mission and growing to maturity in Christ through the ministry of pastors and leaders who believe, teach and live by the word of God.

Our mission is to strengthen the ministry of the word of God through:
- nurturing national movements for biblical preaching
- fostering the creation and distribution of evangelical literature
- enhancing evangelical theological education

especially in countries where churches are under-resourced.

Our ministry

Langham Preaching partners with national leaders to nurture indigenous biblical preaching movements for pastors and lay preachers all around the world. With the support of a team of trainers from many countries, a multi-level programme of seminars provides practical training, and is followed by a programme for training local facilitators. Local preachers' groups and national and regional networks ensure continuity and ongoing development, seeking to build vigorous movements committed to Bible exposition.

Langham Literature provides Majority World preachers, scholars and seminary libraries with evangelical books and electronic resources through publishing and distribution, grants and discounts. The programme also fosters the creation of indigenous evangelical books in many languages, through writer's grants, strengthening local evangelical publishing houses, and investment in major regional literature projects, such as one volume Bible commentaries like the *Africa Bible Commentary* and the *South Asia Bible Commentary*.

Langham Scholars provides financial support for evangelical doctoral students from the Majority World so that, when they return home, they may train pastors and other Christian leaders with sound, biblical and theological teaching. This programme equips those who equip others. Langham Scholars also works in partnership with Majority World seminaries in strengthening evangelical theological education. A growing number of Langham Scholars study in high quality doctoral programmes in the Majority World itself. As well as teaching the next generation of pastors, graduated Langham Scholars exercise significant influence through their writing and leadership.

To learn more about Langham Partnership and the work we do visit **langham.org**